JAMÓN AND HALAL

JAMÓN AND HALAL

LESSONS IN TOLERANCE FROM RURAL ANDALUCÍA

CHRISTINA CIVANTOS

Amherst College Press

Copyright © 2022 by Christina Civantos
Some rights reserved

This work is licensed under the Creative Commons Attribution-NonCommercial 4.0 International License. To view a copy of this license, visit http://creativecommons.org/licenses/by-nc/4.0/ or send a letter to Creative Commons, PO Box 1866, Mountain View, CA 94042, USA.

The complete manuscript of this work was subjected to a partly closed ("single-blind") review process. For more information, visit https://acpress.amherst.edu/peerreview/.

Published in the United States of America by
Amherst College Press
Manufactured in the United States of America

DOI: http://doi.org/10.3998/mpub.12404742

ISBN 978-1-943208-36-4 (paper)
ISBN 978-1-943208-37-1 (OA)

Table of Contents

List of Figures   xi

Preface: My Family Narrative   xiii

1   Introduction   1

    The Setting   1
    The Back Story: al-Andalus, Convivencia, and Andalusian Nationalism   6
    Historical Memory and Contemporary Conflicts: Narratives about al-Andalus in Immigration and Cultural Politics   14
    The Methods behind this Narrative   26

2   Tolerance, Power, and Civilizational Discourses   31

    Recognition and Sustainable Tolerance   31
    Recognition, Toleration, and Power   37
    Toleration and "Civilization"   41

3   Written Narratives about the Alpujarra and Órgiva   45

    Early Modern to Late Modern Travelogues, Ethnographies, and Histories   45
    Late Modern Memoirs and a Collaborative Community History   54

4   21st-Century Televisual Narratives about Órgiva   81

    The Maghrebian Connection as Strictly Part of the Past   82
    Órgiva as a Site for Contemporary Islam: The Titillation of the Return of Islam vs. a Continuation of the Convivencia   88
    Convivencia-Washing for Regional and National Audiences   94

5 Oral Narratives about Órgiva   113

"The Locals": Alpujarrans and Andalusians Who Have Lived
    in Órgiva for a Generation or More   113
The First of Recent Incomers: Lifestyle Migrants and Alternatives
    from Northern Europe and Metropolitan Spain   120
Spiritual Chain Migration: The Influx of Converts to Islam   136
The Other Muslims in Órgiva: Migrants from the Maghreb   151

6 Bridges between Parallel Worlds: The Creation of Shared
   Narratives Via Estrangement   181

7 Conclusions: Accepting Estrangement, Building Bridges,
   and Two-Way Tolerance   205

Notes   215

Bibliography   229

Acknowledgements

First and foremost, I am grateful to my relatives in Órgiva and especially *la Superprima*, for all the leads and contacts that she supplied and a million other forms of inspiration and logistical support that she provided.

I also owe a debt of gratitude to my dear friend Karen Rignall, who served as the intellectual midwife for this book, reading an early draft and suggesting astute, elegant, and creative ways to reshape the project when I wasn't sure how to make it viable. I thank Beth Bouloukos at Amherst College Press and the anonymous external readers, all of whom provided valuable critiques and suggestions. The organizers and other members of the Fieldwork in the Humanities Interdisciplinary Research Group at the University of Miami Center for the Humanities enriched this project greatly. The readings, speakers, and discussions organized by this group helped me refine my methodology. Of course, all shortcomings are my own responsibility.

At the University of Miami, Nada Naami was an excellent instructor of Moroccan *Darija* who patiently helped me to connect *Darija* to standard written Arabic and the other colloquial dialects that I speak. During that course and previously as the teaching assistant in the summer study abroad program that I led in Morocco, she taught me a great deal about Moroccan and North African culture. Yolanda Martínez-San Miguel, my chair in the Department of Modern Languages and Literatures, and the College of Arts and Sciences supported some of the *in situ* research and provided funds for a research assistant. I thank Aya Hamza, Lina Jardines del Cueto, and Zayer Baazaoui for help with gathering source materials. I thank my *primo granaíno* Mario for connecting me with Saad Ben Tahayekt Ben Tahaikt, who proved to be an amazing on-the-ground research assistant.

For the use of their maps, to which I added the location of Órgiva, I thank the Wikimedia Commons users Xufanc (Alpujarras-Location1) and NordNordWest (Spain location map).

For salvaging my low-quality photos and making them usable, as well as enhancing the dpi of the maps, I am very grateful to my cousin on the Cuban-Puerto Rican side, Ana Rodríguez-González.

My beloved family has tolerated my travel and long hours at the computer keyboard. But best of all, when they have been able to travel too, they have thoroughly enjoyed the Alpujarra with me! And my father-in-law, through cohabitation, has taught me a great deal about tolerance.

I thank all of my interlocutors in Órgiva for the time and viewpoints that they shared with me. It's possible that some of them may feel that I misrepresented or inexplicably excluded a statement they made, or have done a disservice to the people and place about which I am writing. Please forgive any errors or inadvertent repercussions and know that, as Karen pointed out, this project has been a labor of love whose only intention is to empathically analyze and thus better understand Órgiva's confluence of cultures and the much sought after respectful coexistence.

Dedication

Para Pipo, Mima y Papá

To all the seekers whose journeys led them to leave the Alpujarra, or drew them (back) to it.

List of Figures

FIGURE 1: One of the roads heading out of town between farmhouses, with olive groves ahead.

FIGURE 2: A map indicating the location of Órgiva within Spain (with the coast of Morocco and Algeria below).

FIGURE 3: A map indicating the location of Órgiva within the Alpujarra (darker in the larger map) and Andalucía.

FIGURE 4: The sign on one of the main roads into town, announcing "Órgiva, Pura Alpujarra [Pure Alpujarra]."

FIGURE 5: A detail of the entrance to the town church; the sign states that it was built upon a former mosque.

FIGURE 6: A slice of life in the "New Age Alpujarra": a detail of the bulletin board at the main halal restaurant, Café Baraka, announcing alternative and Muslim activities and services.

FIGURE 7: A member of the alternative community passes next to the town hall (inside the 16th-century palace of the Condes de Sástago) and the church.

FIGURE 8: The *Ermita de San Sebastián*, a Catholic chapel on the edge of town that may have once been a *ribat* (a combination of Muslim monastery and military outpost) and some believe to be the tomb of a Sufi saint.

FIGURE 9: The entrance to the Sufi *dargah* on the outskirts of town; the flyers on the right announce a concert of Turkish Sufi music benefitting the children of Palestine, and a lecture on permaculture and the Muslim agricultural tradition of al-Andalus.

FIGURE 10: A North African immigrant, wearing a longer headscarf and long skirt, passing in front of the town library.

FIGURE 11: The Arabic graffiti stating "al-ghurba saʿiba" meaning "life as an émigré/being a stranger is difficult."

FIGURE 12: An *orgiveño* and a convert to Sufi Islam wait their turn at the meat counter of a local grocery store that sells both cured *jamón* (hanging from the wall behind the counter) and halal meat.

Preface: My Family Narrative

My great-grandfather left a small village in the Alpujarra region of Andalucía to fulfill his military service. Since those were the days of the Cuban War of Independence (1895–98), Cuba's final push for independence from Spain, he was deployed to Cuba. He returned to the Alpujarra to marry, but soon went back to Cuba with his bride. The next two generations of the family crisscrossed the Atlantic, with some being born in the Alpujarran town of Órgiva and some in Havana, until the time of the Spanish Civil War, during which my family definitively left Spain. However, my grandparents and their children maintained contact with relatives in Órgiva and Granada through letters, phone calls, and visits. Due to these family ties, I have visited Órgiva regularly, staying with second cousins there, for more than 30 years, often spending several weeks there during successive summers.

During my childhood, my paternal grandparents, who were both raised in Órgiva, would travel there whenever they could to see their siblings and then my parents started to visit to see my father's only aunts, uncles, and first cousins. As a result, I grew up seeing photos of *orgiveño* relatives and hearing stories about the town, many of which highlighted the ways in which it seemed to be frozen in time and cut off from modernity: that my father as a baby there had been fed by a wet nurse while his mother was ill, that through the 1970s the only bathroom at my great aunt's large house was an outhouse, and that she and her family had to go to a store on the town plaza if they wanted to use a telephone. My grandfather built two identical rabbit hutches, one at his sister's house in Órgiva and one at our house in Miami, but the similarities were superficial. We were the only people I knew in Miami who kept rabbits outdoors. For my siblings and me they were pets, but for my grandparents they were livestock. I cried when my grandfather prepared some of them for dinner in a moment of culture clash that intensified the sense that we were more "modern" and "civilized" than those "backward" *orgiveños*. At the same time, though, my grandparents' sweet affection and their amusing stories about life in Órgiva—like the local priest who made the rounds among Alpujarran villages on his motorcycle, or the former wet nurse who greeted my awkwardly shy father with effusive affection in the middle of the town plaza when he returned to the town for the first time in decades—endeared the town to me.

When I first visited Órgiva as an 18-year-old, there were no traffic lights in the town and every afternoon herds of goats filled the side streets as they returned from the day's grazing. I started to visit regularly in search of the slow pace and natural beauty that the town offered: an ancient whitewashed house full of photos of my father and two generations of paternal ancestors, a tranquil garden behind the house with a grapevine trellis, laundry drying on the line, and a spectacular view of the mountains, as well as walks between and up those mountains. The first few times that I visited the town, my grandfather's sister, Tía Paca, was still alive.[1] Tía Paca was a wisp of a woman, but astonishingly spry. One day, as I sat reading in the backyard orchard, or *huerto*, I witnessed this tiny octogenarian, eternally clad in a black dress and apron, pop out of the kitchen door and into the animal pen. She delivered a solid thwack with the edge of her hand to the scruff of a rabbit that she was holding by its ears and then hung the rabbit by its hind legs from the low branch of an orange tree, as the first step toward that day's lunch. It was probably that morning, as I read, looking up occasionally to catch the incongruous sight of what appeared to be a rabbit bounding down from an orange tree, that my ideas about pets and food preparation expanded.

Cousins my age also lived in the same ancient house with thick, cool walls and rustic wooden doors and shutters, and I set out with them on many adventures: Vespa rides around town, cookouts at a friend's farmhouse, and the open-air summer discotheques. My *orgiveño* relatives had started a business in town, but they still kept working their small plots of land on the side. Depending on the time of year, during some visits I was able to help with the olive, orange, or almond harvests. In the *huerto*, sitting in a circle of local women hulling and shelling almonds, or in the kitchen brimming with blue and green accented ceramics, cooking with my father's cousin, *Tía* Paca's daughter whom I refer to as *Tía* Conchita, I took in many stories. There was the latest town gossip—Manuel up the street has accused another neighbor of stealing water by not following the rotation of water rights from the *acequia*, the community-operated irrigation channels—and there were tales about my father's early childhood— one time at the beginning of the Civil War he was out playing in the street with other children when a bomber flew overhead and though he hid quickly the explosion sprayed shattered glass, a piece of which cut his leg. This explained why, as I had heard in Miami, while he was

FIGURE 1: One of the roads heading out of town between farmhouses, with olive groves ahead.

a 4- and 5-year-old in Havana he would hide anxiously whenever he heard a plane fly overhead. *Tía* Conchita also showed me the wood and leather trunk that my great-grandfather José had used to carry his belongings across the Atlantic. His wife, my great-grandmother Nieves, developed a mysterious ailment which she insisted required that she stay in Órgiva with their children while José returned to Havana to work. Nieves had found a crafty way to put an ocean between her and José, whose overbearing personality was legendary. But then again, perhaps my back troubles were related to the ailment that led to Nieves spending so many hours in a rocking chair that she left the impression of the foot that she pushed off of in one of the terracotta floor tiles, where it can still be seen to this day. The experiences and bits of family lore that I gathered in Órgiva built new narratives that added facets to my identity.

Considering that my parents had only been in the US for a decade when I was born, and that I grew up in a very new city as part of a community of immigrants who rarely visited their island of origin (first because it was prohibited and later because of logistical and ideological barriers), Órgiva offered a sense of history and rootedness (and an escape from Cold War politics) that I enjoyed. Later, I brought my children there to extend that family connection, to enjoy the mountains, and to boost their proficiency in Spanish. But with time, along with the installation of a few traffic lights and a reduction in goat sightings, English began to be heard in Órgiva with increasing regularity and a Sufi center was established near my *orgiveño* cousins' home. When I visited with my children, I realized that I was wary of the amount of English spoken in the town and I was faced with my own intolerance toward a process that could be understood as a loss of cultural authenticity, or as an organic shift that is part of long unfolding changes—changes that are sometimes only visible over a millennium, sometimes readily apparent over only a few generations. What follows is my attempt to carry out a compassionate critique of a place that is close to my heart.

CHAPTER 1
Introduction

THE SETTING

The weekly Thursday market in Órgiva is a kaleidoscope of regional, national, religious, and ethnic origins, as well as of lifestyle choices.[1] At one stand, in this town about 60 km southeast of the city of Granada, an older woman speaking Spanish with the local Alpujarran accent and wearing a black skirt, short-sleeve floral print blouse, and gold crucifix buys vegetables from a local farmer. Nearby, a group of teens browses an array of knock-off sneakers sold by a West African immigrant who travels for hours to sell his wares at different Andalusian markets. Elsewhere, a man with an Italian accent wearing a cotton tunic and an embroidered kufi cap (the brimless, cylindrical hat also known as a topi or taqiya) sells incense and hand-crafted soaps.[2] In front of a stand displaying dozens of bins full of aromatic spices, a Moroccan family confers in Arabic about what to purchase, and one of them places their order in Spanish. At a series of small tables, people sporting eclectic, mostly bohemian, clothes, piercings, and sometimes dreadlocks, many of whom arrived on foot from neighboring hippie communes, sell handmaid jewelry and pipes for smoking marijuana, with signs advertising their wares in a mix of Spanish and English, and bilingual brochures for a local exchange trading system, an alternative economic system based on barter.

Órgiva, a town of approximately 6,000 inhabitants nestled between the southern slopes of the Sierra Nevada and the smaller Sierra de Lújar mountains in the Alpujarra region of the province of Granada, boasts residents of nearly 70 nationalities and practitioners of various spiritual and healing traditions.[3] With so much diversity tucked between terraced almond, olive, and orange groves, Órgiva has been called "the little Manhattan of Andalucía" (Sánchez Alonso 2015a).[4] How does a small town in rural Spain come to be known as a literal global village distinguished by its harmonious cohabitation (*convivencia*)? How do narratives about this town represent its multicultural, multi-ethnic, and multi-confessional fabric, and what gets erased from such representations? How do its residents conceive of the town's diversity and enact tolerance? What can the narratives about the town—both outside representations of it and residents' stories about their lived experience—tell us about the workings of tolerance? Through an analysis of written, visual, and oral narratives about the Alpujarra and specifically the town of Órgiva, this interdisciplinary inquiry responds to these questions and considers their broader implications in an increasingly globalized, yet conflict-ridden world.

With the intensification of intercultural contact that we know as globalization, which produces increased commonalities and increased inequalities, comes an intensification of the need or desire to assert specific identities. The Mediterranean region in particular is one of the hotbeds of such issues. As Natalia Ribas-Mateos, a specialist in North–South Mediterranean migration explains, the Mediterranean is "one of the most active friction-planes when considering North-South imbalances in the globalized world" (2001, 22). For this reason, various scholars have turned their attention to literary and cultural aspects of migration from North Africa to Spain.[5] Spain, and in particular the region of Andalucía, is home to many European converts to Islam, which adds another layer of complexity to this interfaith and intercultural confluence.[6] In articles and book-length studies, various anthropologists have examined the workings of tolerance, or the lack thereof, in the context of migrants, converts, and/or Catholic nationals in Andalucía.[7] Much of the work on Muslim converts and immigrants has focused on the city of Granada, but the traditional place of refuge of Granada, the Alpujarra, had yet to be studied in this light.[8] Due to Órgiva's position as the largest municipality in the Alpujarra region and a gateway to its more remote villages, it has long been known as "the capital of the Alpujarra." In keeping with this, Órgiva is the epicenter for late 20th- and early 21st-century changes that are also seen, though to a lesser extent, in nearby areas of the Alpujarra.

Given the Alpujarra region's particular and evolving role in Spanish cultural history, there are layers of narratives about the Alpujarra and Órgiva. Historically, the Alpujarra has been the site of the entrance and exit of various empires, an intercultural contact portrayed particularly in works of historical fiction about the Moorish Other. Fittingly, the Alpujarra has also been frequently represented in travel narratives and ethnographies that spring from other types of cultural contact. More recently, Órgiva itself has been represented via memoirs, a collaborative collection of residents' testimonials, and various television shows. Taking Órgiva as a case study, this book has two goals: (1) to situate the latest written and televisual narratives about Órgiva against the backdrop of earlier narratives and analyze the portraits of Órgiva that they offer, and (2) to examine, in light of the silences in these recent narratives, the workings and texture of coexistence in the town—including its tensions and conflicting stories—by means of the narratives that those who live in the town tell about it. I use the residents' expressions of their lived experience to consider how those with local roots integrate the transformation of their town, how the more recent arrivals portray their presence in the town, and how both groups negotiate difference and produce conceptions of coexistence. This allows me to analyze how representations of the town and everyday lived experience across difference formulate tolerance, in particular as it pertains to the various forms of migration that are part of the life of this Andalusian town. These narratives about coexistence have implications on the level of the autonomous community of Andalucía, the Spanish nation, and beyond.

The manifold narratives about Órgiva sometimes run counter to each other, but these ambivalences and contradictions reveal how tolerance is worked out and how more sustainable tolerance can be achieved. A deeper form of tolerance that is more likely to endure is based on both the recognition of mutual worthiness as human beings and of each side's compromises, interests, and types of power. The various communities that live in Órgiva are engaged in a process of assessing the gains and losses of different ways of coexisting. Although written and especially televisual narratives about the town use terms such as "tolerance" and "multiculturalism" to mask tensions and power differentials, by recognizing that toleration is an ongoing negotiation of what will and will not be accepted—of what is established as *halal* versus *haram* to use Islamic terminology—we can identify the points of contact that create robust, respect-based tolerance.

FIGURE 2: A map indicating the location of Órgiva within Spain (with the coast of Morocco and Algeria below).

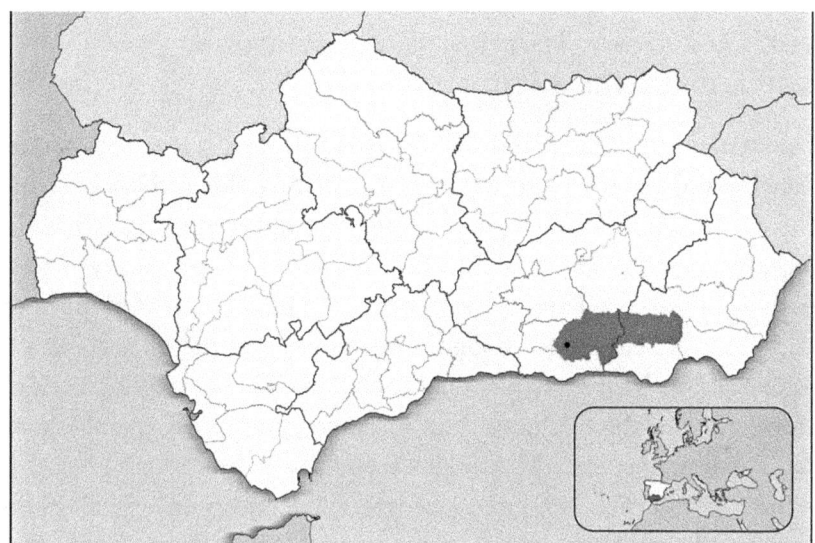

FIGURE 3: A map indicating the location of Órgiva within the Alpujarra (darker in the larger map) and Andalucía.

FIGURE 4: The sign on one of the main roads into town, announcing "Órgiva, Pura Alpujarra [Pure Alpujarra]."

THE BACK STORY: AL-ANDALUS, *CONVIVENCIA*, AND ANDALUSIAN NATIONALISM

Understanding Órgiva and the Alpujarra in the present requires reviewing the region's lingering past: al-Andalus, the Reconquista, and the consolidation of the Spanish state through measures such as the expulsion of the *moriscos* (Muslim converts to Christianity) in the early 17th century. This historical backdrop is still present in the body of written narratives (travelogues, memoirs, and the like) about the Alpujarra, at least in works published through the 1950s, in television episodes about Órgiva, and in some community members' attachment to the area. Al-Andalus refers to the intersection between a time period (711–1492) and a geographic territory (nearly all of the Iberian Peninsula), and thus to medieval Muslim-ruled Iberia. This period of Muslim rule was initiated by the conquests of the Umayyad Caliphate and continued under a variety of often rival dynasties and emirates, some headed by Arabs and some by Amazigh (Berber) leaders. Under Umayyad rule, mostly Imazighen (plural of Amazigh/Berbers) but also some Arabs slowly settled the Alpujarra. As early as the 11th century, the district of Órgiva was mentioned in a text by the geographer and historian al-'Udhri (Trillo San José 1990, 49). The Muslim Arabo-Amazigh conquerors brought agricultural advances to rural areas: Trillo San José (1994) indicates that records from the middle of the 10th century point to the Arabo-Amazigh impact on agriculture in the Alpujarra (175). They instituted terraced agriculture and a system of irrigation channels, both of which are still in use today. Meanwhile, the major cities of al-Andalus, most of them in what is today the region of Andalucía, were home to not only Muslims but Christians and Jews and flourished as centers of intellectual inquiry and artistic production.

Centuries after the political end of al-Andalus, with the Christian conquest of the entire peninsula, al-Andalus still functions as a popular symbol for both paradise lost and religious conflict, depending on whether it is viewed as a time of interfaith tolerance and cultivation of knowledge and the arts, or as a time of intolerance under either threatening Muslim power (Islamic Empire, Islam in Europe, etc.) or threatening Catholic consolidation of power (oppression and expulsion of Jews and Muslims, the Inquisition, etc.). A core element in the question of how to assess Muslim Iberia's cultural legacy is the ongoing debate regarding the place of al-Andalus in Spanish cultural history. One of the key figures in the early 20th-century manifestation of these debates was Américo Castro (1885–1972), a philologist and historian who hailed from Granada and, as a result of the Spanish Civil War (1936–39), carried out most of his professional life in exile in the Americas. Castro is famous for having developed the concept of *convivencia*, literally: "living together." Focusing his interpretation of medieval Iberia on the scholarly and artistic synergy between Christians, Jews, and Muslims that took place there, Castro proposed that these three faiths enjoyed a Muslim-led tolerance that he dubbed "*la convivencia.*" According to this interpretation, tolerance was one of several significant Muslim contributions to Spain's unique cultural history. The main opposing narrative of al-Andalus from Castro's time posited that the authentic Spanish identity was Gothic, Germanic, and Roman in origin—that is, purely European—and that the period of Muslim and Jewish presence was a detriment to the development of Spain that must be overcome.

Built upon Castro's narrative of harmonious coexistence in al-Andalus, the term *convivencia* has taken on a life of its own and is often used to refer to a utopian vision of interfaith harmony. The idea of the "Spain of the three religions" (anachronistic, since it was not yet "Spain") grew out of this and has become a catchphrase that is featured in a certain vein of Spanish historiography and in the promotion of tourism in Spain.[9] The question of how much tolerance, and of what sort, there actually was in al-Andalus has led to many a scholarly study. One conclusion of this research is that the systems of rule in place in al-Andalus (in which conquered areas were given considerable freedom in exchange for taxes paid by non-Muslim religious communities) neither prevented certain kinds of discrimination and occasional religious violence, nor are analogous to modern political regimes. For these reasons, calls to "reinstate" the harmonies of *convivencia* in the present are problematic. However, as Christian Fernández indicates, in both the pre-modern and modern periods, one can find practices that are motivated by "a desire to accommodate rather than eradicate diversity." Thus, while invocations of *convivencia* tend to ahistorically mythify interfaith harmony, they also reflect a persistent desire to find ways in which diversity and harmony can coexist. As contemporary nation-states grapple with tensions within their heterogeneous populations, liberals and progressives look to al-Andalus for inspiration.

The historical movements that are understood as the polar opposites of *la convivencia* are the Reconquista—the process of Christian kingdoms forming, conquering territories in the Peninsula, sometimes fighting amongst themselves, and eventually consolidating into a single kingdom, that was subsequently framed as a holy war of Spanish Catholics against Muslims—and, intertwined with it, the Inquisition.[10] Given the gains of different Christian kingdoms in Iberia, by 1252 al-Andalus was reduced to the Emirate of Granada, an emirate of the Nasrid dynasty that itself was successively reduced from roughly half of today's region of Andalucía and part of the region of Murcia down to about a third of today's Andalucía. Muslim rule in Iberia ended in 1492 with the fall of that final holdout, the Emirate of Granada. As the Reconquista reduced and then eliminated Muslim-ruled areas, more Jews and Muslims lived under Christian rule. Many converted to Christianity in the face of decrees expelling unconverted Jews (1492) and unconverted Muslims (the early 1500s). Eventually, even converted Muslims (*moriscos*) were ousted through the final expulsion decrees (1609–14).

But between the fall of Granada and the final expulsion, the Alpujarra had a prominent role in Spanish history. The Alpujarra region was the first site of exile for the last Muslim ruler of al-Andalus, Boabdil (Abu 'Abd Allah Muhammad XII), and the last site of Muslim uprisings against the Catholic Monarchs: the Rebellion of the Alpujarras (or *Morisco* Revolt) of 1499–1500 and that of 1568–71. During the Catholic Monarchs' battles to conquer the Emirate of Granada (1482–91), the Alpujarra was the only area that was not occupied militarily by Christian forces (Trillo San José 1990, 49). Until the 1500s, the Alpujarra was known for its terraced agriculture and its sericulture: the nobles of the time (regardless of religion) prized the region's silk. These characteristics no doubt made the Alpujarra a worthy consolation prize for the ousted Boabdil. At the time of the Catholic Monarchs' victory over the Emirate, as part of the Capitulations of Granada, Ferdinand and Isabel gave Boabdil as his fiefdom a territory in the Alpujarra, including the village of Órgiva. However, Boabdil only lived in the Alpujarra for a short time. In 1493, he sold his Alpujarran fiefdom back to the Catholic Monarchs and left for Fez.

The Capitulations of Granada also included stipulations protecting Muslims' religious freedom and the continuation of their customs. However, these stipulations were only upheld by the Catholic Monarchs until 1499. In that year, when the Christian authorities broke the treaty of surrender by carrying out forced conversions and public burnings of Arabic manuscripts, Muslims in the Alpujarra rebelled against the Spanish authorities in what is known as the First Rebellion of the Alpujarra. The Castilians quashed the rebellion and bequeathed Órgiva to a Spanish military officer nicknamed "El Gran Capitán," Gonzalo Fernández de Córdoba (1453–1515), for his role in that victory (Trillo San José 1990, 49). The Castilians then gave the Muslims the choice of baptism or exile. Most accepted baptism, although an indeterminate number continued to live in Iberia as crypto-Muslims. That uprising was followed by the Second Rebellion of the Alpujarra and increasing socioeconomic tensions that led in 1609 to the first decree mandating the expulsion of the *moriscos*.

The momentum of the Reconquista and the Crusades created Spain's first footholds in North Africa (Melilla and Ceuta) and when Spain lost most of its New World colonies in the early 19th century, its attention then turned to colonization projects in North and West Africa. Spain's colonial project in North Africa was justified via a concept related to *convivencia*. In a contradictory stance, during the first half of the 20th century, Spanish military and colonial authorities espoused the idea of a Spanish-Moroccan *hermandad* (brotherhood) rooted in al-Andalus as a way to rationalize Spanish presence in the Maghreb. Although the official nationalist ideology of the Franco dictatorship

(1939–75) was based on a rhetoric that explicitly invoked the spirit of the Reconquista and its mission to restore the unity of Spain through Catholicism, the Franco regime also embraced a vein of Spanish historical revisionism that, starting in the 1930s and continuing for several decades, posited that Iberia had been the site of a different type of Islam, one that reflected Hispanic influence. Hence, anachronistic and appropriative terms such as "Muslim Spain," "Spanish Islam," and "Hispano-Arab" became common in academic circles, the media, and popular discourses.[11] The rhetoric of Hispano-Arab *hermandad* was used to support a colonial campaign that resulted in Spain's occupation of the Western Sahara (1884–1976), which has been claimed by Morocco, and Spain's protectorate in two regions of Morocco (1912–56): the northern Rif and the southern strip adjacent to the Western Sahara. Spanish colonization in North Africa included the cultural elements (the colony as the object of academic study and artistic representation) typical of French and British colonial ventures, but with the twist of the *hermandad* rhetoric that positioned Morocco and the Western Sahara as the "little brother" receiving Spanish tutelage.

Alongside the development of Spain's colonial relationship with North Africa, in the late 19th century, Andalusian nationalism (*andalucismo*) arose, demonstrating an equally complex relationship with al-Andalus. The culmination of *andalucismo* during the late 20th-century transition to democracy then led to the return of the open practice of Islam in Andalucía and the Alpujarra. In the 19th century, the Alpujarra experienced some industrialization through the establishment of lead, silver, and fluorite mines that remained active through most of the 20th century.[12] Together with this industry that was dependent on new technologies, the period also saw the burgeoning of new conceptions of political and community identity in the form of regional nationalisms. Spain has a long tradition of strong cultural and/or linguistic regions, many of which espouse forms of nationalism known as *nacionalismos periféricos* (peripheral or non-central nationalisms). Toward the end of the 19th century, many of these regions, among them Andalucía, witnessed Romanticism-inspired regionalist movements that promoted political autonomy on the basis of cultural difference from the other regions of the peninsula. While the *andalucista* (Andalusianist) movement saw different, mostly cultural manifestations during the following decades, it burgeoned after the Franco dictatorship (1939–75).

Spain underwent a deep and rapid cultural transformation in the post-dictatorship period. The Spanish transition to democracy that began with Franco's death in 1975 included the establishment of a new political system and constitution (1978) as well as the outpouring of new and formerly suppressed artistic, social, and ideological movements. This surge of countercultural movements, known as La Movida (the Scene), which began in Madrid in 1980 and then manifested in other parts of Spain, responded to the end of years of oppression and the start of post-dictatorship economic growth with a spirit of freedom of expression that transgressed what had up until recently been taboo. As such, it entailed a reconfiguration of Spanish identity and cultural expression. This movement included, particularly in Andalucía, interest in the practice of Islam, a religious and lifestyle choice that was ideologically intertwined with the more strictly political side of the Spanish transition.

Alongside La Movida, in the post-dictatorship period the various regionalist and nationalist movements, which had been suppressed by the Franco regime, also experienced a resurgence. With the transition to democracy and the preparation of the 1978 constitution, which reorganized the country politically on the basis of Autonomous Communities, in 1976 the *Partido Socialista Andaluz* (Andalusian Socialist Party), later the *Partido Andalucista*, was established with the aim of demanding autonomy for Andalucía. It achieved this goal in 1981. From the perspective of supporters of regional nationalisms, Castilian centralism is a colonizing force. Among the regional nationalisms, that of Andalucía is positioned as both subordinated to centralist Spain and linked to al-Andalus. As a historically economically depressed region, Andalucía has sent laborers to other regions of Spain, where they often experienced the oppression of class and cultural hierarchies. This experience intensified Andalusian awareness of cultural differences from other Spaniards. Although within Europe

Spain's "Europeanness" is questioned, within a national framework, that element of "Africanness" (backwardness, barbarity, etc.) attributed to Spain is ascribed specifically to Andalucía. Hence the Spanish saying that defends against the French adage "Africa begins at the Pyrenees": *Andalucía es África* ("Andalucía is Africa").

With the post-dictatorship period's rise in cultural and political movements centered on regional nationalisms, the invocation of al-Andalus as part of the *andalucismo* movement also intensified. *Andalucismo* includes highlighting and celebrating the characteristics of Andalusian culture that are understood to be a part of its Andalusi heritage. The prevailing ethno-nationalist view of Spanish history, and within it Spanish demography, is that all Jews and Muslims were expelled and the areas they had inhabited were repopulated through a policy of bringing in Christians from elsewhere in the peninsula and distributing the Muslims' confiscated property among them. A contestatory account posits that sizable Muslim and Jewish populations assimilated enough to escape the notice of the Inquisition and stayed in Iberia.[13] According to some of these narratives, the remaining Muslims and Jews were relegated to working the lands of the Christian knights who had colonized the peninsula's last Muslim kingdoms. Thus, *andalucismo* has included an identification with those most famously disenfranchised by powerful Castilians: the Moors.

As an economically depressed region that has been viewed from the outside as an extension of North Africa, the ideologues of *andalucismo* as well as certain veins of popular sentiment have embraced a *moro* (Moorish) connection. Whether by tracing a Moorish genealogy, using the Moor as a figure for the disenfranchised, or only carrying out a class analysis, key *andalucista* writers have pointed to Castilians and the central Spanish government as colonizers of Andalucía. These discourses, together with the partially overlapping geographic location, place names, and famous monuments, forge a strong link between Andalucía and al-Andalus that serves to heighten the perceived connection between the contemporary Spanish region and the former Muslim political and cultural entity. *Andalucistas* have often embraced the cultural achievements and splendor of al-Andalus in order to enjoy the compensatory fantasy of a glorious and powerful past, as well as a fighting spirit.¹⁴ For instance, in 1918, Blas Infante (1885–1936), a musicologist and writer who is seen as the father of Andalusian nationalism, chose the green and white colors of the Andalusian flag because green was the color of the Umayyads and white that of the Almohads, the caliphates that represent periods of grandeur and power in that region.¹⁵

Through at least the 1980s, there was a notably Islamist vein in Andalusian nationalism, as witnessed by the political party *Liberación Andaluza* (Andalusian Liberation), established in the mid-1980s and linked to *La Yama'a Islámica de Al-Andalus* (The al-Andalus Islamic Group), a convert cultural organization that seeks to promote Islam as integral to Andalusian cultural heritage (Stalleart 1999).¹⁶ This link between *andalucismo* and Islam as a religious practice (in contrast with the broader focus on Islamicate civilizations as accomplished) is intertwined with the cultural forces that led to the rise of Spanish converts to Islam in the post-Franco period.¹⁷ Christiane Stalleart indicates that the "neoconversos," (in reference to, and contrast with, the earlier converts in medieval Iberia) while not forming a uniform group, arose as a phenomenon of the first years after the dictatorship, as part of the ideological opening of the newly democratic Spain (Stalleart 1999, 189).

Given the groundwork laid by *andalucismo*, during the intense social and economic changes of the transition to democracy, the early convert movement was particularly strong in Andalucía. Charles Hirschkind, in his work on converts to Islam in the city of Granada, states that many *andalucista* activists themselves converted to Islam and that "today Andalusia has the most rapidly growing community of converts in all of Europe" (Hirschkind 2014, 234). As Beebe Bahrami explains, those southern Spanish converts were "almost all middle-class intellectuals who, dissatisfied with Catholicism and secular ideologies, and alienated by Spain's sudden rapid economic and political changes, sought a new yet not entirely foreign ideology to offer meaning to their lives" (Bahrami 1998, 126). The convert community is particularly active in the city of Granada (Hirschkind 2014, 234) and that community has links to the Alpujarra. Rosón Lorente explains that the development of the Muslim convert community in Granada, which took officially recognized form in the mid-1980s, ran parallel to, and was intertwined with, the development of hippie communes in the Granadan Alpujarra (335).[18] Specifically, a number of hippies (or "alternatives," as some of them prefer to be named) from the Alpujarra converted to Islam and moved to Granada to join the convert community there (336–38). Based on what converts in Órgiva told me, some of these hippie converts to Islam later returned to the Alpujarra. As noted by Bahrami (1998, 127) and others, the familiarity of Spaniards and particularly Andalusians with Islam, albeit filtered through Orientalist and political *andalucista* lenses, has made them more likely, when searching for a meaningful ideology, to choose Islam.[19]

HISTORICAL MEMORY AND CONTEMPORARY CONFLICTS: NARRATIVES ABOUT AL-ANDALUS IN IMMIGRATION AND CULTURAL POLITICS

The narratives about medieval and early modern Spain that constitute Spanish historical memory contribute directly to current sociopolitical tensions surrounding immigration, the practice of Islam, and nationalism. Another aspect of Spain's transition to democracy was the negotiation of its political and cultural relationship with Europe, and Spain's migration history has a central role in this relationship. In 1982, amid heated debate within Spain, the country joined the North Atlantic Treaty Organization (NATO) decades after its founding. Similarly, Spain was a relative latecomer to European integration. It was not part of "the inner six" who established the European Communities in 1951, nor "the outer seven" who formed the European Free Trade Association. Rather, it joined the European Communities (which later developed into the European Union) in 1986.

Amid the other transformations witnessed in late 20th-century Spain, within the framework of human mobility, the country rapidly changed from being a sending country to being a receiving country, and Andalucía in particular shifted from being a region of out-migration and emigration to one of immigration. Until the late 1970s, Spaniards, and especially those from rural areas, were migrants. As part of the late 19th-century European emigration to the Americas, many Spaniards left for Hispano-America. Later, in the 1950s, an intranational migration wave saw many leave impoverished rural areas for work in large cities. When the Franco government legalized extranational emigration in 1959, the trend of migrants leaving Andalucía and other depressed regions to work elsewhere in Europe continued until the early 1970s. Experiences as labor migrants elsewhere in Europe often served to heighten awareness of civilizational hierarchies within Western Europe itself. But the direction of movement switched as a result of Spain's economic boom ("The Spanish Miracle" of 1959–74) and entry into what would become the European Union.

In the 1980s, a rise in North African immigration to Spain added to the questioning of Spain's relationship to Europe and the legacy of al-Andalus. Before 1985, Moroccans did not need visas to enter Spain, and many young Moroccan men went to Spain temporarily to work in agriculture and industry. Paradoxically, Spain's integration into the European Union led to a dramatic rise in North African immigration to the country. The European Schengen Convention, a 1990 supplement to the earlier Schengen Agreement, dissolved internal European borders, thereby making entry through Spain even more desirable for migrants who could then use the country as a stepping stone to other points in Europe. With time, many new migrants decided to stay in Spain, and in the 1990s, the number of Moroccan migrants in Spain began to rise significantly. For this reason, until 2002, Moroccans were the largest immigrant group in Spain. Since then, in yearly statistics they have typically been the second largest group, closely following Romanians or Ecuadoreans, and occasionally still are the largest group (*España en cifras*).[20] These changes led the European Union to pressure Spain to intensify its policing of borders, a material expression of the broader pressure for Spain to "police" its cultural borders in terms of building and maintaining a European conception of national identity.

In *The Return of the Moor*, Daniela Flesler explains the particular cultural location of North African migrants in Spain as follows: "the current rejection of Moroccan immigrants is related to the fact that they are the one group most directly implicated in the question of Spanish identity in relationship to Africa" (3). On the one hand, as Flesler notes, the rejection of Maghrebi immigrants is a manifestation of what scholars such as Étienne Balibar, Martin Barker, Paul Gilroy (1990), and Pierre-André Taguieff have defined as cultural racism, new racism, or differentialist racism, terms used to name prejudices and discrimination that are based on cultural rather than biological differences. Although biological racism is generally rejected today in Western Europe, expressions of cultural racism point to some cultures being superior to others and certain cultures being intrinsically incompatible. Muslim immigrants in particular are seen as holding values and following traditions that are understood as being incompatible with democracy, modernity, and secularism. On the other hand, the rejection of these immigrants also results from their perceived connection to Spain's past: "in the Spanish collective imaginary," North African immigrants "become the embodiment of everything there is to fear from their history, the ghosts of a past that has not stopped haunting them, the return of the repressed" (Flesler 80). As Flesler skillfully argues, this haunting consists of both the perception of Maghrebi immigration as a return of the invaders of old as well as anxieties regarding how to establish clear boundaries with an Other that is so similar to the Self (195–96). Since at least the 1990s, right-wing Spanish populists have exploited and exacerbated this troubled relationship with Maghrebis by fomenting fears of a Muslim reconquest of Spain, primarily in the form of Maghrebi immigrants. With regard to Andalucía in particular, Mikaela Rogozen-Soltar (2017), in her study on relations between European converts and Maghrebi migrants in the city of Granada, points out that Andalusians' marginality within Spain and Europe makes religious affiliation and immigration more sensitive topics, as there is a heightened desire to differentiate from those viewed as marginal (13).

In comparison with France, whose *foulard* affair has become known internationally, in Spain there have only been a limited number of issues regarding Muslims of immigrant origin being prohibited from wearing a hijab or headscarf to school. However, there have been violent manifestations of anti-immigrant sentiment, namely, in February 2002 in the town of El Ejido, a 75-minute drive from Órgiva, and in other towns in surrounding southwestern Almería. Western Almería province is known for its greenhouses made of plastic sheeting, where much of Spain's fruits and vegetables are grown. This agricultural work is largely carried out by migrants, most of whom are Moroccan.[21] After two murders were committed by Maghrebi migrants within a few days, another fatal incident led to an aggressive outpouring. The protests reacting to this third incident, in which a Moroccan with mental health issues killed a young Spanish woman in El Ejido, developed into 24 hours of violent xenophobic unrest that included the vandalism of a mosque and immigrant businesses and the burning of cars. Residents of Spanish origin also attacked Maghrebi immigrants with rocks, bats, and metal bars. Riot police had to come in to quell the situation and there were 22 wounded—yet no out-of-control protesters were arrested (Constenla and Torregrosa).

A bit further from Órgiva, about a 3-hour drive away in Córdoba, there is an ongoing ideological conflict centered on Christian/Muslim use of a historical monument that conservative discourse has connected to North African immigrants. Since the early 2000s, Muslims have been petitioning Roman Catholic authorities to allow them to pray in the Cathedral of Córdoba, a former mosque still known popularly as *la mezquita de Córdoba* (the mosque of Córdoba). In 2010, a fight broke out when a group of Austrian Muslim tourists began to pray in the cathedral and guards tried to stop them. When the Austrian Muslims were acquitted of injuring the guards, conservative commentators accused the Spanish justice system of bias. The Spanish clergy and the Vatican have continued to deny requests to allow Muslim prayer, which primarily come from Spanish converts to Islam. Conservatives frame this issue within the debates regarding immigration policy and concerns about terror threats which rose after the 2004 Madrid train bombings. Consequently, Muslim North African immigrants have dissociated themselves from the efforts to allow Muslim prayer, fearing negative repercussions.[22]

Closer to Órgiva, less than an hour's drive away in the city of Granada, there is a similar ongoing tension regarding *El Día de la Toma*, the annual celebration of the Catholic Monarchs' capture of Granada and defeat of Muslim rule in Iberia. This event commemorates the public ceremony of January 2, 1492 (known as *La Toma de Granada*), in which Boabdil handed over a set of keys to King Ferdinand and Queen Isabella. The commemoration, in keeping with the Catholic Monarchs' rule, blends Catholicism and military pomp and circumstance. First, a procession of officials carries the standard of the Catholic Monarchs from the city hall to the royal chapel (*la Capilla Real*) that is part of Granada's cathedral. This is followed by a Mass in the cathedral, the offering of flowers at the tombs of the Catholic Monarchs, the continuation of the military parade carrying the flag of the Catholic Monarchs, and the grand finale of *la tremolación*, the waving of the military flag from the city hall's balcony.

While some Granadans see this flag waving accompanied by a military band playing the national anthem as an expression of local tradition and Spanish pride, others see this homage to Ferdinand and Isabella as a distasteful glorification of the genocide of Muslims and Jews that the monarchs undertook soon after capturing Granada, one that threatens pluralism. As a result, as Rogozen-Soltar explains, in 1995 "a group of artists, professors, and generally elite intellectuals of Granada formed the 'January 2nd Collective,'" and published a statement proposing that the *Día de la Toma* be replaced by a celebration of tolerance. Although the movement gained support, it was rejected by local and national government officials (Rogozen-Soltar 2007, 877–78). Since then Granada Abierta, a coalition of various associations that oppose the celebration, has continued to argue that the event is offensive and supports xenophobic, ethno-nationalist agendas. While the coalition has moved forward with alternate celebrations of multiculturalism and egalitarian pluralism (www.granada-abierta.org/), no political party has dared to suggest ending the celebration of the *Día de la Toma* and heightened security is needed at the event due to the presence of protesters and counter-protesters.

Rogozen-Soltar explains the connection between conceptions of European identity and this struggle over historical memory:

> a contingent of the city finds the racist undertones and the implicitly Christian and triumphalist religious message of the *Día de la Toma* not only offensive, but also embarrassing and harmful to Andalusia's entrance into an enlightened, European sphere of secular modernity. This attitude is clear in the official publications and website of the Collective, including the main document to which adherents sign [. . .] The document goes on to state that "we understand that the [events of the festival] do not contribute to the consolidation of sentiments of reconciliation to which the city should be committed in its aspiration for progress" (Collective website). Moreover, the movement's documents deploy the specter of backward, unmodern, presecular Spain, constructing members of the anti-festival collective as secular, modern, rational subjects of the enlightenment, as opposed to President Aznar, the local Andalusian government, and supporters of the festival" (Rogozen-Soltar 2007, 879–80).

For those against the celebration, what is at stake is not only putting an end to a display of military power against Muslims and Jews, but the desire to display their modernity—expressed in the form of secularism and tolerance, and thus their Europeanness.[23]

Another contentious issue in the city of Granada is centered more specifically on the presence of Islam as a religion currently practiced by residents. In 2003, after a 20-year struggle, a new mosque opened in Granada in the historic Albaicín neighborhood overlooking the Alhambra. Named the "Great Mosque of Granada," the opposition to its construction came from Spanish Catholic residents of the Albaicín and Catholic authorities, who expressed concerns regarding whether the mosque's minaret would be higher than the bell tower of a nearby historic church, whether there would be windows facing a neighboring convent, and how the facility would affect tourism in the area

(Rogozen Soltar 2017, 163–65 and 168). Some supporters presented the mosque project, led by the convert community, as an opportunity for Spain and Granada to showcase its tolerance (Rogozen Soltar 2017, 168–69). However, now that the mosque is open, it contributes to tensions between European converts to Islam and migrant Muslims (Rogozen Soltar 2017, 179).

The increasing reevaluation of local customs on the part of progressive Spaniards who wish to foment a more egalitarian culture and construct a tolerant, secular, European identity (as witnessed by the *Día de la Toma* and Great Mosque of Granada controversies), together with the rise in numbers of Muslim converts and North African migrants, has sparked a linguistic reevaluation. The term *moro*, or Moor, is emerging as another controversial remnant of al-Andalus and the Reconquista. Etymologically, *moro* comes from the Latin term *maurus*, meaning Mauritanian, which, in turn, comes from the Greek μαῦρος *(maûros)*, meaning "dark" (*Diccionario de la lengua española*). Although in certain contexts *moro* is used to refer to a dark color, primarily it is used to refer to people from North Africa, in reference to their darker skin and hair, and by extension to Muslims. In that sense, the term doesn't distinguish between ethnicities (Amazigh vs. Arab), but rather is vaguely centered on geographic, religious, and cultural origins—all figuratively associated with skin and/or hair color. In Ross Brann's essay on the cultural history of the term "Moor," he demonstrates that the term has been "unstable" (317) since the medieval period. First used in the Iberian context in the 8th century to identify Imazighen, by the 12th century, there are examples of Christian texts in which the term is used to refer to all Muslims (Brann, 311).

Today the term *moro* is used for people from the Maghreb or anywhere in the Arab world, and even *all* Muslims, carrying with it all the baggage from medieval and early modern usage. The register of the term is informal; it is not one that would be used in an academic or official setting, but rather in conversational contexts and in certain types of media. When used to refer to immigrants from the Maghreb, as Flesler indicates, the term serves to establish an identification between the contemporary migrants and those who invaded, Arabized, and Islamized Iberia; in so doing, it transfers to the immigrants the negative affect associated with those seen as the enemy of Catholic Spain and the immigrants "become conceptually collapsed into this category of the imaginary and threatening 'Moor'" (Flesler, 4). Moreover, these immigrants symbolize not only the historical Moor and the Moor of the Spanish national imaginary, but they also "embody the non-European, African, and oriental aspects of Spanish national identity," and in that sense they are the carriers of the problematic aspects of Spanish identity and, too close for comfort, they are rejected (Flesler, 9).

The debate that is beginning to emerge regards whether or not the term is necessarily pejorative and offensive. There are certainly established uses of the term (e.g., to refer to a jealous, domineering man, regardless of origin) and colloquial expressions including the term that point to its derogatory nature. But it was not until 2014 that the term *moro* was officially questioned and hence became a topic on the national level. That year, Hilal Tarkou, a lawyer who had moved from Morocco to Catalonia decades before, made an official request to the director of the *Real Academia Española* (the national institution that sets the norms of the Spanish language) that the Academy add to its dictionary entry for *moro* the term's use as a discriminatory and racist appellation. The request was not granted and at least one prominent Spaniard, the author Arturo Pérez-Reverte (b. 1951), who is himself a member of the *Real Academia Española*, responded quite dismissively to the request, describing it as "cheap demagoguery."

Pérez-Reverte, a novelist and former foreign correspondent, argues that the fact that the term is sometimes used pejoratively should not be detrimental to "those who use it in its straightforward [recto] sense and need it to express themselves with efficacy [con eficacia]." Pérez-Reverte contends that *moro* is of the same ilk as "Black" as a reference to race and thus censuring someone for using *moro* would be as absurd as censuring someone "for calling Black someone who is of the Black race [(por) decir negro a quien es de raza negra]." Thus, he completely misses the fact that these categories based on physical traits are social constructs with negative social, political, and economic consequences. Additionally, even within today's commonly accepted logic of racial categories organized according to perceived traits, there is no "North African" or "Muslim" race and this understanding of race harkens back to medieval and early modern Iberian conceptualizations of difference that are equally entrenched in biological essentialism. Using the deep cultural history of the term *moro* in Spain as a justification (rather than seeing it as an impediment), Pérez-Reverte insists that, regardless of what the Academy decrees, he will continue to use the term *moro*.[24]

Pérez-Reverte's reaction, while presented as a commonsense attitude, is connected to the historical roots of the term in Spain. Brann explains that

> Because of its potent connotations, *Moor* arguably served as the principal linguistic vehicle for suppressing the indigenous nature of the Andalusi Muslim cultural heritage in Iberia and rendering Andalusi Muslims as others in a projected Christian Iberia. It enabled Christians in thirteenth century Castile to dismiss as "foreign" the substantially mixed Andalusi Muslim population to their south, as well as Castile's own Mudejars, and to disregard the extent of social and cultural ties among all Andalusis, including Muslims from Africa (Brann 313).

Pérez-Reverte and those who share his stance of insisting on continuing to use the term *moro* are seeking, through a highly imprecise term, to define that which is and is not "Spanish," understood as ethnically European and Catholic, whether in practice or as a cultural background. In the process, they exclude Arab and North African immigrants and their descendants, as well as those of other faiths, from a sense of belonging and from a sense of legitimacy as Spaniards.

Although the nascent debates regarding the term *moro* have not yet made it to the Alpujarra, confusion regarding the parameters of the term—i.e., to whom it applies—certainly has. After the Spanish expulsion decrees of the 1600s, outside of the Alpujarra, Spanish and European lore connected the isolated region to crypto-Muslims who stayed in Iberia. In this way, the cultural location of the Alpujarra vis-à-vis Andalucía and all points beyond is analogous to that of Andalucía vis-à-vis Spain and beyond, and Spain vis-à-vis Europe. Thus, the Alpujarra in particular has a role in the contested narratives regarding Spanish national identity and the shifting definitions of what counts as European. Through at least the mid-20th century, Spain was seen from the outside as part of the Southern Mediterranean or even Africa. But nationally that identity as somehow *morisco* and backward was attributed to Andalucía and especially the Alpujarra.

In the 19th century, the Alpujarra's supposed primitiveness and Moorishness attracted tourists from Spain and other European countries who sought a quaint, or even exotic, bucolic experience. Today Alpujarran villages such as Pampaneira, Bubión, and Capileira have become picturesque tourist destinations. Órgiva, the largest town in the Alpujarra, serves as the service and commercial hub for visitors to the western Alpujarra and also as the focal point for those seeking a variety of alternative lifestyles. Among the various spiritual traditions active in Órgiva, the town is home to the largest Sufi community in Spain, made up of some 35 families of European converts to Islam, most of whom are affiliated with the Naqshbandi order, a major Sunni Sufi group.[25] These modern-day converts were drawn to the area in part due to the lasting image of medieval Muslim Iberia as a space of religious tolerance and *convivencia*. There are also other Muslims in the town: more recently, a small Maghrebi migrant population has settled in Órgiva. While their numbers are small, they are highly significant due to the intensity of the Maghrebi immigration issue throughout Andalucía and Spain, as well as the tensions surrounding Muslim immigrants in general in Europe as a whole.

These tensions arise from regional, national, religious, and civilizational identities. For instance, some of Órgiva's residents of local origin still take pride in the region's role in the Reconquista's last stages, which also saw the rise of the Spanish Inquisition (established in 1478). Those who were trying to escape judgment by the

Inquisition attempted to prove that they were genuinely converted *moriscos* (rather than crypto-Muslims) by drinking wine and eating pork. Similarly, after the 17th-century expulsion edicts, *moriscos* used pork and wine to demonstrate that they were Old Christians and avoid expulsion from Spain.[26] Thus, enjoying wine and pork became a way to ostentatiously demonstrate that one was an Old Christian and eventually became intrinsic to Spanish foodways and social life.

Indeed, the Alpujarra is one of the centers of the iconic dry-cured ham produced in Spain, specifically the type known as *jamón serrano* (from the *sierra* or mountains).[27] These ham legs, which can be seen hanging from the rafters in restaurants and bars all over Spain, are cured and dried in the Alpujarra because of its unique climatological conditions. Although technological advances in climate control have made it possible to cure the ham elsewhere, Alpujarran *jamón* establishments still pride themselves in curing the ham in the traditional manner. Now, though, in contrast with other areas of the Alpujarra, Órgiva is becoming more well-known for halal foods than for *jamón*. In another part of Andalucía, an enterprising Tunisian has actually created "halal *jamón*": lamb or beef cured in the same process as the famous Spanish *jamón*.[28] But, as put forth here, so far Órgiva is more about maintaining separate yet linked spheres, than about creating a fusion (or simulacrum?) that allows all groups to follow the same gastronomic pursuits.

While other Andalusian cities and towns are known for tensions between local inhabitants and North African migrants or Muslims in general, Órgiva has gained notoriety as a place of harmonious convergence. There are certain factors that make Órgiva different from the places in Andalucía and elsewhere in Spain where anti-migrant or anti-Muslim sentiment has been expressed violently; however, what interests me most is how this difference and Órgiva's relative harmony are constructed and questioned in narratives about the town. In contrast with the city of Granada, in Órgiva the lack of any major heritage site (such as the Alhambra or the Albaicín) means that Maghrebian immigrants are not part of the performance of exoticism that takes

FIGURE 5: A detail of the entrance to the town church; the sign states that it was built upon a former mosque.

place in the Granada tourism sites. The main vestiges of the past in Órgiva's built environment are the church and a chapel (previously a mosque and a Muslim monastery, respectively), a modest palace, and the ruins of a Muslim fortress.[29] Tourism in Órgiva either caters to Spaniards and foreigners looking for easy access to nature and charming villages, or Muslim tourists interested in the historical and contemporary ties of the town to Islam—including access to a delicious halal meal.[30]

Additionally, as a rural town Órgiva doesn't offer the same number of job prospects as a large city. This means that, on the one hand, the *orgiveños* (the demonym for Órgiva) seeking jobs gravitate to big urban centers and aren't likely to perceive that immigrants are competing with them for the same jobs, while, on the other hand, the economic migrants in Órgiva have sought out the town because of the lifestyle—not the job opportunities—that it offers.[31] In one way or another, Órgiva's residents are there by choice: whether they chose to stay there or to seek it out. For Maghrebi migrants and converts, Órgiva is a refuge from the tensions surrounding the celebration of *El Día de la Toma* and the new Grand Mosque of Granada. For migrants, it is also a refuge from the sometimes violent demonstration of anti-immigrant sentiment in other areas of Spain. For both incomers from large European cities and *orgiveños*, it is an alternative to industrialized, urban life. These circumstances lead to various questions: how is the town's diversity portrayed for international, national, and regional audiences? What do members of its different communities say about the town and each other? How do they narrate the way the inhabitants coexist? How do the dynamics of Órgiva's new *convivencia* provide insight into interfaith and intercultural contact in other parts of the world? Now that Spain has established itself as (politically) European, what it means to be Spanish and European is being redefined by immigrants and converts to Islam. This larger dynamic can be seen on the micro-level in Órgiva's negotiation of erstwhile Moorish, Spanish, Muslim, and European identities.

THE METHODS BEHIND THIS NARRATIVE

With the unique perspective of my insider/outsider status, witnessing Órgiva's transformation from a remote, monolingual village steeped in Catholicism and local traditions to an international, multi-faith town that hosts many alternative lifestyles, made me wonder how this shift had come about, how this convergence of cultures had not produced the violent conflict seen nearby, and how certain groups within this human potpourri viewed each other and narrated their experience of cohabitation. No doubt inspired by my grandfather's tales about Andalucía and my mother's obsession with Washington Irving's *Tales of the Alhambra* (which she read in Spanish translation in Cuba), before stepping foot in Spain I had started studying Arabic and the Islamicate world in college. Like the legacy of al-Andalus, would Órgiva have lessons to offer regarding tolerance? This led me to start taking notes on my incidental participant observation and carry out background reading, and to do targeted field research in Órgiva during the summers of 2019 and 2021.

My methodology can best be described as a combination of literary analysis, television studies, critical discourse analysis (the study of spoken and written discourse centered on examining the relationship between societal power relations and language use) and, to borrow from Shalini Puri and Debra Castillo, humanities-based fieldwork. As explained by Puri and Castillo (2), this type of fieldwork is ethnographic in many of its methods, but not meant to necessarily produce an example of the genre of writing known as ethnography (9–10). My qualitative, humanistic fieldwork consisted of participant observation, interviews, and the collection of oral narratives, followed by the interpretation of statements made and behaviors observed. To carry out this work, I drew not only on my experience in literary and cultural studies, but also on graduate coursework in ethnic studies, rhetoric, and oral narrative that included the critical assessment of ethnography. My approach rests on the understanding of stories not as direct records of reality or sources of truth, but as a means for social actors to express their lived experience and negotiate its meaning. As Marita Eastmond observes: "In the dynamic interplay between experience and expression, experience gives rise and form to narratives, but it is also organized and given meaning in the telling" (249). Each story is a construction of past experience conditioned by the circumstances in which it is produced and researchers must interpret these mediated expressions of experience, identifying organizing themes and metaphors. As Eastmond notes, individual stories may draw on collective ones and their underlying ideologies, or may push against them, in the effort to construct meaning (253). Either way, individual narratives reveal how people make sense of their experience and the world around them.

In my fieldwork, through a mix of participant observation and interviews, I interacted with a variety of *orgiveños* (many with community leadership positions), residents of British origin, members of the Muslim convert community, and North African immigrants living in the town.[32] I met some of these Maghrebi migrants through mutual friends and acquaintances, and another migrant by requesting help with learning more of the Moroccan dialect of Arabic (*Darija*). Subsequently, one migrant would introduce me to another, following the normal rhythms of small-town life in the summer in Spain, where socializing occurs as people stroll through plazas and outdoor cafes. I primarily elicited their perspectives on Órgiva and its inhabitants, using open-ended questions to allow interlocutors to take the lead in structuring their responses. Given that the precarity of immigrant life does not provide a context conducive to more formal interviews, with the North African migrants I chose to use targeted interactions in the form of semi-structured interviewing. As a woman researcher, social norms would make it more difficult to have extended conversation alone with male migrants, and I wanted to compensate for the deference effect and social desirability effect that could make interlocutors reticent to share negative views with me. For these reasons, I also employed a research assistant who, as a male Moroccan immigrant residing elsewhere in Andalucía, was close to an insider interviewer. The migrants in Órgiva readily viewed this interlocutor as someone who was part of their in-group of Moroccan immigrants in Spain and these interactions took the form of something in between informal interviewing and semi-structured interviewing. Overall, I combined narratological and rhetorical analysis of both written texts about Órgiva and oral statements about the town that create narratives about it in order to identify recurring concepts, categories, and tropes, and to draw conclusions about their ideological charge.

Paul Atkinson observes that "Ethnographers—or qualitative researchers more generally—too often claim to be special and different" (187). While I certainly don't want to commit that mistake in an effort to claim authenticity and ethical superiority, I do bring an unusual positioning to this project. Although this is certainly not an example of insider fieldwork, it also is definitely not the classical type of fieldwork in which the researcher has no previous relationship with the community studied. Along with Ruth Behar and many others, I have reflected upon my situation vis-à-vis the paradox of traditional fieldwork that called on the researcher to share the "native" perspective while maintaining objectivity. Like Behar, I am "between places, between identities, between languages, between cultures, between longings and illusions, one foot in the academy and one foot out" (162). While insider/outsider status offers the benefits of ease of connection and of insight tempered by the ability to also evaluate from an external perspective, I recognize that one drawback is the accompanying emotional ties. This relationship to the site being studied no doubt led to particular conscious and unconscious choices in how I pursued and wrote about my research. To invoke Steinar Kvale's metaphors about interviewers, although at certain moments I felt like a miner who had found a valuable "nugget" of meaning, I was also aware that I had an active hand in the construction of that nugget's significance. Thus, I endeavored to approach my fieldwork as a traveler who sought to share experiences and listen, in order to weave that journey into a narrative:

> The alternate traveler metaphor understands the interviewer as a traveler on a journey that leads to a tale to be told upon returning home. The interviewer-traveler wanders through the landscape and enters into conversations with the people encountered. The traveler explores the many domains of the country, as unknown territory or with maps, roaming freely around the territory. The traveler may also deliberately seek

specific sites or topics by following a method, with the original Greek meaning of "a route that leads to the goal." The interviewer wanders along with the local inhabitants, asks questions that lead the subjects to tell their own stories of their lived world, and converses with them in the original Latin meaning of conversation as "wandering together with" (Kvale 4).

CHAPTER 2

Tolerance, Power, and Civilizational Discourses

RECOGNITION AND SUSTAINABLE TOLERANCE

Much scholarly ink has been spilled on the topic of tolerance. Reviewing those "ink blotches" and connecting them to each other and other lines of inquiry point to ways of reconceptualizing tolerance that can establish more worthwhile societal goals. It also reveals what is at stake, and what may be obscured, when people and places are labeled as "tolerant," or related terms such as "multicultural" or "cosmopolitan." Some theorists question the desirability of tolerance, while others try to refine definitions of the term and consider how practices that seek peaceful coexistence can be better understood and made more equitably effective.

As stated earlier, *convivencia* means living together, getting along with each other, or coexistence; however, due to the work of Américo Castro and the usage of the term that it launched, the term has become tightly linked to certain kinds of discourses about medieval Muslim Iberia—a vision of al-Andalus as a time of religious communities harmoniously living together.[1] While the term "coexistence" also means the state of living together peacefully in spite of differences, unlike the Spanish *convivencia*, the word "coexistence" does not carry the connotation, or cultural baggage, of a particular interpretation of history. In contrast, the term "tolerance" refers to an attitude of acceptance, typically understood as a virtue, held on a personal level toward other individuals or groups, whereas the related term "toleration" is used in political science and related fields to refer to a set of practices in the social or political realms.[2] Significantly, the *con-* and *co-* prefixes of *convivencia* and coexistence indicate mutuality, but in the case of the term "tolerance," one party tolerates (puts up with) another, who is tolerated. The active and passive roles inherent in the idea of tolerance reflect a disparity in the power of the tolerator and the tolerated. Thus, the question that emerges is: how can societies move along the continuum of interactions between diverse groups that ranges from outright violence to underlying hostility to peaceful, respectful coexistence with difference, when the very attitude that is supposed to cultivate such coexistence—tolerance—is built upon disparity? In other words, coexistence refers to a healthy state of tolerance, one without the inequity and lack of mutuality inherent in the term "tolerance" itself. And here the ambiguities of tolerance and toleration begin to emerge.

Tolerance and toleration are such slippery concepts that Rainer Forst has categorized toleration as "a normatively dependent concept," that is, one that requires further specification in order to be evaluated as a virtue and have defined limits (Forst 2004, 314). Part of what makes the concept of tolerance so difficult to separate from the opposing ideas of peaceful respect and tense aversion, is the number of paradoxes that constitute it. Primary among them is the paradox that limitless tolerance will most likely severely limit tolerance. In other words, if a society freely tolerates the intolerant, intolerance will dominate. This leads to a related paradox: to maintain a peaceful and predominantly tolerant society, there must be intolerance in specific contexts—hopefully carried out with civility. Forst in particular has explored the process of drawing the boundaries between what can and cannot be tolerated.

The traditional understanding of tolerance as permitting that which is considered reprehensible has, in fact, been rejected by many thinkers as intolerable. Slavoj Žižek contends that tolerance, when practiced, is only done so in a limited and superficial manner (Daly and Žižek 122–24; Žižek 674). Wendy Brown argues that tolerating is tantamount to conditionally allowing that which is viewed as abhorrent and abject, thus marginalizing the tolerated and, especially in colonial and neocolonial contexts, labeling the intolerant as barbaric.[3] The dynamic of one group allowing something of which it disapproves in another group—and thereby establishing a hierarchy, has been labeled by others the "permission" conception of tolerance.[4] The disapproval inherent in permission tolerance is at the center of many critiques regarding the means and even the desirability of promoting tolerance. Forst distills the crux of the issue when he writes that, within a permission understanding, toleration can come to be "a word signifying power, domination and exclusion" (Forst 2012, 3, cited in Verkuyten and Yogeeswaran 85).

Before returning to the issue of power, what can be done with this stalemate regarding tolerance? Levinovitz's observations help us out of the impasse by shifting the focus to the goals of tolerance: "The ultimate end of tolerance is not actually toleration, but the realization of specific ideals: human dignity, autonomy, reduced pain, diversity, recognition of the Other, etc." On a day-to-day level, this includes the realization of cohabitation without violence or aggression. The question then becomes: what conceptualization of tolerance can help us coexist with difference, as well as with dignity and well-being? How can we cultivate peaceful coexistence while we avoid erasing difference in the name of a false universality, promoting the privileging of one group as arbiter of what should/should not be tolerated, or heightening a rigid sense of boundaries between in-group and out-group that leads to violent conflict? Can an equitable and socially empowering tolerance be conceptualized and put into practice?

The response that various thinkers have offered is the "respect" conceptualization of toleration.[5] Respect-based tolerance seeks to respect each person's right to hold a particular view, even when others do not agree with that view. In so doing, this conception tries to counteract asymmetrical power via mutual respect (Forst 2004). Levinovitz warns that we should not reduce tolerance to respect, because they are not equivalents. I agree that tolerance is not the same as respect, but I would argue that respect and recognition are crucial elements in deeper, more horizontal forms of tolerance, that is, in sustainable tolerance.

In some contexts, conviviality is used to denote a sustainable type of coexistence. The dictionary definition of conviviality is friendliness, sociability, and/or merrymaking, which makes conviviality and *convivencia* false friends (the linguistic term for a pair of similar-sounding words that may be etymologically related but have different meanings). But starting in the late 20th century, the proximity in meaning and the etymological relationship between the two terms led to a reworking of conviviality in social movements that critique industrial development and the overconsumption of natural resources, and in scholarly work on issues of coexistence and cosmopolitanism. The Austrian philosopher and social critic Ivan Illich first used the term "conviviality" in his influential critique of industrialized societies, *Tools for Conviviality* (1973), to refer to a type of society in which individual autonomy and creativity flourish. However, Paul Gilroy later retooled the term as an alternative to "cosmopolitanism," which he saw as having been coopted by Western neo-imperialism. In *After Empire: Melancholia or Convivial Culture*, Gilroy uses *conviviality* to describe the lively multiculturalism that he observes in young, urban, post-imperial Britain, a state of being that is at ease with diversity. Here conviviality points to the commonalities between people in spite of difference—what Gilroy describes as the "recognition of mutual worth, dignity, and essential similarity" that "imposes restrictions on how we behave if we wish to act justly" (2004, 4). Subsequently, conviviality has been taken up by social scientists to analyze forms of human interaction across difference that result in a coexistence based on respect and mutuality.[6]

In Kwame Anthony Appiah's efforts to rescue the term "cosmopolitanism" in order to formulate an attitude supportive of coexistence to which humans can aspire, he seems to refer to—and reject—a permission-based conception of tolerance, while naming a recognition-based tolerance "cosmopolitanism." Appiah formulates cosmopolitan communities as those defined by interpersonal relationships built upon respect and ongoing conversation across boundaries of difference: "cosmopolitanism [...] begins with the simple idea that in the human community, as in national communities, we need to develop habits of coexistence: conversation in its older meaning, of living together, association" (2006, xix). When discussing relativism versus objective moral "truths," Appiah asserts that "there are some values that are, and should be, universal, just as there are lots of values that are, and must be, local. We can't hope to reach a final consensus on how to rank and order such values. That's why the model I'll be returning to is that of conversation and, in particular, conversation between people from different ways of life" (2006, xxi). As he delves further into the fact that "beliefs are subjective," he states that "even on the Positivist view there is no route from the subjectivity of value judgments to a defense of toleration. Toleration is just another value" (2006, 25). Here, Appiah echoes Brown to some extent in her rejection of tolerance on the grounds that it is the imposition of a set of values. At the same time, Appiah's call for dialogue based on mutual respect "not because cultures matter in themselves, but because people matter, and culture matters to people" (2008, 88) is parallel to calls for mutual recognition. Whether we call it conviviality, cosmopolitanism, or recognition-based toleration, humans need to aspire to find ways to coexist harmoniously and in a sustainable manner.

Various thinkers have considered the necessity and complexity of recognition in the context of human rights and interpersonal relationships: Hannah Arendt's "right to have rights," Martin Buber's "I-Thou [*Ich-Du*] relationship," and Thich Nhat Hanh's "interbeing," to name a few. But the anthropologist Elizabeth Povinelli has questioned whether recognition can actually be achieved. In her study about aboriginal land rights legislation in Australia, Povinelli points out that the legal system employed is based on normative European ideas about aboriginals' relationship with land. As a result, aboriginals must uphold stereotypically authentic ways of being. Liberal multiculturalism relies on the law, but by the same token the recognition granted is only a legal one. Within the framework of Hegel's master–

slave narrative, recognition takes place only in the master's terms. This creates a situation in which aboriginals serve to demonstrate that Australia is a multicultural nation but as part of the process they must "protect the liberal subject from suspecting the (ir)rationality of their intolerance" (109). Analogous to Gayatri Spivak's famous "Can the subaltern speak?," Povinelli wonders if the tolerated subaltern can be recognized. As de Boever has pointed out, the pragmatic response has been that this recognition, limited as it may be, is necessary for legal protection and an effective political process (41). Thus, a questioned recognition is our best available option.

One of the last times that I went to visit *Tía* Conchita in the Alpujarran nursing home where she has lived ever since she began to need 24-hour care, after our initial greetings, my cousin asked *Tía* Conchita if she recognized me. *Tía* Conchita, still holding my hand, contemplated my face for a moment and said, with great certainty "eres la cubana [you're the Cuban woman]." My cousin and I laughed, unsure about whether my Cuban accent or my physical resemblance to my grandmother who had left Órgiva to live in Cuba with my grandfather, *Tía* Conchita's uncle, had led her to place me correctly without being able to recall my name, whether my resemblance to my grandmother had made her think—through the logic of senility—that I was my grandmother, or whether the accent had just led her to state the one conclusion that she could draw, which remained a generic one. Had she recognized me, mistaken me for another family member, or not recognized me at all? My cousin and I had also laughed because, having been born and raised in the US—albeit a very Cuban corner of the US, I'm clearly not only/simply "*cubana.*" Had *Tía* Conchita never really grasped this even before senility? Had she forgotten the details of my family's journey? Or had she not even placed me as a relative? There was no way to know, but we still kept holding hands and talking. Whoever she thought I was, she seemed happy to see me. Recognition has its limits and may be built upon a flawed, one-sided logic, but we need to sit with the uncertainty, hold hands if possible, and practice the most self-reflective recognition that we can manage.

RECOGNITION, TOLERATION, AND POWER

Axel Honneth (1995, 2012) and Anna Galeotti have established the importance of respect and acknowledgement as equals, that is, the importance of social recognition. Galeotti explains why "the symbolic meaning of public recognition" is crucial by stating that the symbolic dimension of toleration

> depends on a conjectural causal chain linking the lack of public visibility of "different" identities with the lack of public respect for their bearers and their consequent incapacity to develop adequate self-esteem. Given the public invisibility of their identity and its social stigmatization, self-esteem is often pursued at the price of rejecting difference, resulting in humiliation and the loss of self-respect. If this causal chain holds, and if public toleration of a certain trait symbolically entails public acceptance and the legitimization of the different identity, then this very gesture of symbolic toleration will signify public respect and consideration for minorities as well as for the majority. This, in turn, should help members of minorities to build up an adequate reserve of self-esteem and self-respect (Galeotti 12).

While recognizing that there have been few studies on "the social-psychological implications of being the object of toleration," Verkuyten and Yogeeswaran similarly propose that being the object of permission toleration may have negative consequences for the individual and their community (86). They explain that "What is being tolerated transgresses or deviates from what is considered appropriate and normative and this implied deviance and inferiority thereby threatens a valued group membership among the tolerated. Such an identity threat may negatively impact (collective) self-esteem [. . .] and well-being [. . .] among the tolerated" (Verkuyten and Yogeeswaran 86). Additionally, they observe that in permission toleration "the tolerated can feel a decreased sense of control over their own lives [. . .] Such a lack of perceived control may undermine personal and group efficacy" (Verkuyten and Yogeeswaran 86). Furthermore, "research on identity denial has demonstrated that denying one's social identity leads to negative emotions and attempts at proving one's belongingness in the group [. . .]" (Verkuyten and Yogeeswaran 84).

The importance of identity in toleration becomes clear when we acknowledge that the cultural practices involved in tolerance are entwined with the concept of assimilation—whether sought, rejected, or managed via hyphenation—in social contexts with immigrants or with other ethnic, racial, religious, or linguistic minorities. W. E. B. DuBois explored one aspect of this dynamic through the concept of "double consciousness," which explains the burden of viewing oneself both from one's own eyes and from the eyes of the dominant white world. This double awareness can lead to the internalization of racist beliefs or to the tactical use of racist rhetoric, which, at least in the short term, upholds the racist belief system. Social psychologists have pointed to the dangers of internalized essentialist beliefs. In the absence of the affirmation of their identities, minorities turn to essentialism to establish belonging (Morton and Postmes 2009; Verkuyten 2003, cited in Verkuyten and Yogeeswaran 82). This essentialism, albeit strategic, can lead to heightened tensions between in-group and out-group and assertions of identity that are neither civil nor tolerant. In contrast, through social recognition, the process of respect-based toleration can take place in a less hierarchical, more mutual fashion and thus one that has fewer negative consequences.

But how mutual can toleration be on an uneven playing field? Who is positioned to tolerate and to define what is, or is not, tolerable? Various scholars have noted that to tolerate one must have power: "one can only speak of toleration where it is practiced voluntarily and is not compelled, for otherwise one would speak of 'suffering' or 'enduring' certain things which one rejects but against which one is powerless" (Forst 2004, 315).[7] Galeotti, rather than referring to "suffering" or "enduring," notes that without power, instead of toleration, there is "acquiescence" (22). While I agree that power is a central factor in toleration, I find that the use of the terms "suffering," "enduring," and to some extent "acquiescing" confound the situation because to tolerate is precisely to suffer through something of which one disapproves—even if one decides to suffer through it on the basis of respect and recognition. Moreover, it leaves open the question of whether a disadvantaged minority can exercise tolerance, or if only the powerful can bestow the gift of tolerance on others.

If power is understood as only being top-down, as only residing in structural centers of power and always being repressive, then the act of toleration is a gift—understood as an item of value bestowed on another to indebt that other toward oneself and establish one's superiority. Marcel Mauss explained gift-giving as an act that establishes honor and status via a reciprocal exchange in which the gift creates a social bond built on the obligation to reciprocate. Building on Mauss, but with an emphasis on the role of the social agent over and above the societal structure, Pierre Bourdieu (1977, 1991, 2014) viewed gift-giving as an act of taking possession of the receiver that is disguised as generosity. He developed this conception of the gift as concealed oppressive power into his concept of symbolic violence.[8] This understanding of the bestowal of gifts is analogous to Brown's understanding of the act of tolerance: a mechanism through which the powerful establish and maintain power in a concealed fashion. Yet this understanding is based on a static, structured, unidirectional conceptualization of power.

Catriona McKinnon suggests another way to understand the power dynamics inherent in toleration when she states that among the "essential structural features of toleration" are "Power: the tolerator believes herself to have the power to alter or suppress what is tolerated," and "Non-rejection: the tolerator does not exercise this power" (14). She explains further that these features "relate to the control the tolerator believes herself capable of exercising over what she tolerates" (15). The belief in one's ability to exercise power, to carry out the steps necessary to exert control over oneself or one's social environment, is also known as self-efficacy. When recognition and consequently self-efficacy are part of social dynamics, even those on the margins can enact power, albeit in a limited way.

Foucault's decentralized, mobile conception of power elucidates how power operates in such a space of (recognition-based) toleration:

"Power is exercised through networks, and individuals do not simply circulate in those networks; they are in a position to both submit to and exercise this power. They are never the inert or consenting targets of power; they are always its relays. In other words, power passes through individuals. It is not applied to them" (Foucault et al. 2003, 29). Elsewhere, Foucault speaks of "a web of microscopic, capillary" power (2000, 86) to elucidate how power is not centralized and confined to structures, but rather includes a fluid network of multiple, smaller loci of power outside of government and religious institutions. Although oppression is pervasive, so too can resistance be found everywhere (Foucault 1980). Power is not possessed, but is exercised, passing from one person to another. Thus, the subject is both oppressed and exerts power, is both constituted by power and produces knowledge. Based on this conception of power, I contend that community members that are further from the main loci of power can still exert power and still bestow the gift of tolerance on others. This understanding of power allows the symbolic power of toleration to be reciprocal across asymmetrical power relations. It also allows room for power over the self, the power to develop a sense of self and will that are distinct from those imposed by the dominant culture, because when an individual is so marginalized, or unrecognized, that they have no means by which to enact refusal, the situation referred to by Bernard Williams can arise: the individual can still be aware that, if s/he were in a position to enact refusal of a disapproved-of behavior, s/he would intervene and be intolerant (or, inversely, would choose not to do so and tolerate) (19).

Generally, in the scholarly literature, it is acknowledged that toleration is about accepting something disliked in order to attain the reward of greater harmony, but there is emphasis on allowing without interfering for a broad societal gain, not on the rewards received in exchange on the individual level. Although Forst and others stipulate that tolerance by definition must be voluntary, not compelled, (2004, 315), once there is some form of recompense, due to the workings of power, ambiguity arises regarding voluntariness or choice. Brown notes the role of compensation, but considers that it irreparably taints the toleration process: "As compensation, tolerance anoints the bearer with virtue, with standing for a principled act of permitting one's principles to be affronted; it provides a gracious way of allowing one's tastes to be violated. It offers a robe of modest superiority in exchange for yielding" (Brown 2006, 25). While "[m]agnanimity[,] in the case of tolerance, [. . .] disguises power" (Brown 2006, 26), the magnanimous position created by tolerating can also confer power on the more marginalized and contribute overall to a more peaceful state of coexistence. By understanding power as centralized and unidirectional, Brown sees the rewards of toleration as only being enjoyed by those with the highest status in society. I would like to propose that by recognizing other rewards in the forms of opportunities for recognition and quality of life (the overall goal of a peaceful society, but also the desire to live with a high level of recognition-based acceptance), we can better understand the dynamics of toleration, who partakes in them, and the extent of toleration's positive potential. Even social actors who are marginalized and seen as Other have the power to tolerate and are part of the dynamic of gifting tolerance.

The ideal of tolerance is free of compensation, but rarely, if ever, is the process of toleration that innocent of power. The dynamic of toleration is a gift exchange, but, unlike Mauss's understanding of gift-giving, it is not ritualistic and structured, but a fluid dynamic in which many have at least a modicum of power. Like gift-giving, the bestowal of tolerance rewards the giver with status. In many contexts, identifying as tolerant and being recognized as tolerant becomes a desired status that is often the main recompense, but there can be others as well. Tolerance as an ideal may be sought without any type of reward, but, in practice, rewards, even if only in the form of an identity as "civilized" (that is, tolerant), motivate tolerance and the willingness with which it is enacted.

TOLERATION AND "CIVILIZATION"

The association between tolerance and the concept of "civilization" requires further commentary. The term "civilize" means "To bring (a person, place, group of people, etc.) to a stage of social development considered to be more advanced, esp. by bringing to conformity with the social norms of a developed society; to enlighten, refine, and educate; to make more cultured and sophisticated" and is etymologically related to "civil," "citizen," and "city" (*Oxford English Dictionary*). Thus, while "civilization" is associated with farming settlements that grow into cities and the centralization of authority, it is also closely tied to ideologies regarding progress and superiority. The term rests on an implicit comparison and a teleology of what is defined as development and, as a result, is inherently hierarchical. Reflecting the concept of progress characteristic of the Enlightenment, the period in which the term first circulated in French and English, civilizational hierarchy opposes cultures understood to be advanced to those seen as primitive or barbaric, without acknowledging the culturally determined definition of advancement.[9] The civilizational hierarchy constructed by communities contributes to the formation of the types of capital that Bourdieu (1991) put forth in *Language and Symbolic Power*: cultural capital (one's knowledge, skills, and education), symbolic capital (accumulated prestige or honor), and the distinction (self-presentation of status and distancing from "lower" groups) that both of these types of capital can be used to create. Civilizational hierarchy has been used to justify European colonialism and, in turn, the cultural capital and symbolic capital that link a person to Europe create the Occidental distinction that is part of the discourses and power dynamics of Orientalism, as laid out by Edward Said and further nuanced by others. Until today, civilizational hierarchy intertwined with Orientalism has established an association between the Middle East and North Africa and barbaric violence, on the one hand, and between Europe and civil tolerance, on the other.

Hirschkind reminds us that, as Said established, "the idea of Europe as a civilizational unity was constructed in [a] way that was dependent on a principle of differentiation opposing a Muslim Orient to a Christian Europe" (2014, 229). In the process of the construction of these civilizational units, Christianity, tolerance, Europe, and civilizational superiority became intertwined. For this reason, Brown asserts that "tolerance has become a discursive token of Western legitimacy in international affairs [...] the identification of liberal democracies with tolerance and of nonliberal regimes with fundamentalism discursively articulates the global moral superiority of the West and legitimates Western violence toward the non-West" (37). This "exclusive identification of the West with tolerance, and of tolerance with civilization," not only gives the West the power to determine what is intolerable (37), but results in "Islam, in that same discourse," being "relentlessly identified with intolerance" (Brown and Forst, 19).

Hirschkind goes on to explain how even ideologies regarding European identity that apparently eschew religion point to values, including secularism and tolerance, that are deemed to be rooted in Christianity. In the current socio-political climate, concerns regarding how to maintain the identification between Europe and Christianity in the face of Muslim immigration, as well as conversions to Islam, have taken on renewed force:

> The demand to include a reference to Europe's Christian character within the 2003 Draft Treaty establishing a Constitution for Europe, a position strongly championed by [then president of Spain] Aznar, is one symptom of this project, though it is also evident in claims that Europe's secular traditions are an extension of its own forms of Christianity. Thus, for [French intellectual] Marcel Gauchet (1999), it is Christianity alone among religious traditions that has the theological resources to achieve its own self-overcoming and thus set in motion the processes that lead to secular modernity and the autonomous subject of modern democratic political life. Accounts of this sort introduce religion into the conceptual vocabulary of modern political life in a way that simultaneously naturalizes one particular religious tradition (Christianity) and secures the civilizational boundaries of modern Europe (Hirschkind 2014, 229).

In this identity narrative of European secular modernity, one of the cornerstones of which is tolerance, non-Christians are either not tolerated at all or considered a threat. Thus, the limits of the toleration process in Europe (understood as essentially and preferably Christian) are found in the inclusion of non-Christians. On the one hand, as Hirschkind suggests, this conception of Europe belies Spain's long history of entanglement with the Muslim world. On the other hand, the toleration dynamic in Órgiva brings to the fore and further complicates this contradiction between Europe as tolerant and as essentially or exclusively Christian.

Invocations of medieval Iberia as a space of carefree *convivencia* and especially the idea of a cross-confessional tolerance under Muslim rule destabilizes the conception of a modern Europe whose secularism or Christianity is the source of its tolerance. But drawing on the myth of idyllic interfaith harmony without digging deeper maintains a shallow and ultimately harmful (in that it entails marginalization) conception of tolerance. Both models, that of Muslim-led *convivencia* or that of European civility (whether Christian, secular, or pseudo-secular), are built upon the belief that to be tolerant is the hallmark of an advanced civilization (whether al-Andalus or contemporary Europe is taken as the setpoint for civilization). This overarching civilizational framework and the place of tolerance as a value within it is part of the broader context within which residents of Órgiva interact. Thus, the residents of the town are aware that intolerance is not tolerated. The issue that is up for grabs is where and how the limit between tolerant and intolerant is established.

In what follows, Chapters 3, 4, and 5 examine how civilizational hierarchies, the *convivencia* imaginary, tolerance practices, and conceptions of coexistence arise in written and televisual representations of Órgiva and in individual oral narratives about it. Overall, the televisual narratives invoke the cross-confessional interaction associated with *convivencia* and reference cosmopolitanism, while simultaneously eliding certain groups or tensions. In contrast, most of the written and oral narratives demonstrate that the residents of the town view their cohabitation as one characterized by separate realms, the negotiation of boundaries, and ambivalence, yet also reciprocal benefits.

CHAPTER 3

Written Narratives about the Alpujarra and Órgiva

A fair amount has been written about the construction of the Alpujarra region's image as a space of pre-modern primitiveness, an image that predominated through at least the 1980s. However, to my knowledge there has been no analysis of the discourses about the "New Alpujarra"—or perhaps the "New Age Alpujarra." These new representations consist of journalistic pieces published on the Internet that often reflect the increasing overlap between travel narrative and travel industry publicity, as well as more extensive works: memoirs, a collaborative collection of local narratives, and (as will be discussed in the following chapter) various television narratives about Órgiva.[1] In the 21st century in particular, Órgiva has been the subject of written, televisual, and multimedia storytelling that has contributed further to drawing attention to the town and fashioning particular narratives about it. In order to contextualize these narratives about the new Órgiva, first we need to understand how the town and its region have been presented in early modern to late modern texts.

EARLY MODERN TO LATE MODERN TRAVELOGUES, ETHNOGRAPHIES, AND HISTORIES

As witnessed by the references to the Alpujarra in Voltaire's *Dictionnaire philosophique* (1764), at the end of the early modern period, the region was already known beyond Iberia as an inaccessible enclave of rugged mountains interspersed with delightful valleys in which the descendants of Moors who were forced to convert to Christianity still worked the land (volume XIX, 297–98). In "La invención de la Alpujarra," Baumann (1996) refers to "the myth of the Alpujarra that is sold for tourism" and analyzes travel narratives to better understand "how such a mysterious image of an isolated Alpujarra has been invented, severed from history and completely closed in on itself" (89). After addressing Voltaire's lines about the Alpujarra, Baumann notes that throughout the 19th century foreign travelers "emphasize the draw of a visit to the Alpujarra for its evident Arab traces" (90). Baumann points to a constellation of associations between paganism or Islam and barbarity that underlie the discourses that emerged depicting the Alpujarrans as ignorant. In 19th-century European travel narratives that describe the inhabitants against the backdrop of the rise and fall of the local mining industry, the poor, "backward" villagers remain conflated with the marginalized, barbarous *moriscos* that had inhabited the area before them (Baumann 1996, 92–93). Northern European historiography had established the sense that the Middle Ages continued to endure in locales outside of the Northern European, Christian, industrialized world.[2] This served to construct the very idea of modernity and in the process perpetuated a vision of the Alpujarra as still medieval and Moorish.

In the mid-20th century, the Alpujarra experienced a resurgence in British travel literature through the work of Gerald Brenan (1894–1987), a fringe member of the set of British writers known as the Bloomsbury Group. Fresh out of serving in the British army in World War I, Brenan began traveling in Spain and in the 1920s he spent several years living in Yegen, a village in the Alpujarra. Brenan's account of life there, *South from Granada: Seven Years in an Andalusian Village* (1957) is a travel narrative in which he describes local customs and cuisine, as well as visits to his home by core Bloomsbury members Virginia Woolf, Lytton Strachey, and Dora Carrington. In addition to several passing references to Órgiva, the text includes various references to Moorish heritage and legends.[3] Brenan, who recounts spending his time in Yegen reading and throwing dance parties attended by the villagers, frequently refers to Yegen as "my village," and emphasizes the poverty and blissful ignorance of the villagers.[4] Altogether, this creates an image of the Alpujarra as charmingly primitive and Moorish, while it positions Brenan as the modern, colonizing subject who takes ownership of the village and of knowledge about it.

As Lisa Lowe notes in her examination of 18th-century French and British travel narratives, travel writings often function to address internal national struggles, "by transfiguring internal challenges to the social order into fantasies of external otherness" (31). No doubt texts such as Voltaire's and those of the 19th- and 20th-century European travelers from beyond Iberia had a role in the definition of their own national identities, largely through the creation of the Black Legend (*la leyenda negra*). While Spain has produced various forms of Orientalism, it has also been the object of Orientalist essentializations, particularly in the form of anti-Spanish rhetoric known as the Black Legend, which traced the perceived greater barbarity of Spaniards (understood to be manifested in the Inquisition and in the treatment of the indigenous peoples of Spain's colonies) to their contact and mixture with North Africans. The discourses of the Black Legend first arose primarily in Britain and France during the Reformation and then started up again in the late 18th century, gaining momentum with the ideas of scientific racism.[5] While within a Euro-American frame of reference Spain's level of civilization has been questioned because of the "Africanness" (backwardness, barbarity, etc.) ascribed to it, within a national framework Moorish backwardness is ascribed specifically to Andalucía. And within Andalucía, the area seen as primitive and premodern (though rustically ignorant, rather than barbaric) has typically been the Alpujarra.

Hence, the Romantic, Orientalist mystique of the Alpujarra was created not only by French, Swiss, and British writers, but by Spaniards as well. Indeed, many Spanish legends and then literary works (often inspired by legend) focus on Boabdil, the last Muslim ruler of Granada, as a primary or secondary character and are set in or refer to the Alpujarra.[6] These narratives no doubt helped to fuel those produced outside of Spain. The most famous of the legends, one that has circulated far beyond the Mediterranean and is still well-known today, is the legend of *El suspiro del moro*, or the Moor's last sigh. According to this legend, when Boabdil and his entourage were leaving Granada for his fiefdom in the Alpujarra, Boabdil paused at a mountain pass to look back at the Alhambra and cried. His mother then said, "Cry like a woman for what you were not able to defend like a man!"[7] Other legends tell that Boabdil never actually left Granada or the Alpujarra because an enchanted Boabdil still lives in the Alhambra or inside a mountain in the region. Still others narrate that before Boabdil or other wealthy Muslims left, they hid treasures of gold and precious gems in the Alpujarra. In the late 19th and early 20th centuries, new life was breathed into these legends when caches of intricate gold jewelry from Nasrid artisans were found in three different villages of the Alpujarra (as well as other parts of the peninsula).[8]

As part of the 19th-century redefinitions of Spanish identity, the Alpujarra region was the subject of various literary works by Spanish writers. Most notably, the Romantic play *Aben Humeya o la rebelión de los moriscos* (Aben Humeya or the rebellion of the Moors; 1836) by Granadan Francisco Martínez de la Rosa (1787–1862) presents Aben Humeya, the historical leader of the second Rebellion of the Alpujarras, and his wife as betrayed, melancholic figures.[9] Two decades later, following the trends of Romantic *costumbrismo*, Sevillan author Manuel Fernández y González (1821–88) published the novel *Los monfíes de las Alpujarras* (The outlaws [from the Arabic *manfiy*] of the Alpujarras; 1856), which blends the historical and adventure novel genres to depict the exiled outlaws of the Muslim kingdom of Granada who sought refuge in the Alpujarras as charming bandits who resisted authority. These two works linked the Spanish Romantic vision of the noble, valiant Moor to the Alpujarra region in particular.

The Alpujarra was also featured in domestic Spanish travel literature. Most famously, Pedro Antonio de Alarcón (1833–91), a Romantic writer of a more realist vein from the province of Granada, travelled through the Alpujarra after serving as a soldier and journalist in *la Guerra de África*, the Hispano-Moroccan War (1859–60) that initiated Spain's colonial project in North Africa. In fact, as González

Alcantud, Lorente Rivas, and Correa Ramón point out, Alarcón was inspired to travel through the Alpujarra because of his contact with Muslims in North Africa and his struggle to define the role of the Moor in Spanish culture (26). Alarcón's travelogue, *La Alpujarra: sesenta leguas a caballo precedidas de seis en diligencia* (The Alpujarra: sixty leagues by horseback preceded by six in stagecoach; 1874) contributed to the interest in the local color of the Alpujarra as a remote region with historical ties to al-Andalus.

The Spanish historical novels and Alarcón's travelogue, by attaching a Romantic Orientalist mystique to the Alpujarra, piqued the interest of other writers and also the nascent field of anthropology. The renowned poet Federico García Lorca (1898–1936), in part through his mother's visits to the Alpujarran town of Lanjarón's therapeutic springs and in part through his collaboration with the Andalusian composer and pianist Manuel de Falla (1876–1946), sought out the Alpujarra as a source of traditional Andalusian culture. Between 1917 and 1934 Lorca visited the Alpujarra, including Órgiva, multiple times to gather legends and poems from the oral tradition and to write. On a postcard from Lanjarón, in approximately 1927 Lorca wrote to a Catalan friend:

> In the middle of Sierra Nevada one is in the heart of the soul of Africa. All eyes are already perfectly African, with a ferocity and poetry that the Mediterranean makes resistible [. . .] Andalucía strange and Berber [. . .] [En plena Sierra Nevada se está en el corazón del alma de África. Todos los ojos son ya perfectamente africanos, con una ferocidad y una poesía que hace resistible el Mediterráneo [. . .] Andalucía extraña y berberisca [. . .]] (González Blasco 2004, 674).

In the same year he wrote to another Catalan intellectual:

> Here in Lanjarón I'm working. The Moorish accent resounds on everyone's tongue. A wind from Africa comes through, whose haze we can see in plain sight. There's no doubt that here there is a *blueprint of nostalgia*, that is anti-European, but that is not Oriental. Andalucía [Yo aquí

en Lanjarón trabajo. El acento morisco suena en todas las lenguas de la gente. Viene viento de África, cuyas brumas podemos ver a simple vista. No hay duda de que aquí existe un *esquema de nostalgia*, que es antieuropeo, pero que no es oriental. Andalucía.] (678).

Drawing from this passionate North African ethos that he perceived in the Alpujarra, Lorca composed in the Órgiva area some of the emblematic poems of his *Romancero gitano* (1928), known for their twinning (conflation?) of gypsy and Arab cultures.[10]

Also in search of an authentic Andalucía, but in the name of science rather than poetry, in 1894 the Granadan medical doctor and anthropological researcher Federico Olóriz Aguilera (1855–1912) arrived to study the physical types and health conditions in the Alpujarra.[11] Having chosen to study the Alpujarra because he deemed it to be one of the "least known" among the regions of Spain that are of the "greatest ethnic interest" (Olóriz Aguilera 135), in Órgiva and various other villages Olóriz took body measurements and photographs of the residents, observed their cultural practices, and gathered demographic information. He explains that the purpose of this "scientific mission [empresa científica]" was to define "the natural constitution of the natives, recognize their diverse ethnic types and investigate the races that had contributed to creating the current people [la constitución orgánica de los naturales, reconocer sus diversos tipos étnicos e indagar las razas que hayan contribuido a formar el pueblo actual]" (135).

Olóriz's measurements focused on the inhabitants' cephalic index (or cranial index), a measurement of the head that was commonly used by late 19th- to early 20th-century anthropologists in an effort to categorize human populations and thus support the development of racial categories. In addition to comments on each village's personal hygiene habits, common illnesses, and temperament (what he deemed to be the violent or reserved and distrusting character of some of the Alpujarran villages), Olóriz also took notes on customs such as games and festivals and married women's use of head scarves. Additionally, Olóriz used church records, property records, and the like to determine how many inhabitants during earlier periods were of *morisco* origin and how many were re-populators from Galicia and other parts of Spain.

A section of Olóriz's notes consisting of information from historical sources and his comments on these sources (130-34), sheds light on his interest in race and the *morisco* presence and demonstrates that these are the driving questions motivating his project. Olóriz's historical notes all have to do with how many Muslims there were in the area in the late medieval and early modern periods, how many of them were actually Christians who had recently become Muslim, how many Christians were killed by the Moors during the Rebellion of the Alpujarra, details regarding the rebellion in each village, and similar topics. In separate sections on his visits to particular towns, Olóriz references these Reconquista-era events. For instance, in the section on Órgiva when he mentions the village's church tower he points out that a heroic act had occurred there during the siege of the church that was part of the Rebellion of the Alpujarra (155). In Olóriz's last comment on a historical source, he explains his concern regarding whether or not the inhabitants can be classified as *morisco* versus non-*morisco*:

> It seems that the kingdom was cleansed of the "Moorish race" but from the ethnic point of view it is very doubtful that there would be essential organic differences between the expelled and those who persisted or Christians; since it would be necessary to find out first: if the Mahomedans in the time of the Arabs were or were not the same group as the Mozarabs and of the same blood as that of other Christians; if those that passed as Old Christians actually were that; and if the natives of the country could be classified with accuracy into *moriscos* and non-*moriscos* at the time of expulsion [Parece que el reino quedó limpio de "raza morisca" pero desde el punto de vista étnico es muy dudoso que hubiera diferencias orgánicas esenciales entre los expulsados y los persistentes o cristianos; pues sería preciso averiguar primero: si los mahometanos en tiempo de los árabes eran o no los mismos mozárabes y de sangre igual a la de otros cristianos; si los que pasaban por serlo viejos lo

eran realmente; y si podían clasificarse con exactitud en moriscos y no moriscos los naturales del país al hacer la expulsión] (Olóriz, 134).

Although Olóriz distinguishes between religion and biological origin, he does so in search of a more precise way to determine the ethnicity or "blood" of the Alpujarrans and even when he concedes that such a distinction may not be possible, this gives Olóriz's expedition an underlying purpose: to attempt to answer these questions via modern science. In Olóriz's work, the Alpujarra is clearly positioned as the primitive object of study that gives science an opportunity for advancement and his engagement with the Alpujarra is threaded through with concern about events and human categories from some 300 to 400 years earlier.

Olóriz and Lorca's interest in the Alpujarra was followed by 20th- and 21st-century travel literature and histories that continued to establish the link between the Alpujarra and al-Andalus and historical and ethnographic works focused on the traditional Andalusian culture maintained in this mountainous region.[12] In the mid-20th century, the prominent Spanish anthropologist, historian, and linguist Julio Caro Baroja, as he led an official Spanish exploration mission in the Spanish Sahara (later known as the Western Sahara), wrote *Los moriscos del reino de Granada* (The *moriscos* of the kingdom of Granada; 1957). This history of the Kingdom of Granada added to the Spanish reading public's association between the Alpujarra and the last rebellious Moors of al-Andalus. The Andalusian writer, journalist, and painter Francisco Izquierdo Martínez's *El apócrifo de la Alpujarra Alta* (The apocryphal of the high Alpujarra; 1969) presents, along with the author's travels over a 12-year period in the 1950s and '60s, various legends about the region, many of which involve its Moorish past.

Spanish imaginaries about al-Andalus, the Reconquista, and the *Morisco* Revolt continue to have a role in the construction of the Alpujarra, as witnessed by more recent works of travel literature, popular history, and historical fiction. In 2017 Eduardo Castro, a writer from Motril, published *La Alpujarra en caballos de vapor* (The Alpujarra via mechanical horsepower), a play on the title of Alarcón's 1874 travel narrative. Based on a 1984 car trip, Castro's narrative retraces Alarcón's journey, with passages steeped in lore from the era of Muslim rule and a chapter dedicated to Brenan. The interest in the past takes over and there is no mention of the hippies or late 20th-century Britons who had already begun to settle in the area.

The 2013 *El país perdido: la Alpujarra en la guerra morisca* (The lost country: the Alpujarra in the Moorish war) is a history with elements of travelogue by Granadan novelist and poet Justo Navarro Velilla (b. 1953). *El país perdido* focuses on the 16th-century second Rebellion of the Alpujarras (or *Morisco* Revolt) as the end of the Reconquista and thus a turning point in Spanish history. But Navarro's text insists on portraying the 21st-century Alpujarra as hermetic and still transmitting the echoes of its Muslim past, without mentioning its Muslim present. The visual imagery of this book reinforces this attachment to the past: the images consist of contemporary photos of landscapes and villages seen from afar and reproductions of 16th- to 19th-century drawings and paintings of people in the region. There are no images of 20th- to 21st-century inhabitants of the region, and thus the text avoids having to grapple with the presence of the eclectic newcomers to the Alpujarra.

The fascination with the *Morisco* Revolt also arises within the broader phenomenon of Spain's boom in historical novels since the last decades of the twentieth century.[13] Among those historical novels, there are several set in the Alpujarra of the 15th- and 16th-century *morisco* rebellion. These include the bestselling *La mano de Fátima* (2009; The hand of Fátima) by Ildefonso Falcones (b. 1959) which includes as a secondary character Abén Humeya, the leader of the revolt who was immortalized by Martínez de la Rosa's 19th-century play *Aben Humeya o la rebelión de los moriscos*. The protagonist of Falcones' *La mano de Fátima* is the son of a Christian priest and a Moorish woman, a tortured soul who struggles to reconcile and live with the two sides of his heritage. Another of these historical novels is specifically focused on Órgiva: *El secreto de la Alpujarra* (2019, The secret of the Alpujarra), self-published by José Antonio Porras Carrión

(b. 1961), who was born in the Alpujarran village of Pampaneira and raised in one of the rural hamlets that is part of the municipality of Órgiva. This pulp fiction recounts the love and intrigue between a young Arab woman and a Spanish soldier who meet in the church of Órgiva while it is besieged by *moriscos*.[14]

These novels are part of a slew of highly popular historical novels focused on medieval and early modern Christian-Muslim contact in Iberia that demonstrate an interest in grappling with interfaith and intercultural contact through the distance and sense of safety offered by the past and the grandeur attached to it, rather than present-day challenges. In keeping with this, the Alpujarra-focused works demonstrate a continued Spanish interest in Orientalizing the Alpujarra and viewing it as the culmination of the Reconquista, rather than the start of a new experiment in coexistence. On the whole, Spanish authors are more interested in the era of the Rebellion of the Alpujarras than in the new, highly diverse Alpujarra, epitomized by Órgiva. Spanish literary, ethnographic, and historical discourses have established and maintained the association between the Alpujarra and a particular vision of Arabs and Islam—one linked to Spanish nationalism and the Spanish colonial enterprise, even when infused with romanticized Orientalism, the association between the Alpujarra and discourses of primitiveness and authenticity, or a combination of the two.

LATE MODERN MEMOIRS AND A COLLABORATIVE COMMUNITY HISTORY

More than 40 years after the publication of Brenan's *South from Granada*, another British author, Chris Stewart (b. 1951), started to write about the Alpujarra and Órgiva more specifically. As Stewart was one of the first in a trend of Northern European settlement in the area, his texts also contributed to drawing more people to the area. After Stewart's three memoirs (1999, 2002, and 2006) two other memoirs by British incomers appeared in 2020, and a few years before the 2020 texts a process-based community narrative was published in Spanish. The memoirs in English and the collection of local narratives in Spanish address different audiences, but all move away from presenting Órgiva as insular and wary of outsiders, as predominately poor and ignorant, or as Moorish or "Oriental." Instead, they consider, to differing degrees, the contact between tradition and modernity as well as between local and incomer lifestyles in the new Alpujarra that still maintains a role as a refuge from modern, urban living, but now not only for transient travelers or sojourners (such as Brenan), but for many incomers who are sojourners or permanent residents, as well as for return migrants. As witnessed in these new narratives, in many ways Órgiva serves as an open refuge for these incomers and returnees. But what are the constitutive elements of this literal global village that these recent written narratives highlight, and what are the elements that they obscure?

When Stewart arrived in 1988, newcomers had just begun to settle in the Alpujarra. The confluence of Andalusian emigration, farms purchased by British expats, and the changing cultural landscape in Ibiza—Spain's erstwhile hippie haven—was starting to transform Órgiva. Taking advantage of the properties vacated by *orgiveños* who had emigrated to major urban centers in the previous decades or had simply given up on farming, starting in the late 1970s British and other Northern Europeans began to purchase at low prices land and often dilapidated houses in Órgiva and the surrounding area. They sought a "back to the land" experience, or simply a way to enjoy a lower cost of living in a warmer climate.

As that trend commenced, another type of settlement began, that of hippies or "alternatives." By the late 1970s, Ibiza, once a mecca for alternatives, had become too commercialized and pricey and some of those looking for a new environment settled in abandoned farmhouses and hamlets in the Alpujarra, heading to the nearest town, Órgiva, whenever they needed to buy provisions. With time, various alternative communities were established in the area. Most notably, a small group of Britons and Catalans used purchased farmland to establish the alternative community named Beneficio. This organized community in the tradition of the Rainbow Family was founded about 3 km from the center of Órgiva and, according to Sánchez Alonso (2015b), is the oldest in the Peninsula and the largest in Europe.[15]

The transformation of the Alpujarra accelerated in the 1990s. It so happens that a young Catalan, Felipe Margarit, who was living the hippie life in the environs of Órgiva, met a follower of Naqshbandi-Haqqani Sufism in the area, and traveled with him to the headquarters of the Sufi order (*tariqa*) in Cyprus, where Margarit converted to Islam, taking the name Umar.[16] After being appointed the head of the Naqshbandi-Haqqani Sufi order in Spain, in the 1990s Shaykh Umar returned to Órgiva, where there were already some other Muslim converts, to establish a Naqshbandi-Haqqani center. In turn, this center and the increasing number of European converts to Islam in the area drew more converts to Órgiva. The 1990s also saw an intensification of the influx of British expats. This increase in the number of Britons and other Europeans was propelled by Spain's 1986 entry into the European Communities, which in 1993 developed into the European Union, and was also boosted by the popularity of Stewart's writings. By 2010, 21 percent of the population of Órgiva was from outside Spain and of those about half were from Great Britain.[17] Through this convergence of economic, cultural, and political factors, a town that was once considered a sort of time capsule of traditional Andalusian culture became an international village immersed in some of the latest global trends in healing and spirituality.

Before the upsurge in incomers, Chris Stewart, a rock musician turned sheepshearer who had grown up in a boarding school in Surrey (a county bordering Greater London), became interested in the Alpujarra after hearing a couple of friends talk about the region's landscape and reading Brenan's *South from Granada*. This led to Stewart and his wife Ana buying an old farm on the outskirts of Órgiva in 1988 and beginning a new life as farmers.[18] Stewart wrote a memoir about the experience, *Driving over Lemons: An Optimist in Andalucía* (1999, later published with the subtitle "An Optimist in Spain"), which was followed by two sequels: *A Parrot in the Pepper Tree* (2002) and *The Almond Blossom Appreciation Society* (2006). *Driving over Lemons* and

FIGURE 6: A slice of life in the "New Age Alpujarra": a detail of the bulletin board at the main halal restaurant, Café Baraka, announcing alternative and Muslim activities and services.

its sequels are often categorized as "travel literature"; however, considering that Stewart arrived with the intention of settling permanently in the Alpujarra and his third book on his life in the region appeared almost 20 years after settling there, the works seem closer to memoirs, although certainly intercultural ones. Addressing this formal ambiguity, Beaven notes that Stewart's *Driving over Lemons* is neither a tourist, sojourner, nor immigrant travel narrative and proposes categorizing it as a "settler narrative," given that the narrator did not move due to political exile or economic need, but out of a desire to settle abroad (189–90). Whatever label we give the text, the overlapping genres of travel writing and autobiography offer both a construction of self and an interconnected construction of the self's environment. Although these narrative constructions are interwoven, I will focus here on the image of Órgiva and its inhabitants that these memoirs create.[19]

In contrast with the tone in Brenan's work, Stewart, whose goal was to farm, recounts his experiences with wry, often self-deprecating humor and presents a variety of personalities among the *orgiveños*, often lauding them as having tremendous knowledge and resourcefulness. Amid stories about deep friendships as well as conflicts with *orgiveños*, the narrator recounts moments in which tradition and modernity collide and local and incomer eating habits are incompatible.[20] Stewart's introduction into the Alpujarra of mechanical sheepshearing (a skill he had acquired in England in his twenties) brings to the fore questions about insider/outsider status and the desirability of modernity.

When Stewart is hired to carry out his first mechanized shearing job, he is thrilled because "No longer would I be an outsider observing, but I could step inside the scene and become one of the observed" (1999, 98). After a humorous take on his shearing debut as a low-key success in proving himself to the *orgiveños*, the narrator recounts being criticized by another foreigner—"one of a small band of New Age travellers" who was living in an old truck parked in a riverbed—for ending local sheepshearing traditions (109). Although the narrator himself admits to having qualms about his effect on the social side of gathering to hand shear with scissors, he and the local shepherds are well aware of the physical advantages of mechanical shearing, for both the shearers and the sheep. All the same, the narrator notes that "the eco-fundamentalists of Órgiva" continued to criticize him for months for "the havoc I was wreaking in the delicate balance between man and nature" (110). Through humor, Stewart's text raises questions about who should be the arbiter of whether change is desirable— the local agricultural workers who had been doing the heavy labor of hand shearing or incomers who have no experience with caring for livestock but an interest in maintaining the traditions of their new environment. Interestingly, the local shepherds welcome the change— the narrator reports that they seek him out to shear their sheep mechanically, but other incomers are intolerant of it and the narrator suggest that it is because it disturbs their romanticized image of the area as one steeped in "natural," traditional ways. Indeed, throughout Stewart's three memoirs centered on Órgiva, there are about as many examples of recognition-based tolerance, permission-based tolerance, and outright intolerance between himself and alternatives living in the area as between himself and *orgiveños* and other locals from the Alpujarra.

An encounter between different dietary habits and perceptions in *Driving over Lemons* is a forerunner to the topic of food as the site of cultural and religious difference in Stewart's subsequent memoirs. In the first memoir, Stewart's first mechanized shearing job takes place at a farmhouse near the O Sel Ling Buddhist monastery, founded in 1982, about a 35-minute drive further up in the mountains from Órgiva. This leads to a vignette in which a local shepherd's wife asks Stewart to explain to her why, when she offers food to the exhausted travelers that get lost looking for the monastery, they push aside what for her are the best parts—different types of fatty pork—and only eat the bread. In the ensuing conversation, the shepherd's portly wife says that she feels sorry for these foreigners who only eat rice and vegetables, but wonders if doing so would help her slim down (1999, 106). The comical incompatibility of foodways is a theme that is extended and sometimes developed further in Stewart's next two memoirs.

As the internationalization of Órgiva increased, the two sequels to *Driving over Lemons*, published in 2002 and 2006, make more reference to the various communities in the area. In *A Parrot in the Pepper Tree*, when discussing the decision regarding whether his daughter should take the religion or ethics course at the Órgiva public school, Stewart's narrator describes the religion textbooks. These schoolbooks included culturally and racially stereotyped drawings of practitioners of religions other than Catholicism, but gave scant attention to Islam because it is "too close for comfort in Andalucia" (2002, 157). This leads the narrator to note that "These books were obviously not produced with the Alpujarras in mind [. . .]. All the oriental religions are well represented here and within ten kilometres of Orgiva there are more cults and sects and sub-sects than you can wave a joss stick at" (157). Having fun with the idiomatic expression "wave/shake a stick at" by making the stick a stick of incense, precisely what would be used in an Asian religion, the narrator plays with the uniqueness of the Órgiva area and the ignorance regarding the religious plurality of the area on the part of outsiders, who in this case are the Spanish textbook authors from outside of the region.

Later in *A Parrot in the Pepper Tree*, there are passing references to Muslim friends and neighbors, and, when Stewart seeks help from an environmental activist in the area to oppose a proposed dam project that would likely have a negative effect on his property, Muslims come up again in the description of the activists' fundraiser party. At the event, Stewart drinks wine while he works the grill in the kiosk for skewered pork, or *pinchitos*, and "I drained my paper cup again and again, keeping pace with Abu Bakr, opposite, who was gulping mint tea at the halal *pinchitos* stall set up for the Muslim contingent" (2002, 212). With this detail, the memoir highlights the unusual contrasts found within Órgiva's diversity—the strange bedfellows that the town creates, but also the separateness, or side-by-sideness, that this diversity entails, since the very definition of halal depends on separation to avoid cross-contamination.

The issue of halal foods and dietary restrictions in general is developed further in Stewart's third memoir centered on Órgiva, *The*

Almond Blossom Appreciation Society.²¹ Amid tongue-in-cheek moments in which Stewart tries to prove his acculturation to *orgiveños* by correctly using local greeting idioms, managing to skillfully drink from a *bota* or wineskin, and passing commentary on local wines, the issues of labor migration, cultural authenticity, and food are interwoven. A chapter about a group of young undocumented Moroccan immigrants who arrive at Stewart's farmhouse searching for water as they make their way—on foot—to El Ejido to look for work, establishes links between these migrants and Alpujarran migrants. Stewart and his wife Ana take the risk of helping the clandestine migrants, knowing that it is illegal to do so, but the food they are able to offer the famished youths is an egg omelet because the only meat that Stewart and his wife have on hand is pork. Later, the narrator is surprised to find that many others in the area are willing to take the risk of a prison sentence to help such migrants. He recounts that when he talks with a local goatherd about the group of Moroccan migrants, the goatherd spoke about them with "an unusually compassionate tone" and said

> that many of the farmers in the remote *cortijos* [farmhouses] will do what they can to relieve the misery of migrants who come their way–not much, of course, for they haven't much to give, but they will give them bread and olives and a safe place to rest. "Some of the old people have seen their children walk away to find work," he explained. "Maybe not quite so desperate–but people here know about poverty and what it drives you to" (2006, 72).

This reminds the narrator of a conversation he had once had with his good friend and neighbor Domingo, in which Domingo "mentioned that he'd gone to Barcelona as a young man to work in a bottle factory. It was *muy mal*, he had said, and then sharply changed the subject as if unwilling to linger. I realised that, although he often speaks of Catalunya, he'd never again made the slightest reference to having lived there himself" (2006, 72). Through this narration of an encounter with desperate Moroccan migration, the memoir highlights the local labor migration history and the compassion as well as traumatic silences that it produces.²² The unexpected compassion toward the desperate migrants reveals that the authentic Alpujarran experience is just as much about the Alpujarra as it is about labor migration.

After his contact with the Moroccan youths headed to work "in dire conditions" in El Ejido (69), Stewart decides to bring awareness to the plight of undocumented migrants by walking in the footsteps of those young migrants; that is, he and another British writer set out to hike the same path that the young men had walked from Algeciras toward El Ejido and then publish an essay about the experience. From the start, the project is plagued by issues of authenticity, but the chapter's title, "Authenticity Will Out," suggests, by rewording the common expression "truth will out" (meaning "the truth will become public"), that authenticity is irrepressible, and thus, that, according to other criteria, the project was actually quite authentic. The narrator questions the expedition's authenticity from the beginning, not only because their footwear and his backpack are much more comfortable than the inadequate gear of the Moroccan migrants he met, but because of the haram food that Stewart and his companion are enjoying en route: "a shadow of concern that the purity of our expedition was being compromised by a very un-Moroccan feasting on ham and wine," (89) and "Once again, though, I couldn't help noting that few genuine arrivals from North Africa would fancy pig-fat butter at the start of their day" (90). Later, when Stewart reports that he complained to his travel companion, Michael, that they were eating too much pork—"'Surely we ought to make some efforts to be a little more authentic. No?'"—Michael replies: "'It depends what you mean by authentic. Five hundred years ago converted Muslims and Jews were obliged to display a *jamón* swinging from their rafters as proof that they had genuinely adopted Christianity. Otherwise, they'd have been slung out of the country by the Inquisition. Why do you think the meat has achieved such iconic importance in this country?'" (Stewart 2006, 99). In this passage, conceptions of authenticity, which are fundamental to outsiders' fascination with the remoteness of the Alpujarra as well as efforts to demonstrate acculturation to the ways of "the locals," are turned on their head. As Michael asserts, perhaps the most authentic thing a clandestine Muslim migrant (or someone trying to recreate their experience) can do in Spain is eat copious amounts of pork.

Another chapter, entitled "Salad Days," raises once again differences in diet, but this time in the context of alternative diets. Stewart's narrator recounts the challenges he faced in trying to plan a birthday bash because

> a good many of our friends do not eat meat. All of the local Spaniards do, but the expat community of Órgiva is engulfed in a raft of alternative diets, from straightforward vegetarianism through to vegan, ovo-lacto-vegan, macrobiotic and ayurvedic. There is also a small but significant minority of crudo-vegans, who eat only raw food–a fad which seems to be sweeping the alternative Alpujarras [. . .] Not surprisingly the issue of what to serve a crudo-vegan guest is a vexed one (Stewart 2006, 197).

This ironic account of new food trends demonstrates another facet of difference in Órgiva. The leitmotif of differences in diet foregrounds the multiplicity of definitions of what constitutes a "clean" diet and the contrasting definitions of authenticity, related to both the entrance of modernity (mechanized sheepshearing), migration experiences, and dietary restrictions. The result is a set of memoirs that constructs an image of Órgiva and its environs as an eclectic, quirky place that offers unusual challenges, unexpected bonds, and redefinitions of authenticity. Thus, literally and figuratively, Stewart's memoirs provide food for thought regarding what it means to coexist.

By the mid-2010s, Órgiva's diversity had increased and was recognized nationally and across Europe, and in 2020, another longtime British resident, Andy Bailey, self-published an account of his experience as an incomer in the town. In *Órgiva: A Chancer's Guide to Rural Spain*, Bailey offers a humorous memoir mixed in with detailed practical tips—ranging from the horticultural information pertinent to each season, to the construction materials needed to build a farmhouse, to the ins and outs of raising cows, goats, mules, and sheep—for anyone considering embarking on a similar adventure. This material is interspersed with chapters organized around the feast days of Catholic figures (various saints and the image of Jesus known as the *Cristo de la Expiración*): background information on the saint's life or the venerated statue, how the feast day is celebrated locally, and how Bailey has been involved, often first-hand, in these events. For these reasons, in many ways the text reads like a farmer's almanac mixed with a *santoral* (sanctorale, or calendar of Catholic saints). In contrast with Stewart's memoirs, Bailey's text focuses on *orgiveños* and presents them as "tolerant" without opening the concept for questioning. Bailey's *A Chancer's Guide* highlights that, among the many cultures coming together in Órgiva, the contact between rural and urban ways of life and bodies of knowledge plays an important role. From the author's rural, agricultural lens, the book asserts a vision of Órgiva as tolerant, while it simultaneously foregrounds the local Catholic community and places other constituents in the background.

Bailey himself was raised in a small, rural town, but one located in Cornwall. After spending his youth on farms, he was working as an agricultural technician and consultant when he and his wife Sarah went on vacation to Órgiva and decided to pursue their dream of being self-employed in southern Spain, instead of in southern England.[23] In 2000, he moved to Órgiva with Sarah and their 6-year-old daughter and eventually he wrote *A Chancer's Guide*, his account of his experiences, which features two recurring motifs: taking risks in pursuit of one's dreams and the welcoming tolerance of the *orgiveños*. The memoir explains that as the narrator and his wife struggle to learn Spanish, they are intent on pursuing "integration" with "the locals" (terms that reappear in the text). They become friends with the owner of their favorite bar and spend time playing *rentoy* (a Spanish card game), hunting, and preparing *choto* (goat) from scratch with *orgiveños*. This leads to Bailey becoming the first (and, to date, only) *guiri*, or Northern European incomer, to belong to a *cofradía*, one of the associations dedicated to a particular image of Christ, apparition of the Virgin Mary, or saint whose members participate in a yearly procession carrying the statue of the holy figure. At one point in the memoir, the narrator describes Órgiva as "a bustling busy town with a very cosmopolitan, bohemian atmosphere" (12–13) and throughout he highlights local tolerance: "we could feel the warmth and friendliness of the local parents with children of a similar age" (12); "Communication was difficult, but tolerance was there in abundance" (33); "Playing bingo in Spanish is a challenge [. . .] But tolerance is an enduring quality of the folk around here" (62). When invited to join a *cofradía* or brotherhood, the narrator responds to his local friend "It would be a great honour" (90) and says of the brotherhood's practice sessions for the procession "all of them accepted me as a friend and a member of the team" (91). The memoir closes with an acknowledgments section in which Bailey thanks "All the wonderful tolerant Spanish friends that have looked after us during these years of discovery" (225).

As I explain in subsequent sections, this level of immersion into *orgiveño* life on the part of a Northern European or metropolitan newcomer is rare, as is this type of recognition-based tolerance between these incomers and *orgiveños*. Bailey's small-town, regional agricultural background certainly motivated and facilitated his interest in delving into local social life. In *A Chancer's Guide*, he recounts stories from his childhood in Cornwall, where he grew up farming in a town about the size of Órgiva. This rural upbringing also took place in a part of Britain with a distinct regional identity. In conversation with Bailey, he noted that in Cornwall people see themselves primarily as Cornish, not British, and remarked that it's similar to the situation of the Alpujarra: the area where he grew up, also reliant on mining and agriculture, has traditionally been "very much an enclosed society," his hometown is similar to Órgiva in that everyone is related to each other, and people in his hometown and in Órgiva have "the same sort of mentality." Bailey added that "You felt an empathy and a unity with the people here that I had in Cornwall."[24] Bailey's familiarity with small-town rural life, and appreciation for it, led him to seek out the same kinds of relationships and pastimes in Órgiva, and to present his relationship with *orgiveños* as an example of toleration.

The distinction between rural know-how and urban, bookish knowledge is clear in a passage in *A Chancer's Guide* when the narrator states that their first Christmas in Spain was unexpectedly busy because they were housesitting for someone who had a vacation rental business and "ten people turned up from all over the world: Sweden, the Hague, South America and France. All lovely people, but all academics. Not a practical bone in their bodies. We had to show them how to light the fires every evening" (Bailey 32). In contrast, when Bailey asks a local goatherd to sell him a goat to cook and the fellow arrives with the animal alive, the slaughter of the goat becomes an initiation rite of sorts through which Bailey cements his bonds with the *orgiveños*: "So, off we went to dispatch the creature. When in the woods Antonio offered me the knife to do the deed. No problem. The look on his face was one of amazement. I explained my farming history. I think the story circulated quite quickly as I started to get lots of 'holas' from the locals" (44). According to Bailey's narrative, demonstrating farm-life know-how resulted in admiration and respect from the *orgiveños*. In other words, what may have been a form of permission-based tolerance or indulgent curiosity (reflected in Bailey's joke about having been adopted as a "pet foreigner" by an *orgiveño* [183]), becomes a tolerance based on mutual recognition. As a result, in contrast with Brenan's references to "my village," which, especially in the context of that narrative, convey individual possession, Bailey uses the plural possessive—"our Brotherhood" (80), "Around our town [. . .]" (96), and "our town opens [. . .]" (Bailey, 111), creating turns of phrase that project a shared sense of community.

With its focus on immersion in the local culture, *A Chancer's Guide* makes sparing reference to the contemporary Muslim presence in Órgiva, but gives some attention to the abundance of alternative lifestyles in the town, including manifestations of Muslimness among those. In addition to a few brief references to the historical presence of Muslims in the Alpujarra—the Moorish origins of the irrigation system and a key Spanish word's Arabic origins, the memoir-cum-incomer's guide makes two very brief references to Muslims in Órgiva: "a Bangladeshi builder who also knew the Halal method of slaughter" (46) and, within a list of the variegated clothing styles one can see in Órgiva: "from kilts, jellabiya, cravats, sports jackets, top hats to baggy trousers" (217). The text's focus on the local also leads to a remark about there being only one place of worship in the town, in reference to the Catholic church.

The narrator's affiliation with a traditional version of the local leads to a particular perspective on the relationship between *orgiveños* and the more extreme forms of alternative lifestyle that have arrived in the town. In the same chapter that presents the celebration of the *Cristo de la Expiración*, Bailey devotes a paragraph to the Dragon Festival (an alternative event that I return to subsequently). He mentions this spring equinox festival and states:

> Unfortunately, this often clashed with the El Cristo celebrations. The tolerant folk of Órgiva put up with this invasion of thousands of festival goers at a time when many normal Christian devotees were visiting the town. Obviously, it had its financial benefits and the supermarkets did a roaring trade in festival refreshments. A few attempts were made to make the festival illegal and get it banned but, in the end, nature provided the solution (Bailey, 89–90).

Bailey then explains that the combination of a municipal tree-planting project and a heavy rainfall led to the festival site being flooded and the relocation of the festival to a new site closer to the city of Granada, "to the relief of the town hall but not the supermarket owners" (90). Curiously, this interpretation of the festival's relocation, which differs significantly from the accounts of the festival organizers and the local mayor, places all agency in the hands of Mother Nature. That is, Bailey's narrative downplays considerably the tensions between the local authorities and the festival organizers and, to maintain the tolerant portrait of the *orgiveños*, disassociates *orgiveños* from the ousting of the festival by attributing it to factors outside their control. In this way, Bailey avoids presenting the more radical alternatives as the object of *orgiveños*' intolerance and is able to join *orgiveños* in their demarcation of what is (not) acceptable in "our town." Like other 21st-century narratives about Órgiva, Bailey's erases certain differences and tensions in an effort to portray the town as overwhelmingly tolerant.

Another narrative about the Alpujarra and an incognito Órgiva that presents a very different perspective on the area appeared later in the same year as Bailey's account. In spite of vast differences, both texts emphasize agriculture, such that the second one might be considered a white Muslim version of the Alpujarran farmer's almanac. In late 2020, Medina Whiteman published *The Invisible Muslim: Journeys Through Whiteness and Islam*, a memoir of her experiences as someone of Anglo-American and British origins who was born into Islam through her convert parents; though born in the city of Granada, she was raised in England and later settled in Spain, first staying in Órgiva in 2005 and settling there permanently in 2009.[25] Within her memoir, Whiteman dedicates a chapter to her experience as a white Muslim in the Alpujarra, emphasizing links to al-Andalus while also pointing to racist thinking and questioning ethnicity-based constructions of identity and romanticizing impulses.

In the chapter entitled "A Blessed Tree: Digging for Andalusian Roots," Whiteman presents her experiences as a white Muslim living in Órgiva, although she never names the town. On the chapter's second page, she identifies the region of Spain to which she moved as "the Alpujarras" (126) and continues to reference this region throughout the chapter, although she only mentions by name the neighboring town of Lanjarón (154). To refer to the town in which she resides, at one point she uses "my town" and "our town" (154). Given the book's focus, the chapter says little about the local Spanish residents of the Alpujarra, aside from references to instances of stereotyping and othering of Muslims. In this sense, indirectly the chapter points to the limited contact between *orgiveños/alpujarreños* and the local Sufi community. But it also directly points to manifestations of intolerance on the part of Alpujarrans toward both Muslims (regardless of origin) and Maghrebis, as well as on the part of European converts to Islam toward Muslims from Asia and Africa.

The chapter consists of historical and social commentary sections interspersed with sections that reflect upon how moving to Granada and then the Alpujarra have shaped Whiteman's identity. The more outward-looking sections address the history of al-Andalus and the so-called Reconquista, with an emphasis on the Alpujarra, the presence of al-Andalus in contemporary Spain, and the rise of contemporary Spanish conversion to Islam, commenting upon Andalusia's "ambivalent relationship to its Muslim past" (136) and Spain's "ambivalent relationship to non-Europeans in general" (153). While exploring these topics, the narrator highlights the presence of living, breathing Muslims in the contemporary Alpujarra and the different types of intolerance in which they are involved.

On the one hand, the mosque where she prays draws "the usual crowd of happy misfits from the world over" (152). On the other hand, she recounts instances of Spanish discrimination against Muslims and especially Muslims of color: "a long-term Spanish resident of Senegalese origin, told me that while Spanish people generally treat him respectfully, he's seen plenty of *racismo maquillado*: 'racism wearing make-up'" (149–50); "A couple I know, a half-Sudanese, half-Spanish woman and the son of Spanish converts, were about to take an apartment in my town, but when the landlord saw their names on the contract—three out of four surnames Spanish but, crucially, Arab sounding first names—he refused, saying he preferred 'people from here'" (154); and "When a country lane near our town was blocked, for once not by goats, but by an Arab man who had driven into an *acequia*, a neighbour of mine who happened to be passing shook his head and muttered so that only I could hear: '*Estos moros*.' These Muslims" (154–55). Whiteman also notes a problematic attitude of superiority on the part of European converts to Islam toward Muslims from Muslim-majority regions of Asia and Africa: "a Moroccan who has lived for many years in Spain, told me that he has met plenty of Spanish Muslims who disdain to be around North Africans" (149) and at her local mosque "the daughter of [a] Spanish convert family" recounts that her father, after spending time in various Muslim-majority countries,

> was not attracted to Islam until he returned to Spain. "He found a purer Islam here" [...] I have noticed that converts, perhaps over-eager to claim Islam as their own, can sometimes tout this apparently "pure," sanitised

version of European Islam, reduced to abstract concepts and stripped of distasteful cultural clutter. While the appeal of a diverse global *ummah* might be attractive to Westerners like me, the desire for belonging can make European Muslims cling together in white gaggles. I myself am not immune to this (Whiteman, 152–53).

Thus, the portrait that emerges of the Alpujarran Muslim community is one of a highly diverse, yet separate group that, in search of different forms of belonging, experiences occasional instances of discrimination—both as the object *and* the agent of othering.

Agriculture has a prominent place as the unifying thread throughout Whiteman's chapter and the core symbol within that running theme is the olive tree. Through a mix of humor and poetic imagery, Whiteman presents the region's millennial olive trees as a natural, living link to the period of Muslim cultural ascendancy in the area. The chapter's opening lines evoke the olive tree: "In the mountains around Granada there are millennial olive trees. No, they aren't Instagram influencers, though you might scrabble to take a selfie with one if you saw their sinuous figures rippling out of the earth" (125). Soon after, she connects these olive trees and agriculture more broadly to the southern Mediterranean and Muslim roots of Spain:

> The Phoenicians initially brought juicy olives here from the Levant to improve the varieties eaten by Celtiberians [. . .] In the Muslim period we know as Al-Andalus, Spain—particularly the south, climatically and geologically similar to North Africa—was extensively developed. Agriculture contributed decisively to the economic and cultural renaissance that took place here during almost 800 years of European Muslim history (Whiteman, 126).

The olive and farming are also a catalyst in her personal growth. Whiteman observes that returning to Spain after university led to a

> personal revelation of nature's staggering, humanity-eclipsing beauty. From getting up early to pick ice-cold oranges from the trees, and tend-

ing wood fires on crisp, star-studded nights, to irrigating olive groves at 3 a.m., barefoot in August, and gorging myself on mulberries, figs or pomegranates straight from the tree, the natural world was no longer a distant, uncomfortable reality, held at a hygienic distance by civilisation, but tangible and dripping with juice (Whiteman, 126).

This passage points to the place of Alpujarran agriculture in providing an antidote to modernity and noxious conceptions of civilization.

The text moves on to focus on the religious and spiritual impact of life amid the olive groves of the Alpujarra: "My experience of Islam evolved, too" (126). In contrast with the narrator's "entirely urban" (126) experience of Islam in Britain, "Here in my new hispanically Wild West home, I attended *dhikrs* held in a round wooden yurt set deep in an olive grove, with a candle in the middle and the hypnotic soundtrack of cicada song. Like most people living here, the local Sufi community has a high proportion of cottage gardeners, proud to use their own cold-pressed olive oil throughout the year" (126). Yet Whiteman recognizes that her affective ties with the region are tinged with Romantic notions: "Romanticism it may be, but as a European Muslim living in Spain, it is spine-tingling to run my hand over the rutted bark of a millennial olive tree knowing that it was planted by a Spanish Muslim. There is something compelling about the idea of Spanish Muslims recuperating the *filahah* (husbandry) of their spiritual forebears" (127).

Her use of "Spanish Muslim" is quite literal: Whiteman presents a revisionist history explaining that "the majority of the so-called Moors [...] were descendants of indigenous Celtiberians, Visigoths, Slavs and Jews who converted to Islam over nearly a millennium of Islamic hegemony" (129–30).[26] She goes on to assert that "Islam became fully indigenised in Spain" (135). However, as heralded by the chapter title, she also suggests that her interest in medieval Iberian Islam is part of a search for roots, a way to anchor and give meaning to her identity as a European Muslim: "I can't help but feel that there is some resonance today with the roots that this religion held firmly in Spanish soil for nearly a millennium and in extremis for another 500 years. Or am I merely romanticising, looking for roots on which to graft my own European Islam?" (150). Whiteman closes the chapter by using the olive tree, as presented in a Quranic verse, to define Órgiva and its environs as a third space, one that encompasses elements of both "East" and "West": "One of the best-loved verses of the Qur'an can be found in *Surat an-Nur*—the Chapter of Light—which likens Divine Light to a lamp kindled by oil from a 'blessed olive tree neither of the East nor the West.' Every time I pass one of these gorgeous, mute giants, I'm reminded of how this place is neither. And both. Such a place I could call home" (158). In this way, Whiteman consciously constructs her identity as a European Muslim through the living remnants of al-Andalus and establishes the Alpujarra as a place that accommodates and nourishes this identity so well that it has become her home, her space of belonging—and of awareness of the unsavory elements (forms of othering) that are part of the production of belonging.

Between the publication of Stewart's third memoir in 2006 and Bailey's and Whiteman's texts, a work appeared that narrates the newly transformed Órgiva through local collaboration. Given the many kinds of narratives about Órgiva produced from primarily outside perspectives, from the gaze of the anthropologist or traveler, or from the vantage point of a newer, Anglophone resident, and primarily for outside readers, the *Proyecto Municipio Andaluz Sostenible* (Sustainable Andalusian Municipality Project) is a refreshing departure ripe with possibilities. This initiative not only includes the portrayal of the new Órgiva that was beginning to emerge when Stewart arrived, but does so by pooling residents' voices. The project produced a collaborative, community oral history, published in 2012 as a book entitled *Hablamos de Órgiva: Historias y reflexiones de la gente de Órgiva, sus anejos y sus cortijadas* (We're Talking about Órgiva: Stories and Reflections of the People of Órgiva, Its Annexes, and Its Farmhouses). In a sense, this text can be understood as an attempt at homegrown narrative, a pastiche tale told with material from the residents of Órgiva themselves and for these residents, though assembled by non-Alpujarran Andalusians.[27] According to the PASOS website, the project was initiated by *Federación Andaluza de Ciencias Ambien-*

tales (FACCAA—the Andalusian Environmental Science Federation) with funding from Ciudad 21, a joint program of the government of Andalucía (*la Junta de Andalucía*) that promotes sustainable development.[28] FACCAA selected various towns that fit certain size criteria and four of these municipalities expressed strong interest in being the site of the project. Representatives of FACCAA visited the four towns and chose Órgiva as the one best suited for the project. Once selected, the municipal government of Órgiva also became one of the project's sponsors. The team of coordinators from FACCAA took on the name PASOS, from the first syllables of the Spanish words for "participation" and "sustainability" (PASOS website).[29]

Conceived of as a pilot citizen participation project, it was meant to increase "environmental, social, economic, and cultural sustainability," through the townspeople "becoming aware of the reality of their surroundings" and through "the steps and proposals generated by them" (PASOS website). To that end, in 2009 the PASOS team moved to Órgiva to start gathering residents' statements about a variety of topics under the umbrella of community sustainability. The introductory chapter, "Para entender mejor el libro" (To Better Understand the Book), explains that for over more than two years the team collected statements from the residents through interviews and group meetings and this was followed by an editing process in which community members also participated. Almost 400 residents of Órgiva contributed with statements and/or via collaboration in the editing stage. The statements are organized by topic into the 17 chapters of *Hablamos de Órgiva*, each one bound and numbered separately with the idea that one could move through the chapters of the book in any order (*Hablamos de Órgiva*, "Para entender mejor el libro" 10).[30] Some of the titles of the chapters are: "Celebrations and Gatherings," "Those Who Left and Those Who Arrived," "Beliefs and Spirituality," "Life in the Streets and Plazas," "The Mountains, Sierra Lújar, and the Mines," "The Fields," "Health and Drugs," and "Water." In each chapter, the residents' statements are preceded by a short introduction from the PASOS team and occasionally the team also adds linking sentences between statements or subsections. Even within the separate chapters, there is no unifying narrative arc and there are no concluding statements after the last quote from a resident.

Moreover, although this decision is not addressed in the introductory chapter, the contributors' statements are not only presented anonymously, but with no direct indication of the speaker's background. Often, but not always, the content or the language (non-standard Spanish and/or phrases in other languages accompanied by Spanish translation) of the piece of testimony suggests what community the speaker is part of. But in many cases, the positioning of the speaker arises at the end of the quote or not at all, such that there is no way to contextualize the perspective or identify the "we" established by the contributor. Organizing the comments according to topic, rather than community group, and only including the contextualizing and identifying information afforded by the quote itself, results in multiple, unknown narrators. Given that these narrators often present opposing perspectives on the town and its inhabitants, this creates a fractured multi-perspectivity. On the one hand, akin to the workings of postmodern aesthetics, this collection of unmarked, often dissenting voices creates a guesswork-based reading experience and forms a loose, conflicted "we," or cacophonic collective voice, for the town that includes old and new residents alike. But, on the other hand, this way of presenting the testimonies also entails a loss of specificity in which there is no way to gain insight into why a particular perspective is expressed or what the relations are like between particular groups. Who is characterizing the town as tolerant and who is establishing the limits of tolerance? Other editorial decisions also added to this loss of specificity.

The introductory chapter addresses some of the editorial decisions faced by the coordinating team, which included the removal of certain markers of localness and all expressions of anger. The PASOS team explains that whenever possible they collected "the words" of the residents "literally, trying to respect to the fullest the different forms of expression, the localisms (words from Órgiva and the Alpujarra) and the oral character of the discourse. Nonetheless, at the request of the majority of the residents who participated, we have dispensed with the pronunciation and accent characteristic of each person, inserting between quotation marks the few 'spoken' words that we have maintained" ("Para entender mejor el libro" 11). This "cleaning up" of the orality of the statements demonstrates just how sensitive the issue of the local accent is. While local vocabulary items and expressions were included, the local pronunciation of standard Spanish words was not. The fact that the participants themselves requested this speaks volumes (no pun intended!) about the residents' awareness of the negative connotations of ignorance attached to this accent outside of the region. Another form of suppression goes beyond the form and flavor of the utterances to affect the content itself (if, indeed, they can be separated). The PASOS team notes that in their introductions and connecting paragraphs they aimed for neutrality ("Para entender mejor el libro" 20). And this approach bled into one of their editorial decisions: "One of the greatest dilemmas arose regarding the elimination or changing of utterances that could be hurtful or accusatory [. . .] In the end we opted to not leave them that way so as not to create a confrontation" ("Para entender mejor el libro" 20). This, of course, leaves one to wonder what was deleted from the testimonies.

The testimonies, in the form in which they are included, contain many references to different forms of separation and exclusion, as well as to "nationalities," "religions," "diversity," "tolerance," and "coexistence" [*convivencia*]. Some refer to the lack of interaction between the incomers and the *orgiveños* (e.g., "Many of the British don't do their part to assimilate and although we're together, we don't mix [Muchos ingleses no ponen de su parte para integrarse y aunque estamos juntos, no nos revolvemos]" ("Los que se fueron y los que llegaron" 17), while others see this as exclusion on the part of the *orgiveños*—for example:

The relationship between them is stronger, it's something you can't achieve . . . When there are two people from Órgiva, you're excluded; they arrive at their understandings, and there is a respect among them and you don't have a role to play, you're on the outside [Es superior la relación que tienen entre ellos, es algo que no consigues . . . Estando dos de

Órgiva, tú estás fuera; llegan a sus acuerdos, y hay un respeto entre ellos y tú no intervienes, estás fuera] ("Los que se fueron y los que llegaron" 14).

Or there is specifically the *orgiveños*' rejection of those living alternative lifestyles (e.g.: "People from Órgiva don't enjoy diversity, they're very opposed to the hippies [La gente de Órgiva no disfruta de la diversidad, es muy reacia a los hippies]" ("Los que se fueron y los que llegaron" 11), and the persistence of stereotypes (e.g.: "I would like for [the people] of the town to take some interest in looking this way, toward [the alternative community in] Morreón and shatter their stereotypes [A mí me gustaría que (la gente) del pueblo se preocupara un poco de mirar hacía aquí, hacía el Morreón y romper sus estereotipos]" ("Cómo se vive en Órgiva, sus anejos y cortijadas" 102).

However, many of the other contributors describe Órgiva with references to "tolerance" and "coexistence" [*convivencia*]. Although one contributor, who identifies him or herself as being from outside Spain, refers to tolerance in the context of *orgiveños* "tolerating" more noise pollution and litter ("Los que se fueron y los que llegaron" 14) and another reframes what may be seen as tolerance on the part of the local authorities as negligence by stating that "There's carelessness, it's not tolerance, and a lack of respect [Hay una dejadez, no es tolerancia, y una falta de respeto]" ("La política de partidos" 16), others describe the town—though not necessarily *orgiveños*—as a space of tolerant coexistence. For instance: "In Órgiva there's a unique tolerance [En Órgiva existe una tolerancia única]" ("Los que se fueron y los que llegaron" 11), and "The coexistence with the foreigners is very good [La convivencia con los extranjeros es muy buena]" ("Cómo se vive en Órgiva, sus anejos y cortijadas" 65). These comments indirectly define "tolerance" as mutual respect and the ability to have power over one's lifestyle: "There has to be respect for people who have chosen a different way of life, as long as these people respect you, of course. A mutual respect [Hay que respetar a la gente que ha elegido una forma de vivir distinta, siempre que esta gente te respete a ti, claro. Un respeto mutuo]" ("Cómo se vive en Órgiva, sus anejos y cortijadas" 86), and "I think that the people from outside want to be in charge of their own lives and here they can, in that sense Órgiva is very tolerant [Yo creo que la gente de fuera quieren ser protagonistas de su propia vida y aquí pueden, en ese sentido Órgiva es muy tolerante]" ("Los que se fueron y los que llegaron" 7).

Some contributors presented the arrival of the newcomers as what had made the local inhabitants more tolerant of difference:

> It's probably because of the hippie communes, but we've lived with them since we were little and we've experienced it as something normal; that's why this town is more special in this way, we know how to tolerate people from other countries more. That's why here there is so much diversity that coexists perfectly [Será por las comunas hippies, pero hemos convivido con ellos desde pequeños y lo hemos vivido con normalidad; por eso este pueblo es más especial en este aspecto, sabemos tolerar más a las personas de otros países. Por eso aquí hay tanta diversidad que convive perfectamente] ("Los que se fueron y los que llegaron" 11).

Although one local contributor laments that the town has "lost its identity" because of these newcomers ("Los que se fueron y los que llegaron" 11), another sees the town as having benefitted from them, explicitly connecting the values of the newcomers (in this case in regard to recycling), to European cultural advancement:

> I remember when they came and were starting to talk about recycling 30 years ago [...] I didn't understand it culturally [...] We've gone from being a society isolated from the world to being among the most culturally advanced of Europe [Yo recuerdo cuando vinieron y empezaban a hablar del reciclaje hace 30 años [...] no lo entendía culturalmente [...] Hemos pasado de ser una sociedad aislada del mundo a ser de lo más avanzado de Europa culturalmente] ("Los que se fueron y los que llegaron" 16).

Here the civilizational prestige of the newcomers vis-à-vis the *orgiveños*, and the latter's pride in becoming more "European" and "advanced" is clear.

Hablamos de Órgiva addresses the Muslim communities in the town in the chapter on "Beliefs and Spirituality," which includes extensive material on Islam as a religion (its basic principles and forms of worship) and one testimony addressing how ignorance about Islam makes some *orgiveños* assume that all Muslims are bad people ("Creencias y espiritualidad" 12). Nonetheless, the book contains only a few references to intra-Muslim differences. The one testimony that is obviously from a Maghrebi migrant says a lot about how some Maghrebis in the town view the Sufi converts.[31] In the chapter's opening section, which focuses on beliefs in general and is not yet divided by religion, this North African states:

> When I was in Algeria, I was only familiar with Islam, I didn't know anything about the outside world. But since I arrived here, and especially in [Café] Baraka, where a lot of Christians, Muslims, Sufis come in—in Algeria I never saw any Sufis—I'm learning lots of things . . . [Cuando estaba en Argelia, estaba metido sólo con Islam, no sabía nada del mundo de fuera. Pero desde que llegué aquí, y más al Baraka, donde entran muchos cristianos, musulmanes, sufíes—yo nunca vi en Argelia a ningún sufí—estoy aprendiendo muchas cosas . . .] ("Creencias y espiritualidad" 4).

It is noteworthy that the Maghrebi migrant speaker categorizes Sufis separately from Muslims. In a more extensive contribution from the same speaker, he describes how Islam is practiced in Algeria versus in other parts of the Muslim world and in an implicit comparison with the Sufi community, the speaker says: "In Algeria we practice 'normal' Islam [En Argelia practicamos el Islam 'normal']" ("Creencias y espiritualidad" 13–14). The migrant's distinction between Muslims and Sufis and then between "normal" and, by inference, "strange" Islam reveals that he does not identify at all with the Sufis and suggests that he sees them as deviating from "correct" or "true" Islam. However, this is not explored at all in *Hablamos de Órgiva*. Similarly, in another chapter, there is one passing reference to immigration from North Africa: an *orgiveño* states that the Moroccans and other immigrants who work in the fields are there because Spaniards don't want those jobs ("El campo" 16). But there are no other comments about migrants and employment, or about illegal immigration, which seems unlikely given the larger context. Perhaps suppression of any such comments was deemed judicious given that the project started about 9 years after the violent anti-immigrant unrest in El Ejido and other parts of neighboring Almería province. Thus, the *Hablamos de Órgiva* project stands out for the local government's and inhabitants' enthusiasm with regard to sharing their perspectives and striving to better the town, but also for the role of the coordinators and the community members themselves in deciding to silence certain elements of difference by neutralizing the contributions in their written form.

Hablamos de Órgiva is fascinating due both to what it accomplished through its innovative format and to what it shied away from—its self-imposed limits. What the PASOS webpage describes as a "participatory diagnostic" was a wonderful opportunity for dialogue in group sessions and for group decision making when they gathered to edit the rough draft. No doubt this focus on the participatory process was an important step in creating awareness and self-reflection, moving towards new ways of seeing and new initiatives, and fomenting a sense of agency. The *Hablamos* project, as a process, may have contributed to the townspeople's desire to tolerate and their awareness of the forces involved in toleration. But, unfortunately, through its omissions, it stopped short of taking the residents a step further and considering how socioeconomic factors and other forms of difference and power are a part of the toleration dynamic functioning—or struggling to function—in Órgiva.[32]

The five memoirs and collaborative community history examined here span a 21-year time period and two languages. As a group, they depart from the textual construction of the Alpujarra as wary of outsiders and marked by primitiveness, poverty, ignorance, and/or stereotyped or romanticized Moorishness. They all register Órgiva's recent diversification, but in different ways. Stewart's memoirs (1999, 2002, 2006) present Órgiva and its environs as eclectically idiosyncratic, a space in which tradition and modernity—and the conflicting dietary goals that they produce—exist in a state of quirky tension, but also as an area with multiple connections to labor migration. Whiteman's text presents the area as a thriving hub of contemporary, yet farming-focused, European Muslim life, simultaneously foregrounding the persistence of Islam in the area, of problematic relationships with the past, and of discrimination against Muslims, and especially Muslims of non-European origin. In the process, both authors demonstrate some of the bonds and tensions that arise in the contact zone that is Órgiva, while also raising questions, often via foodways, about understandings of authenticity and belonging. In contrast, Bailey's memoir downplays differences and tensions in order to emphasize tolerance on the part of the *orgiveños*.

By the time Bailey and Whiteman wrote, Órgiva's image as a tolerant space had already begun to circulate in the media and, in the case of Bailey's text, this may have created a sort of self-fulfilling prophecy in which the narrator views the town a priori as tolerant and as a result excludes or downplays that which would disturb this image and/or complicate common definitions of tolerance. In some ways, *Hablamos de Órgiva* "talks back" to the multitude of authors, Andalusian, Spanish, and from elsewhere in Europe, who have written about the Alpujarra. This collection of narratives by a range of Órgiva's inhabitants blurs and broadens the boundaries of what is "local," and re-presents Órgiva to the Spanish-speakers in the town as well as to potential regional and national readers, allowing many different perspectives to come to light, but also omitting other differences that could shed light on the town's social dynamics. *Hablamos de Órgiva* offered Órgiva's residents an active, primary role in the narration of the town—in the construction of an image that then interacts with the perceptions and realities of the place. However, by not providing any contextualization of the testimonies presented and editing out or avoiding certain issues, the project does not offer a coherent portrait of the town nor of the toleration dynamic within it. It does, however, much like Stewart's memoirs, point to the constant negotiation and questioning that is part of the friction between different value systems and their notions of what is and isn't acceptable. The juxtaposition of these new narratives about Órgiva demonstrates that the struggle over how to represent the voices and positions in the town mirrors the struggle to establish what should and should not be tolerated and what it means to tolerate in and of itself.

CHAPTER 4

21st-Century Televisual Narratives about Órgiva

As word spread about Órgiva, in the 2010s narratives about the town started to appear via television. This set of narratives, like that of Bailey, crafts an image of Órgiva as tolerant, without considering what is meant by "tolerance"—what kinds of tolerance exist, how forms of coexistence are created, and where and by whom their limits are set. All eight of these televisual narratives present Órgiva as a place that draws people who seek an escape from modern, urban life or conventional living, and most present it as a space of tolerant harmony. These television programs feature the town either as one of a set of locales tied to a particular theme, or as the sole focus of an entire episode. Aimed at a Spanish (and in one case a broader Spanish-speaking) audience, these televisual narratives reflect and amplify the layers of written narratives, journalistic pieces, and informal accounts circulated on the Internet or by word of mouth, that establish Órgiva as a haven for alternative lifestyles. In the ultimate rebuttal of the Black Legend, most of these television portraits emphasize the town's tolerance and *convivencia*. In the process, they highlight certain elements that create cohesion in the town, but obscure others that are sources of both friction and more sustainable forms of tolerance.

In keeping with the pattern of travel writing about the Alpujarra, these television shows are forms of 21st-century travel narrative. These small-screen narratives create different visions of the same town. They differ not only in their characterizations of Órgiva, but in their production values and their forms of distribution. Four of these mass-media representations of Órgiva were broadcast by the free-to-air Canal Sur television network, which is part of *Radio y Televisión de Andalucía* (RTVA), the public broadcasting company of the Autonomous Region of Andalucía, while two were broadcast by the free-to-air national public television network *Radio y Televisión Española* (RTVE), and two others by different branches of the international telecommunications giant Movistar (one as Internet television and the other as on-demand Spanish digital television). However, this set of eight shows, broadcast within a 6-year timespan, does demonstrate certain patterns. Aside from one quick visual reference in one of the shows, none of them include any mention of Maghrebi immigration, but almost all mention the Moorish past of the area and most participate in what I call "*convivencia*-washing": erasing or de-emphasizing certain elements in order to create an idealized image of happy cohabitation. Although, as indicated earlier, Órgiva is relatively more diverse and peaceful than other towns in Andalucía, painting a rosy picture results in three key losses: 1) the elimination or minimization of tensions experienced or witnessed by others in the town and thus the negation of their lived experience, 2) the inability to gain a deeper understanding of how the townspeople perceive and navigate these tensions, and 3) the impoverishment of the concept of tolerance via oversimplification.

THE MAGHREBIAN CONNECTION AS STRICTLY PART OF THE PAST

The second of the televisual narratives about Órgiva to appear, and the first of the RTVA episodes to appear, is a 1-hour and 15-minute show from the series *Este es mi pueblo* ("This is my town"), that is dedicated in its entirety to Órgiva.[1] In general, Canal Sur demonstrates lower production values than nationally broadcast shows and this is particularly true of this episode. More importantly, this show stands out from among the eight shows featuring Órgiva in that it is the only one in which Islam and North Africans—presented as *lo morisco*—are only mentioned as part of the past.² In the long-running *Este es mi pueblo* series, the show host, Rafael ("Rafa") Cremades, visits Andalusian towns, getting to know them via interviews with local inhabitants, and, in a thinly veiled fashion, promoting local businesses and/or tourism to the area. In its 11th season, the 9th episode (first aired on October 10, 2015) is dedicated to Órgiva. The episode includes a tour of Órgiva offered by Manuel Hernández Linares, a nationally recognized guitarist whose parents are from the town, an interview with Chris Stewart of *Driving over Lemons* fame, and visits to a local bakery, a local ceramics workshop, and the collection of editions of *Don Quixote* in the local library's Cervantes room, among other points of interest.

At Panadería Galindo, a local bakery, baker Antonio Pérez tells viewers that "within the cuisine of Órgiva, my wife and I will present to you some *morisco* sweets [. . .] There is a wide variety of *morisco* sweets [. . .] [dentro de la gastronomía de Órgiva mi mujer y yo os vamos a presentar unos dulces de elaboración morisca [. . .] Hay una gran variedad de dulces moriscos [. . .]]" (2:06–2:17). He then explains that they have chosen to demonstrate how to make two of the most representative of these sweets: "Mozarab [Arabized Christian] curd and Alpujarran delights [la cuajada mozárabe y las delicias de la Alpujarra]" (2:18–2:24).³ The baker goes on to explain that these recipes are "very ancient [antiquísimas]" and that his family, which has run the bakery for five generations, "found a book, a manuscript [encontramos un libro, un manuscrito]" containing many recipes that they had adapted (2:56–3:08). As the video shows Pérez and his wife, Encarnacion Álvarez, demonstrating how to prepare these sweets, the Chyron graphics at the bottom of the frame state "These recipes have been inherited from the *morisco* era [Estas recetas se han heredado de la época morisca]" (3:00–3:08). Curiously, the show does not mention that similar sweets, made by a North African immigrant living in the town, could be found at the town's halal eatery, Café Baraka. Instead, this narrative marks the sweets as traditionally Alpujarran and linked to a long-gone Moorish past, without noting that in

Órgiva these confections are consumed side by side with their contemporary Maghrebi culinary cousins. Additionally, although the two recipes Panadería Galindo highlights do not contain either oil or lard, many of the *morisco* recipes that are still made in the Alpujarra and Andalucía—such as *mantecados, polvorones, almendrados,* and *perrunas*—have undergone a modification: olive oil and vegetable oils have been substituted with lard.[4] Thus, the sweets of the Alpujarra can lie on either side of the dividing line between haram and halal, thereby constituting separate communities.

Immediately following the segment in the bakery, the show moves to the first of various segments that are a creative way to present more spontaneous, yet elliptical, local perspectives on the town. These segments feature a few alternating small groups of unnamed *orgiveños* (ranging from young adults to some in their 60s) seated on a bench placed next to the town's main plaza and giving their explanations of local vocabulary and customs, their observations on life in the town, and so forth. Although these *orgiveños* included as representative local voices are clearly responding to specific prompts or questions, viewers do not hear these. After the first appearance of these anonymous local commentators, the show moves to an *orgiveño* goatherd and his production of artisanal cheeses, and then, through a local ceramist, returns to the legacy of al-Andalus. When the show host, Rafa, visits the ceramist, Ricardo González, in his workshop, González demonstrates how he makes mosaics and they explain that his work not only recreates the style of the elaborate tilework in Granada's Alhambra palace, but some of his pieces are used in tactile displays within the Alhambra itself. Rafa and the ceramist refer to his craft as "Nasrid ceramics [cerámica nazarí]" (8:58–9:00) and, as the ceramist shows Rafa how to make mosaic tile, Orientalist flute and violin motifs (that is, musical phrases recognizable, partly due to stereotyping, as Middle Eastern or North African) emerge within the background guitar music (8:08–12:58).

Although this narrative of *orgiveño* foodways and artistry emphasizes the Moorish connection and even includes a Quixotesque use of the found-manuscript trope, the Órgiva episode of *Este es mi pueblo* is equally intent on excluding any modern-day Muslims or North Africans from its portrait of the town. The baker's found manuscript serves as a prelude to the show's highlighting of links between Cervantes' *Don Quixote* and Órgiva. Later in the episode (immediately after a segment on tourism that is poorly blended in and seems like an infomercial), the groups of anonymous local commentators read aloud *El Quijote*'s famous opening passages and offer their perspectives on the importance of the town's collection of editions of Cervantes' masterpiece (57:31–58:13). The *orgiveño* observers serve as a segue to Rafa's visit to the Cervantes room in the local public library, which includes more than 300 editions of *Don Quixote* in various languages, the result of the efforts of a former librarian who started building the collection in the 1970s (58:14–1:04:53). Invoking *Don Quixote* brings to mind the uncomfortable relationship between Spanish identity and the Moor. The novel is presented by Cervantes as a found Arabic manuscript that is translated into Spanish by a *morisco* and it features various *morisco* characters. The *moriscos* in the text have been interpreted as either ridiculed or negatively stereotyped figures, or as vehicles for an ironic critique of the nascent modern Spanish nation-state's ethnocentrism, that serves to defend the oppressed *moriscos*.[5] Thus, while the question "What is the place of the Moor in Peninsular culture?" is central to the *Quijote*, there is a great deal of ambivalence regarding how the text responds to the Moorish question and what prevails is an awareness of this identity issue as a source of tension. Through *morisco* and Mozarab sweets, ceramics from the 13th- to 15th-century Nasrid dynasty of Granada, and Cervantes' *Don Quixote*, the Órgiva episode of *Este es mi pueblo* emphasizes Moorishness as part of the past. However, the episode never mentions, verbally or visually, the Muslims or Maghrebis that are part of the town's present.

After the initial visit to the ceramist, the show covers the international and interregional character of Órgiva, still excluding its Muslim and North African elements. The town's international nature is first touched upon via the introduction of Chris Stewart and a visit, in the company of the guitarist Manuel Hernández Linares, to a German luthier who lives in Órgiva.

On the way to the luthier's workshop, Hernández Linares and the show host talk about this German who has chosen Órgiva as the place in which to practice his craft, how often Hernández Linares visits Órgiva, and the town as a source of inspiration for his music. During part of this conversation, the background information about the guitarist that explains his link to Órgiva is presented in a two-line on-screen graphic: "Source of inspiration; Manuel was born in Barcelona because his parents had to emigrate [tuvieron que emigrar]" (22:54–23:01). The choice of wording here—"had to emigrate"—sends the message that labor migration is a necessity or a response to larger forces, not an unjustified choice. The sequencing of this message with the segments that follow is significant. Immediately after visiting the luthier, the show moves to a visit with Hernández Linares' parents, with the on-screen graphics placing them within the realm of migration: "Rafa meets Manuel's parents, return emigrants [emigrantes retornados]" (33:22). The conversation between Rafa, Manuel Hernández Linares, and his parents explains that the parents went to Barcelona in search of work, worked there for many years as manual laborers, visiting Órgiva three or four times a year during that period, and then returned to retire in their hometown. The segment, by mentioning the material and emotional difficulties of emigration, and the broader phenomenon of Andalusians who left the region to work in Catalonia in the 1950s through the '70s (33:22–36:20), sets the stage for a more direct treatment of the newcomers in the town.

After another commercially oriented, tourism-related segment, the groups of anonymous *orgiveño* commentators make another appearance to talk about the high number of different nationalities found in the town. As one trio lists the different nationalities present in the town, one of the participants states that for any country in the world, one will find at least two people from that country in Órgiva (38:19–38:21). In the group of younger commentators, one young woman states "People is [sic] very open [La gente son [sic] muy abierta]" and another in the trio agrees (38:23). Then the anonymous local voices talk about how they manage to communicate with the incomers across language barriers. In spite of the local voices listing many nationalities, there is no reference to Sufi converts or to Maghrebi migrants. Instead, this segment is followed by a conversation with Chris Stewart, in which the show host and Stewart refer to the role of his books and that of Gerald Brenan in attracting newcomers and briefly mention the hippie presence in the town, with Stewart presenting a positive take on the hippie philosophy and lifestyle. The sequencing of these segments that interweave labor migration, return migration, and migration in search of artistic inspiration or quality of life, as well as local voices contentedly describing the town's cultural and linguistic plurality, serves to normalize migration and also paints a harmonious portrait of life in the town. However, this portrait leaves certain groups, namely the large Sufi community, out of the picture. After other segments, including a visit with a local tourist guide to the chapel, the church, and the palace that had a role in the Rebellion of the Alpujarras, and an event of the women's association (*Asociación de Mujeres de Órgiva por la Igualdad*), the episode ends without any reference (verbal or visual) to Muslims of any type in present-day Órgiva, or to frictions between the townspeople and hippies in the area. The upshot is a partial vision of the town that, while normalizing human mobility, ironically presents a *convivencia*-tinged picture of the town without mentioning any of the town's Muslim residents, present-day versions of the hybrid *moriscos* and Mozarabs, and without mentioning tensions with the "alternative" community. This occurs, no doubt, in pursuit of an untroubled image that will support tourism to the area. Given the fact that it is a public television program of the Andalusian government, its aims are to promote cultural and economic development in the region. As a network geared toward traditional television audiences who may be more conservative, the program presents a selective image of Órgiva that primarily serves the economic development goal. In all but one of the other visual narratives about Órgiva, this type of whitewashing is present and even becomes full "*convivencia*-washing."

ÓRGIVA AS A SITE FOR CONTEMPORARY ISLAM: THE TITILLATION OF THE RETURN OF ISLAM VS. A CONTINUATION OF THE *CONVIVENCIA*

In sharp contrast with the *Este es mi pueblo* episode, the Órgiva episode of an Internet television program broadcast almost exactly one year later and directed at a very different audience emphasizes an excitement-tinged fear of the return of Islam to Spain. Part of the Spanish-language arm of the digital media giant Vice Media Group, the *Diario Vice* (Vice Daily News) program is produced by Movistar (a major telecommunications brand, owned by Spain's Telefónica, that operates in Spain and parts of Latin America) in collaboration with Vice News (stylized as VICE News), Vice Media's current affairs channel. Vice News produces daily documentary essays and video through its website and YouTube channel, which are geared toward a youth and young adult audience, and—with a focus on hip, edgy topics (alternative religious practices, fringe groups, etc.)—bills itself as presenting "under-reported stories" in an "unvarnished" manner.[6] Given this profile, the target audience for *Diario Vice* is the polar opposite of the regional, more traditional target audience of *Este es mi pueblo*, and the resulting reportage is also radically different.

The 10-minute *Diario Vice* episode focused on Órgiva is entitled "*Sufís, los místicos del islam en España*" (Sufis, the mystics of Islam in Spain) and was first broadcast on October 26, 2016.[7] From the start, the show seeks to pique the interest of viewers curious about pushing against the status quo and testing the limits of acceptability: against the background of reverberating music with an Orientalist motif, the show uses a cold open that begins with statements from two Spanish converts to Islam about their families' negative reactions to their conversion. From a close-up shot of the second convert, this teaser sequence continues by cutting to an exterior view of the Sufi prayer space (*dargah*) and interior views with details of figures carrying out Muslim prayers, as an off-screen voice (in native Spanish) states: "It might be that we are the answer to the prayers, to that longing for Islam to return to Spain, right [Puede que nosotros seamos la respuesta a las súplicas, de esa añoranza de que el islam volviese a España, no]" (0:10–0:16). During the last second of this provocative statement, the image switches to a close-up of the speaker, a white-presenting young man with a trim beard, tunic top, and taqiya that mark him as Muslim. The image then immediately shifts to a scene of Sufi prayer through movement (a group *dhikr*), focusing on a twirling figure reminiscent of the whirling dervishes whose related religious practice is proverbially associated with Sufism in the European and North American imaginary. A few seconds later, this visual is covered by on-screen graphics showing the black-and-white Vice News logo that then takes over the whole frame, a shift that is accompanied by dramatic music. As this music blends into an Orientalist motif, the title of the episode appears: "*Sufís, los místicos del islam en España.*" Building on the unexpected presence of Islam in Spain that is proclaimed by the title, the next image is a panoramic shot of Órgiva nestled among mountains, looking like any of Andalucía's famous white villages, with on-screen text naming the location (0:25). The reverberating music that continues to play, paired with the contrasting image of a bucolic village, creates a sense of unsettling foreboding.

This teaser and opening title sequence create a titillating threat that taps into what Daniela Flesler identifies as a form of trauma: "Inasmuch as the more than eight centuries of Muslim presence in the Iberian Peninsula are perceived as a breach of the Christian continuum, they constitute a cultural or historical trauma" (57). Thus, the *Diario Vice* episode creates a narrative of a return to Islam in Spain that, for a more nationalist viewer, can trigger Islamophobia, and, for a young thrill-seeker viewer, the rush of brushing up against danger, and, when these viewer categories overlap, a tense mix of the two. Either way, the episode utilizes and intensifies the association between Islam and danger to create a different type of partial portrait, one that situates Órgiva not as the site of *convivencia*, but as the site of a new Islamic invasion.

The rhetoric of Islamic threat is seen throughout the remainder of this *Diario Vice* episode, albeit in more subtle form. After the panoramic view of Órgiva, the show host, Dani Campos, speaks to viewers from behind the steering wheel of a car explaining, as the subtly ominous and Orient-tinged soundtrack continues, that he is taking viewers to remote Órgiva, home of the largest Sufi community in Spain. After talking about Islamic mysticism and austerity, the host launches a very provocative question, shaking his head at the end to emphasize the shock value of his statement: "So I wonder if it's possible to live like in the times of the Prophet in 21st-century Spain [Así que me pregunto si es posible vivir como en los tiempos del profeta en la España del siglo XXI]" (0:46–0:52). Here, the specific fear that is tapped into is that of the incompatibility between Islam, with its Sharia law based on the words and deeds of the Prophet Muhammad, and Europe, with its identification as modern and secular. Given the large number of Muslim migrants from the Maghreb, this question echoes a common concern raised in anti-immigrant discourses in Spain and elsewhere.

The reverberating soundtrack with Orientalist touches continues as the show host interviews Shaykh Umar, the Catalonian head of the Spanish Naqshbandis, and we see the interviewer's subdued skepticism toward one of the Shaykh's statements via the host's facial expression and body language. The sonic ambience becomes specifically Sufi as the show host takes viewers with him to a *dhikr* ceremony and later to a *hadra* ceremony. The Islamic devotional act called *dhikr* (lit., remembrance/reminder, or mention) is the rhythmic repetition of religious phrases or prayers, which in Sufism is done communally and often accompanied by music and movement, while *hadra* (lit,. presence) consists of various forms of *dhikr*, including recitation combined with dance, as well as a sermon and study of a devotional text. Group *dhikr*, especially performed out loud and accompanied by music and dance, is not typically part of mainstream Muslim forms of worship and is seen as heretical by particularly conservative Muslims. The *Diario Vice* host notes that in *dhikr*, Sufis mix prayers with rhythmic chanting through which they say that they can enter a trance state; the host refers to *hadra* as a typically Sufi form of dance, but otherwise does not enter into varying Muslim dogma regarding *dhikr* and *hadra*. He does state that, although he stayed on the sidelines, the rhythmic chanting and drum music were so powerful that he too started to enter into a trance. Given the discursive context of the episode that I have already established, this statement enhances the sense of Islam as an attractive and powerful forbidden fruit and suggests that this Sufi group is cult-like—a powerful yet potentially overpowering fringe group.

The episode then cuts to views of the twin church towers, visually establishing a religious confrontation. After shots of the show host walking through the town, he meets with a series of converts to Islam residing there. This includes visits with the two converts that appear in the teaser sequence, now introduced by name and occupation before longer versions of the statements made in the teaser. (The second of the converts, Qasim Barrio Raposo, is a restaurant owner from the north of Spain whom we will reencounter in subsequent sections.) Then the viewers accompany the host to the *hadra* and at one point in a close-up shot we see that he raises his eyebrows to subtly convey his incredulity toward this Sufi practice (7:53). In the final minutes of the episode, we return to the young man who spoke at the end of the teaser sequence about the yearning for a return of Islam to Spain. He is introduced as Shamsuddin, the son of Shaykh Umar. As the camera alternates between Shamsuddin, panning shots of the olive and orange groves amid the mountains, and herds of goats, we hear Shamsuddin say a longer version of what is presented in the teaser:

> That the Alpujarras was the last place where the Muslims lived is interesting. Eight hundred years here in Spain: they weren't invaders, no, they were people from here who had converted, right. Who abandoned their houses, right, seeing that Spain had been closed off for them, right. It might be that we are the answer to the prayers of those people, right, to that longing for Islam, right, to return to Spain, right [Que las Alpujarras sea el último sitio en el que los musulmanes estuvieron es muy interesante. 800 años aquí en España: no eran invasores, no, eran gentes de aquí que se habían convertido, no. Que abandonaron sus casas, no, viendo que España se había cerrado para ellos, no. Puede que nosotros seamos la respuesta a las súplicas de esta genta, no, de esa añoranza de que el islam, no, volviese, volviese a España, no] (9:33–10:01).

The *Diario Vice* episode ends here, with the credits rolling over the same panoramic shot of Órgiva that was seen at the start, as the last reverberating tones fade out. The episode's circular structure, which kicks off with and then closes with Shamsuddin's statement about expelled Muslims (understood by him as Iberian converts to Islam), creates at once a parallel with the well-known trope of Islam circling back to Spain and also a new twist on this rhetoric of return by presenting the expelled Muslims as originally Iberian. However, the potential for this historical revision to dismantle fixed conceptions of Moorish versus Christian identity and nationalist essentialisms is largely undermined by the sensationalist sonic and visual leitmotif of Islam as a threat and Sufism as cultish.

As if in response to *Diario Vice*'s take on Islam in Órgiva, an Islam-themed series on national television released an episode focused on Órgiva in 2019. *Medina* is a program of 15-minute episodes broadcast on La 2 (Channel Two), a free-to-air television channel that is part of the Spanish public broadcasting company RTVE which is geared toward, or at least more likely to attract, a niche audience: Spanish-speakers already practicing or interested in Islam. Its episode on Órgiva, entitled *"Comunidad sufí de Órgiva"* (Órgiva's Sufi community) was first broadcast on March 3, 2019 and is a clear example of *convivencia*-washing.[8] This type of narrative is evident from the start, when the host and director of the show, Bouziane Ahmed Khodja, a journalist of Algerian origin, states from a studio setting:

> Órgiva, capital of the Granadan Alpujarra, place of refuge of the last Nasrid king, Boabdil, extends into the present part of the multicultural splendor of the past [. . .] This town, of barely 6,000 inhabitants, harbors in its streets more than 70 different nationalities. Perhaps the best manifestation of this diverse blend is the Sufi community of this town [Órgiva, la capital de la Alpujarra granadina, lugar de retiro del último rey nazarí, Boabdil, prolonga en el presente una parte del esplendor multicultural del pasado [. . .] Esta localidad, de apenas 6.000 habitantes, alberga en su callejero más de 70 nacionalidades distintas. Quizá, la mejor encarnación de este variopinto mestizaje sea la comunidad sufí de esta localidad] (0:14–0:45).

This introduction frames the entire episode as a tracing of the continuity of al-Andalus, understood as an example of multicultural harmony, in present-day Órgiva.

In the next segment of the episode, against the backdrop of soothing music with occasional Orientalist phrases, various views of the town (including images of hippies) are accompanied by a voiceover in which a female narrator describes Órgiva as

> a sort of contemporary Babel where more than 60 nationalities coexist in peace and harmony [. . .] Órgiva is, then, a cosmopolitan town. Open to everything and everyone. Where coexisting means exactly that, respect and tolerance towards one another, each other's religion, and way of life. And it is in this environment of tolerance and *convivencia* where one of the most important Muslim Sufi communities not only in Spain but in the world has settled [una especie de Babel contemporáneo donde conviven en paz y armonía más de 60 nacionalidades diferentes [. . .] Órgiva es, pues, un pueblo cosmopolita. Abierto a todo y a todos. Donde convivir significa exactamente eso, respeto y tolerancia al otro; a su credo, a su modo de vida. Y es en este entorno de tolerancia y convivencia donde se asienta una de las comunidades musulmanas sufís más importantes, no solo de España, sino del mundo] (0:46–1:45).

After quoting verses from the famous 12th-century Sufi mystic Ibn ʿArabi, who was born in al-Andalus, the narrator introduces us to Qasim Barrio, the Muslim convert who owns and runs Órgiva's main halal restaurant, Café Baraka. The narrator opens this segment by emphasizing that people from all walks of life are patrons of Qasim's restaurant—from locals to hippies. However, after Qasim speaks about life in Órgiva and its general feeling of "hermandad" (brotherhood) (5:22) and the many spiritual traditions present in the town, he refers to the difficulties inherent in opening a halal restaurant in a societal context in which customers demand alcohol and pork.

The episode then moves to Shaykh Umar who describes Órgiva as "muy cosmopolita [very cosmopolitan]" (9:10). After the narrator describes *dhikr* as a practice common to all Muslims, but distinguishes *hadra* as a specifically Sufi practice, the episode returns to Shaykh

Umar emphasizing the normalcy and even orthodoxy of Sufism within Islam:

> Our practices are the practices of all Muslims. We follow the Sharia [Islamic law]. We follow a school, specifically we follow the Hanafi school. We are within the Naqshbandi *tariqa*, which has been, among the *tariqas*, the one that has most defended the Prophet's Sunna [the part of Muslim law based on Muhammad's words and deeds]. We are at the very center of the heart of Islam [Nuestras prácticas son las prácticas de todos los musulmanes. Nosotros seguimos la sharía. Nosotros seguimos una escuela, concretamente nosotros seguimos la escuela Hanafí. Estamos en la tariqa Naqshbandi, que ha sido, dentro de las tariqas, la que más ha defendido la sunna del profeta. Estamos en el centro mismo del corazón del islam] (11:33–11:56).[9]

After this defense of Sufism's conformity to religious law, the narrator then clarifies that the Sufis do not shun society and use modern technology and media. She closes the episode with an explanation of the quest of Sufism as a search for God in one's heart, while the visuals show Khodja walking and talking with Qasim and sitting and talking with Shaykh Umar, and Sufis gathering together at Shaykh Umar's mosque. The Órgiva episode of *Medina* focuses on presenting the town as a continuation of a Muslim Iberia imagined to be pure tolerance and harmony and within this *convivencia*-washing, the show erases Sufism's often tense relationship with those who see themselves as representatives of Islamic dogma. Based on the show's audience, the episode projects an aspirational *convivencia* that includes intra-Muslim harmony.

CONVIVENCIA-WASHING FOR REGIONAL AND NATIONAL AUDIENCES

In August 2015, two months before the broadcast of the *Este es mi pueblo* episode (making it the first of the eight shows), a show aired featuring a *convivencia*-washed narrative about Órgiva that was directed at a broader national audience. The series *España a ras de cielo* (Spain at sky level—a play on the expression *a ras de suelo* meaning "at ground level"), which is broadcast on the public network RTVE's free-to-air television channel La 1 (Channel One), aims to present hidden corners of Spain, or known areas from a new angle. In the series' second season, the 55-minute episode "*Me voy al pueblo*" (I'm headed to a country town) focuses on the phenomenon of Spaniards moving from urban to rural areas, and one of the four small towns featured is Órgiva.[10] In the teaser sequence that presents snippets about each of the four locations to be visited, the show host, Francis Lorenzo, states "Did you know that the last hippies have transformed a town in the Granadan Alpujarra to the point of turning it into a little Babel? [¿Sabían que los últimos hippies han transformado un pueblo de la Alpujarra granadina hasta convertirlo en una pequeña Babel?]" (0:09–0:15), and we see and hear from Muslim converts in Órgiva and members of a hippie community in the surrounding area. After the title sequence, the host explains that in the last 15 years, the Spanish trend of people moving to major urban centers has reversed; for the first time, there are more people moving from urban centers to small rural towns.

The host's introduction to the segment on Órgiva, which is the first in the episode, includes various images of diversity in the town accompanied by the host's voiceover. The host starts by describing the Alpujarra with a reference to the *moriscos* who didn't want to leave the area:

> We'll set out to the Alpujarra, sheltered by the Sierra Nevada, for our first stop. In this special place, teeming with white villages that dot the landscape, and that the *moriscos* withdrew from only through the imposition of arms, one finds a very peculiar town with the most curious inhabitants of Spain: Órgiva [Ponemos rumbo a la Alpujarra, al amparo de Sierra Nevada, para hacer nuestra primera parada. En esta tierra especial, plagada de pequeños pueblos blancos que motean el paisaje y que los moriscos abandonaron solo bajo la imposición de las armas se encuentra un pueblo muy peculiar con los habitantes más pintorescos de España: Órgiva] (3:15–3:38).

The host's voiceover explains that in the 1970s, many *órgiveños* left for urban centers, while the on-screen graphics display that between 1950 and 2010 the Alpujarra lost 50 percent of its population (3:46–3:53). The presenter then states that in the 1980s, people of various ideologies and religious traditions arrived in the area seeking the tranquility and spirituality of closer contact with nature; he notes "And although at first they made an impact, the locals ended up getting used to their presence and today so much diversity has enriched the town [Y aunque al principio causaron impacto, los lugareños terminaron acostumbrándose a su presencia y hoy en día tanta diversidad ha enriquecido al pueblo]" (4:14–4:21). After this brief reference to shock waves in the otherwise tranquil Órgiva, the show goes on to emphasize happy diversity.

Among the various inhabitants interviewed, Qasim Barrio, the convert to Islam who owns Café Baraka, explains that his spiritual quest led him to Islam and the show's presenter asks what led him to Órgiva. Qasim answers:

> I found Órgiva and saw that there were, shall we say, people with the same profile as me, meaning, Western Muslims [. . .] Let's just say that there's a ton of people the same as me here. There I was a weirdo and here I was a dime a dozen [Encontré Órgiva y vi que había, digamos, gente de mi mismo perfil, o sea, musulmanes occidentales [. . .] Digamos que hay un montón de gente igual que yo. Allí era un bicho raro y aquí era uno más] (5:47–6:04).

I will take up the topic of "weirdness" further on, but it is important to note that indirectly Qasim is stating that being "Western" (that is, from a European-derived cultural sphere) and Muslim is typically a mark of weirdness, but in Órgiva he feels that this is not the case.

After a conversation with Shaykh Umar, the camera pans out over chanting Sufis and the countryside, cuts to the twin church towers, and moves to an interview with the mayor at the time, María Ángeles Blanco, as she and the program's host stroll through the town. The host introduces this segment by saying "We're talking with Mari

Ángeles Blanco, the mayor of Órgiva, to get to know this cosmopolitan town where people from around the world coexist [Hablamos con Mari Ángeles Blanco, la alcaldesa orgiveña, para conocer este pueblo cosmopolita donde convive gente de todo el mundo]" (8:36–8:43). The mayor states "Here diversity is the norm [Aquí la diversidad es la normalidad]" (8:50–8:52). When the host asks why people come to Órgiva, Blanco responds that "it's in our blood [lo llevamos en la sangre]," and indicates that documents from as early as the 1400s mention outsiders arriving and staying for a while, people coming and going, and she ties this to the area's location between the sea and the mountains (9:45–10:05). The mayor's turn of phrase is noteworthy in that it uses biological terms to explain mobility; that is, she expresses the idea that *orgiveños* are already part of centuries of movement in and out of the region, but states this through a figure of speech that indicates that they have movement in their blood, that is, as part of their biological make-up. On one level, the use of the expression "lo llevamos en la sangre" in this context is paradoxical, given that constant movement doesn't lead to genetic similarity in the crossroads locale, but could lead to an accumulation of people who have felt the urge to pick up and resettle. On another level, the use of this biological expression here serves to counterbalance xenophobic thinking by pointing to the long history of population shifts in the area. Using the first-person plural here with this biology-based figure of speech establishes the more recent arrivals in Órgiva (those from Madrid, London, Berlin, and so forth) as part of the same (biological) group as those whose families had arrived in the area generations back. In this sense, here the biological rhetoric usually used to reject newcomers is used by the mayor to embrace them. When the program host suggests that the mayor must be proud to be leading such a place, she states that she's honored and happy to have neighbors from around the world because "always being aware that we all belong to the world and [. . .] spending time with each other and getting to know each other is wonderful [pensar siempre que todos somos del mundo y que [. . .] compartir y conocernos es magnifico]" (10:18–10:34).

After this exchange, the *España a ras de cielo* episode visits the Beneficio hippie commune and the episode closes by emphasizing the common interest in spirituality and nature that unites the residents of Órgiva. Although this episode is focused on people who have chosen rural life, it is important to note that the mayor is the only person among those interviewed who is a born and bred *orgiveño*. Similarly, the *Diario Vice* and *Medina* episodes, given their focus on Islam, albeit from very different angles, do not feature any *orgiveños*. In contrast, the four Andalusian shows from RTVA include and even emphasize the local perspective. In addition to *Este es mi pueblo*, three more recent Canal Sur programs (two from 2021 and one from 2017) have presented Órgiva to the network's regional audience and have done so featuring local perspectives. Tellingly, these additional Canal Sur programs don't dwell on manifestations of difference in the town, but, like all of the other television narratives about Órgiva (except for the *Diario Vice* episode), they still characterize it, albeit with less emphasis, as a space of harmonic multiculturalism.

The cooking show *Tierra de sabores* (Land of flavors), which focuses on traditional Andalusian cuisine, dedicated an entire 55-minute episode to Órgiva, that aired on February 14, 2021.[11] In the episode, the show host and chef Bosco Benítez primarily spends time with the *orgiveños* Carmen Berrio and her husband, Antonio Puerta. Carmen demonstrates how to cook two local dishes and Antonio provides a tour of the town including some of its history. The area's Moorish past is highlighted in the introduction sequence, when the narrator remarks that the town's narrow streets evoke its *morisco* past (1:42–1:46). Later, this past is touched upon briefly when Antonio says that the church was built upon a former mosque and mentions a famous local dish (not one of the two being prepared in the episode) that is of Arab origin. When Bosco asks about what it is like to live in Órgiva, Antonio replies by saying that life in the town in great and the fact that people have come to it from around the world is proof of this. When Bosco says he wants to see this confluence of cultures, Carmen notes that he'll get to do so in the municipal market, where they will go to buy ingredients for the dishes to be prepared. As they speak, the image flips between them and shots of diverse inhabitants of the town, including one in Muslim-associated attire (the clothing typical of the local Sufis). At this point, the voiceover narrator explains that Bosco and Carmen will go to "the municipal market of Órgiva, a multicultural space with many stories to get to know [el mercado municipal de Órgiva, un multicultural espacio con muchas historias por conocer]" (12:07–12:15). The images of the indoor market that follow include two of women wearing North African-style hijab. These visual references are the only mention that the episode makes of the Sufi community or the Maghrebi migrants in the town. After visiting the market, Bosco visits bakers (Antonio and Encarna, the same ones from the Galindo bakery featured in *Este es mi pueblo*) and a potter, and then he and Carmen cook two dishes.[12]

In the closing segment of the show, as Bosco thanks Carmen and says good-bye, he tells her that she has taught him that Órgiva is "una tierra de nacionalidades [a land of nationalities]," as well as a "tierra de sabores [land of flavors]" (53:50–54:00). In sum, this episode of *Tierra de sabores* presents Órgiva as a "multicultural space," but without entering into any detail about the multiple cultures, some of which are very relevant to the oldest traditions of the local cuisine and the newest trends in the food on offer in the town. Thus, this more subtle form of "*convivencia*-washing" wipes away the Muslim presence in the town almost completely, in favor of using the catchphrases of diversity in a superficial manner.

Another Canal Sur series, *Los repobladores* (The repopulators—a play on *repoblar* (to resettle) and *pueblo* (town)) featured Órgiva in its February 20, 2021 episode.[13] The entire series focuses on people who have chosen to move from urban to rural settings and Órgiva is one of three locations featured in this 51-minute episode. The introduction to the episode's segment on Órgiva consists of various shots of the town and its natural surroundings, accompanied by a Spanish pop song and a graphic stating the name of the town and province. In contrast with all the previously mentioned programs except for *Este es mi pueblo*, this montage of views of Órgiva doesn't feature the diverse inhabitants and instead only includes one human figure, that of a man dressed in typical, conservative European clothing seen in the distance crossing an otherwise empty plaza. The show soon focuses on a young man, Antonio Méndez, who had decided to return to his hometown of Órgiva to start an insect-farming business. After Antonio leads the reporter, who always remains off-screen, on a tour of his farm, he takes her to the town church, where they meet an older local woman and the reporter exclaims "Listen to that! Another return rural dweller [¡Cuchen! Otra repobladora]" (37:49). This elderly woman, in response to the reporter's questions, explains that she left Órgiva to work in Barcelona for the same reason as everyone else: because there was no work in the town and they needed to eat. But she wanted to return and encourages young people to remain in their towns "because I was taught to love my town in Catalonia [porque a mí me enseñaron a querer a mi pueblo en Cataluña]" (38:06–38:12). During the scenes at the farm and inside the church, Antonio and the older return migrant emphasize the virtues of small-town rural life and contributing to the development of one's town, a message that the Andalusian government, the source of funding for the station, no doubt would like to amplify.

Immediately after the conversation with the return migrant, an on-screen graphic appears stating "Órgiva is a multicultural municipality where inhabitants from more than 70 different nationalities coexist [Órgiva es un municipio multicultural donde conviven vecinos de más de 70 nacionalidades diferentes]" (38:13). Interestingly, once again this occurs against the backdrop of depopulated vistas of the town. After more coverage of the farm, the show returns to the older return migrant in the church, presenting a longer version of the previous conversation, in which she recounts the devotion and legends surrounding the statue of the *Cristo de la Expiración* and talks about her experiences in Barcelona. At this point, an on-screen graphic explains "Two million Andalusians emigrated to Catalonia in the '60s and '70s" (44:34). In *Los repobladores*, labor migration is normalized and presented in an empathetic light, but put at the service of the series' agenda to encourage a return to small-town, rural life.

Following the extended version of the conversation with the elderly return migrant, Antonio takes the reporter to meet Qasim at an empty Café Baraka. Antonio introduces Qasim as another "*repoblador*" (45:28), and Qasim presents the journey that led him to join the Sufi community there. Then he demonstrates how to make an aromatic tea (a South Asian chai referred to by Qasim as "Pakistani tea"), which he connects to the tranquil life that he was seeking in Órgiva. While he speaks, a few different on-screen graphics appear: one noting that Qasim used to be a "cortador de jamón [master ham carver]" named Pedro in Bilbao, before converting to Islam (45:48); a second graphic stating "The largest community of Sufis (members of a branch of Islam) in Spain is located in Órgiva" (46:38), and two more graphics about tea—the first one presenting it as an expression of Muslim culture. Through Qasim's statements and the on-screen text, the scene focuses on his transformation from a master ham carver to a Muslim and on his search for tranquility in Órgiva. As a musical manifestation of Qasim's transformation, during the scene the muted background music shifts from a guitar-based Spanish pop song to a South Asian pop song meant to invoke the Muslim world.

While the empty public spaces that are seen throughout the show may be related to the fact that it was filmed during the coronavirus pandemic (at certain points, interviewees are seen wearing masks), given the fact that stock footage could have been used to fill the spaces, it is very likely connected to the impetus of the show to draw people to repopulate rural areas—that is, to beckon them to fill empty spaces.[14] The episode closes with a montage of shots of Antonio at work and nearly empty plazas, while a voiceover presents Antonio making a final plug for the return to rural life. In support of this explicit message regarding the virtues of rural life, the plurality of cultures in the town is mentioned, but only demonstrated visually through images of Qasim. Thus, the multicultural descriptor used for the town remains a superficial label and the diversity within the town is kept at a minimum while the tensions caused by difference are completely erased. In this way, the Órgiva episode of *Los repobladores* creates another form of *convivencia*-washing.

An even more food-centered *convivencia*-washing takes place in a short segment of *Andalucía Directo* (Andalucía Live) that was broadcast in 2017.[15] *Andalucía Directo* is an infotainment show that is broadcast on two RTVA channels (one free-to-air and one subscription satellite). A 4-minute segment of the 72-minute episode focuses on Café Baraka and emphasizes sustainability and multiculturalism, but blithely presents the origins of the food served at Baraka as both Arab and authentically Andalusian. This segment opens with an in-studio host announcing that Café Baraka was voted by readers of the British newspaper *The Guardian* as one of the 10 best rural restaurants in Spain, and characterizing the restaurant as "a promoter of all that is eco-friendly and local [una apuesta por lo ecológico y lo local]" (0:17–0:19). Against a background of upbeat Middle Eastern music, the show then moves to on-location interviews of Qasim, the restaurant owner, and his employees and clients. These interviews are prefaced by shots of various dishes served at the restaurant and the reporter's statement that "The aroma of our past and the taste of our history comes together in these dishes [El aroma de nuestro pasado y el sabor de nuestra historia se funden en estos platos]" (0:31–0:34). After this vague reference to Iberia's Muslim and Arab-Maghrebian past, the cuisine served at Café Baraka is referred to as "Arab" once by the reporter (0:56) and for a few minutes through intermittent on-screen text. The segment also includes repeated references to Órgiva as a place characterized by "interculturality" and "something magical," and briefly mentions that Qasim is a Basque convert to Islam. It features images of eclectic clients at the restaurant, including Sufis and a lingering shot of two customers clasping each other's hands—one who looks Northern European and the other sub-Saharan African. The segment also includes shots of the chef at Baraka preparing food, and stating that he has been in Órgiva for 14 years and feels like he is "at home [como en mi casa]" (2:28–2:30). But given his physical appearance and fluent Spanish, and the fact that his Maghrebi origins aren't mentioned (though some restaurant diners are identified as French), his background remains ambiguous. The reporter praises the restaurant's commitment to "that which is autochthonous, local, authentic, and organic [lo autóctono, lo local, lo auténtico, y lo ecológico]" (1:43–1:48) and closes by noting that this food is "seasoned with the best of our culinary inheritance [aderezada con lo mejor de nuestra herencia culinaria]" (3:53). Thus, the segment emphasizes these dishes' authenticity, without specifying whether they are authentically Arab or Andalusian, and claims them as part of "our" culinary tradition, which, given the title of the show and its target audience can be understood as a reference to the cuisine of Andalucía. The result is an ambiguous melding of Arab and Andalusian, and of past and present, that doesn't mention that these recipes were not necessarily prepared in al-Andalus and that Spain's more recent contact with Arab-Maghrebian cuisine results from its colonial entanglement with the Maghreb and from Maghrebi cooks, whether in immigrants' fast-food kebab shops, or in the tea houses and high-end restaurants in Granada, Córdoba, and elsewhere, that try to create a Moorish experience for tourists.

The unquestioned jump from contemporary Arab cuisine to authentically Andalusian cuisine erases the differences between the cuisine of al-Andalus and that of the contemporary Arab world, and the difference between both of these and contemporary Andalusian cuisine. Although a few interviewees mention that no alcohol is served at Baraka, in this narrative no mention is made of the absence of pork—an essential ingredient in contemporary Andalusian cuisine. By vaguely referencing the maintenance of culinary traditions while emphasizing that Baraka's dishes are local, organic, and authentic, and that the restaurant is the center of the convergence of many races and cultures in Órgiva, the segment makes no attempt to explain the relationship between the cuisines of different historical periods and regions, let alone the power relations that are part of foodways. Instead, it pairs *convivencia*-washing with green-washing and uses the rhetoric of authenticity and sustainability to present contemporary Arab food as "organically" Andalusian. This type of erasure becomes stronger in a Moroccan tea-service scene in the Órgiva episode of the show *Radio Gaga*.

Thus far, the only broad audience television series to dedicate an entire, longer-format episode to Órgiva is the highly popular Spanish digital television series *Radio Gaga*, available on demand from Movistar's Movistar+, the largest subscription television provider in Spain. *Radio Gaga* features two witty, yet warm, hipsters, Quique Peinado and Manuel Burque, who visit different communities in Spain with a camper trailer that doubles as a radio station. Upon arrival, they set up localized radio transmission to connect with community members and spend two days drawing them in to share their perspectives on the locale and their life stories, which are heard locally via radio, but are also filmed for the television audience. In addition to what the participants say inside the camper or at the standing microphone in front of it, many are filmed in scenes from their daily lives as they narrate more of their experiences. As seen on screen during the show's opening: "They'll create 48 hrs. of radio searching for the soul and soundtrack of the place [Harán 48 Hs de radio buscando el alma y la banda sonora del lugar]" (00:42).

The 4th episode in the 2nd season of *Radio Gaga* offers a 56-minute multi-media narrative about Órgiva. The episode, first aired on May 3, 2018, portrays the town as a place where people can rebuild their shattered lives, find spiritual fulfillment, and/or escape from the modern rat race in a tolerant space that is, as Quique Peinado puts it, "the theme park of religions and good vibes [el parque temático de las religiones y las energías]" (29:08). As they begin transmitting radio from their camper set up in the town's main pedestrian plaza (Plaza Alpujarra), among their opening remarks Manuel Burque says: "The door of the camper is open. Why? So that you'll enter [. . .] and tell us what makes Órgiva special. Why don't people leave here? [La puerta de la caravana está abierta. ¿Para qué? Para que entréis [. . .] y nos contéis qué tiene de especial Órgiva. ¿Por qué la gente no se va de aquí?]" (3:58–4:08). Among those who come forward and are featured in the episode are *orgiveños* and transplants from other parts of Spain who are rebuilding their lives after trauma or addiction. Fernando, a former drug addict from elsewhere in Andalucía, visits the camper and responds to Burque's question by saying: "The people who sort of aren't interested in the system [que pasan del sistema un poco], well, they hide here. And that's what's special about it" (4:15–5:21). This point is emphasized when, as occurs at the end of most of the participants' visits to *Radio Gaga*'s camper, one of the show hosts asks Fernando for his musical request. Fernando asks them to play "Society" by Eddie Vedder and as this haunting, lyrical anti-establishment anthem plays via the local radio transmission, viewers see the hosts warmly saying good-bye to Fernando and scenes of Órgiva's eclectic inhabitants.

Later, a trio of women—one from Madrid, one from England, and one from Germany—approach the standing microphone outside the camper; the Spaniard explains that, having come from elsewhere alone to raise children in Órgiva, they had to create a new family:

> It's also hard to live here. Because we've all left our families and we've made our own family among ourselves, right? But, for example, those of us who are single moms raising our kids, we've had to set things up among our friends. There's a family bond there, like, we're like sisters, you know [Es duro también vivir aquí. Porque todos hemos dejado nuestras familias y nos hemos hecho nuestra propia familia entre nosotros, no. Pero, por ejemplo, las que hemos criado hijos solas lo hemos tenido que montar entre amigas. Allí hay un vínculo familiar como, somos como hermanas, sabes] (44:03–44:20).

The theme of family ties continues with a young family that is preparing to move from Malaga to the commune of Beneficio in order to leave their jobs and spend more time with their children. The episode closes with Peinado saying that Órgiva demonstrates that one can always start over again, reinvent oneself: "one can always, always, always, start from zero ... [siempre, siempre, siempre, se puede empezar de cero ...]" (56:34–56:40).

The theme of reinvention in Órgiva is also presented via a few of the converts to Islam; one in particular also addresses estrangement. During one of the episode's testimonies regarding a spiritual journey—the theme of existential estrangement, that which drives the convert to embrace Islam—is connected to being a stranger and is intertwined with a statement that highlights the episode's failure to mention Maghrebi migration. Viewers first meet the convert Sonia, who has taken the Muslim name Suniya, through her statement about her feelings of estrangement/strangeness, which is filmed in an olive grove:

> Feeling like a weirdo is a sensation that I had until I found my spiritual family and then . . . everyone was a weirdo, I wasn't the only one anymore. I think those of us that are converts, the Muslims by birth see us as weirdos and those that haven't converted see us as weirdos. So we're the weirdos and then you feel very bundled up and accompanied by weirdos [Sentirme bicho raro es una sensación que he tenido hasta que he encontrado mi familia espiritual y allí ya . . . todos eran bichos raros, ya no era la única. Creo que los que somos conversos, los musulmanes de nacimiento nos ven bichos raros y los que no se han convertido nos ven bichos raros. O sea que somos los bichos raros y entonces te sientes muy arropado y acompañado por bichos raros] (13:33–14:00).

This segment of the episode is significant for two reasons. First, Suniya describes a process whereby she felt estranged from society—strange on the inside—and this led her to make a life choice: conversion to Islam, that, while it provided spiritual solace and enrichment, and the comfort of a community of fellow "bichos raros," also marked her externally as a "weirdo." By resolving her feelings of estrangement, she became a stranger in the eyes of both Muslims by birth and non-convert Spaniards. Unlike immigrants and others who are marked as different, the convert chooses a path that marks him or her as strange in order to resolve inner estrangement. In this sense, a preexisting sense of difference becomes externalized, but within the spiritual community found in Órgiva, Suniya feels at home. Secondly, the way that the scene presents non-convert Muslims is striking because, although Spain has a high number of North African Muslim migrants and their presence is the polemical subject of media and public discourse, in Suniya's statement, at least as it is edited for the episode, the word "immigrant" is never used.

As John Lennon's "Imagine," the song that Suniya requested and dedicated to all those who had come to live in the valley of Órgiva, is fading out, the episode shows a man arriving at the camper with a tray of Moroccan tea. When this participant with a beard, long nose, and olive-toned skin enters the camper and introduces himself as "Amin," Peinado finds a cleverly subtle way to establish whether the guest is a convert to Islam or whether he is of Arab/Maghrebi origin, without having to mention the latter possibility. Peinado asks Amin to say his last names as well because he (Peinado) loves last names. The guest's last names are both clearly Hispanic and this identifies him as, in all likelihood, a convert. The conversation then unfolds with the hosts' questions about how long the guest has been called "Amin," what the name means, and what Muslim names Amin can propose for them—without ever acknowledging other "Amins" in Spain with different kinds of last names. Later scenes filmed outside the camper offer Amin's story of recovery from childhood trauma via conversion to Islam and a new life in Órgiva.

Like other converts featured in the episode, Amin recounts his journey toward spiritual fulfillment, but never addresses the Moroccanness of his tea service (a silver teapot with short Maghrebi-style glasses filled with tea and mint). A perceptive viewer might notice that Amin is wearing an embroidered tunic similar to that worn by the Café Baraka employees seen in earlier scenes of the episode, and (correctly) place him as a waiter from that restaurant. Later scenes do show Amin arriving at work at the café, but at no point is the question of potential appropriation or staging of the "Orient" for customers even touched upon. That is, the episode never mentions either the topic of Spain's historical links to North Africa, or its current migratory links. In keeping with this, the scene with Amin in the camper closes with Peinado raising his Moroccan tea glass and leading the others in an Arabic toast: "As-sahha!" This scene transitions to footage of the sun rising over Órgiva with another convert to Islam belting out the Arabic call to prayer. The religion, language, and cultural accoutrements of North Africa—a large area of which was under Spanish colonial control until 1976—are present in the episode, but not named as such. Thus, *Radio Gaga* portrays and participates in cultural appropriation with no reference to the 19th- and 20th-century Spanish colonial relationship with North African cultures, or the migrants from those cultures whose presence in Spain is well known, and hotly debated.

Within this selective portrait, Órgiva's tolerance is emphasized, alongside the inverted symbolic value of *jamón* in the town. The last group of visitors to the camper is a trio of teenage girls, one of whom is Suniya's daughter, Maryam (who is not dressed in typical Sufi attire). Peinado brings up the topic of body piercings because earlier Suniya mentioned Maryam's desire to get one, and Maryam explains that she had had one before. When he asks what happened to her piercing, her friends jokingly act out her father forcing her to take it off at knifepoint: "you see her dad with the ham knife, 'take that off!' [ves al padre con el cuchillo de jamón, 'quítate eso']," to which Maryam immediately responds "hey, not a ham knife [de jamón, no, eh]." The show hosts build a few humorous comments from this, including Burque saying that her having a ham knife at home would be "an outrage in Órgiva [un escándalo en Órgiva]" (52:17–52:47). Burque then states: "You all seem very tolerant and very activist [Se les ve como muy tolerantes y muy activistas]," and Peinado follows up with "Dude, you have no other choice in this town, if not, you kind of die of boredom [lit., of disgust] if you're not tolerant [Hombre, no os queda otra aquí en este pueblo, sino, te mueres un poco del asco si no eres tolerante]" (53:47–53:54). One of the three teenagers echoes this by saying that if you are "intolerant," you won't be able to leave your house because you'll be offended by everything (53:54–53:55). Paradoxically, through the reenacted figure of the Muslim convert father not tolerating his daughter's piercing, the show presents the town's tolerance as an established fact that is conditioned by the very diversity in the town. Nonetheless, Spain's iconic *jamón*, albeit with an inverted cultural value, still functions as a marker of boundaries.

Radio Gaga's narrative of Órgiva as a space of harmonious tolerance and healing purposely or not omits two significant constituents of this Andalusian "global village."[16] The episode erases the North African immigrants who have chosen to settle in the town and another group of economic migrants: the *orgiveños* who have an intimate awareness of emigration as either return migrants or the relatives or friends of émigrés (a topic I return to later).

On the one hand, considering that contemporary Spanish discourses about North African immigration often use the framework of Muslim conquest, and a seemingly still active Christian Reconquista, to present Maghrebi migrants as dangerous conquerors, the complete omission of North African immigrants, as well as the town's local return migrants, from this television narrative of Órgiva's tolerance is striking. Given the national context of rising and politicized anti-immigrant sentiment, it is possible that the show's producers preferred to leave North African immigration and the period when Spaniards were labor migrants (which recurred to some extent in the wake of the 2008 economic crisis) out of the picture to make the show more palatable to a broader audience. In this sense, these two groups of economic migrants would be left out of *Radio Gaga*'s portrait of Órgiva because they are the uncomfortable truths that would threaten to make the episode unpalatable on a regional and national level. In this reading, economic migration—Spaniards seen as less than European and Maghrebis seen as making Spain less than European—is ignored in favor of a focus on European converts to Islam. In this televisual narrative, tolerance that makes a community feel good about itself is celebrated, while immigration and fragile European identity are too thorny an issue to include in the portrait of the "global village."[17]

On the other hand, the *Radio Gaga* series focuses on listening, and certainly its tone is much closer to the caring cleverness of Stewart that to the imperial attitude of Brenan. Due to the show's format, it is up to the residents whether or not they participate and what they decide to say. Obviously, the most vulnerable (the ones who feel the most "put up with" or tolerated) are not likely to come forward or agree to take part in the show. Thus, if no Maghrebi migrants participated, this in and of itself would be revealing; it signals that they may not have felt secure enough to do so. Either way, this erasure, alongside a Moroccan tea with a toast in Arabic, makes Maghrebi migration the proverbial elephant in the room.

Whether intentional or not, the *Radio Gaga* episode simplifies the Órgiva story by effectively erasing economic migration and the intertwined issues of class, ethnicity, race, and conceptions of European modernity and civilization from the picture. Taking into account all eight of the visual narratives about Órgiva, only two programs address labor migration and two others reference it obliquely. These four are all from the Andalusian television network RTVA. *Este es mi pueblo* and *Los repobladores* highlight Andalusian economic migration, thereby attending to socioeconomic class differences, while the other shows from RTVA, *Tierra de sabores* and *Andalucía Directo*, only hint at Maghrebi labor migration elliptically, through the image of a woman in North African hijab and the chef at Café Baraka, respectively. Of these programs, only *Los repobladores* and *Andalucía Directo* include or even acknowledge the present-day Sufi presence in the town. None of the other four shows, all aimed at a national, or even international, audience make any reference to Andalusian or Maghrebi labor migration, although they highlight the Sufi presence. Given that only one out of the eight programs (*Los repobladores*) addresses contemporary Muslimness—whether in the form of European converts or Maghrebian migrants—together with Andalusian labor migration, one can conclude that acknowledging labor emigration as a Spanish experience alongside the presence of Muslims (largely labor immigrants) in Spain is an uncomfortable proposition. The end result is that none of the eight programs address ethnicity, race, and conceptions of European modernity and civilization, although these are certainly part of the lived experience of the town's residents. In order to present a happy image of effortless tolerance, all eight shows erase or minimize the small but visible Maghrebi contingent and also erase tensions along linguistic lines (primarily Spanish vs. English),[18] substance abuse issues in the town,[19] and friction between the working-class and bourgeois sensibilities of the *orgiveños* and the more alternative elements of the community. In the process, these accounts of Órgiva miss key dynamics in the town's cohabitation dynamic and, thus, any deeper understanding of tolerance is also left out of the story.

The terms "multicultural," "cosmopolitan," *"convivencia"/"convivir,"* references to multiple "nationalities," and—in the case of *Andalucía Directo*—"interculturality," recur in all of the visual narratives about Órgiva, except for that of *Diario Vice*. Yet these same narratives minimize or erase differences and tensions that exist within the town, thus establishing certain experiences as universal and removing from the picture the negotiations and conversations that occur between groups to maintain the level of coexistence present, and the contexts in which coexistence breaks down and a group (the more radical "alternatives") is publicly rejected. Additionally, the shows' recourse to the category of nationality creates dissonance with the purported cosmopolitanism, in which one's identity as a human being and commonality with other humans come before one's identity based on nationality or another type of grouping. Although sometimes the reference to "nationalities" in the television shows is initiated by the show host, often it is the interviewed *orgiveños* that introduce the term, or at least maintain it, building on the phrasing of the reporter's question. This belies the existence of a true cosmopolitan spirit across the town. At the same time, the references to the experiences of Andalusian migrants in Catalonia signal regional *andaluz* and *alpujarreño* identities that trump national identity, let alone a cosmopolitan one. Many of Órgiva's residents—particularly the *orgiveños* and the British residents—still identify along national and regional lines, not as cosmopolitan citizens of the world.

The televisual narratives about Órgiva represent the town as cosmopolitan, multicultural, and/or as an example of *convivencia*, and thus implicitly label it as tolerant, but without any clarification, qualification, or questioning of the terms. The Spanish-language verb *convivir* and the term *convivencia* are in general usage, outside of contexts related to the concept of *la convivencia* or the medieval period, with the sense of amicable coexistence. However, because the concept set forth by Américo Castro has been kept in circulation by various contemporary cultural discourses, within contexts remotely linked to al-Andalus and the *moriscos*, the use of *convivir* evokes *La convivencia*. Thus, harkening back to the discussion of civilizational hierarchies in Chapter 2, the terms used in these television programs serve to identify the town as part of the European modernity and/or local authenticity—the connection to al-Andalus—that the national and regional television networks seek to project as part of their mission to educate and entertain. But they do so without considering the power relations involved, which have to do precisely with the conceptualizations of European, Muslim, and civilized identities. This is an example of what Venegas designates, in reference to Andalusian television, "mass-media *costumbrismo*, a spectacle that dictates rather than debates collective identity" (144). Through a late modern version of *costumbrismo* (the 19th-century subgenre of realism focused on portraying and establishing the customs of a specific country or region), these programs reiterate the liberal discourses of tolerance that, as per Brown, are employed to deflect a deeper analysis of political power dynamics.

Living with difference, even in Órgiva, is not effortless. In all eight television narratives, within this mix of national and regional identities, some form of spiritual identity—Catholic, Sufi Muslim, and/or New Age—has a prominent role. And it is precisely at the intersection of religious and place-based identities that a great deal of the negotiation of difference in the town takes place. For some, this is a matter of reconciling Spanish or *orgiveño* identity with Catholicism vs. agnosticism, atheism, or another spiritual belief system, while for Muslims it is a matter of reconciling this religious identity with European and/or Spanish vs. Arab-Maghrebian identities. In the following chapters, I will delve further into the struggles—and power differentials—involved and how they are negotiated and attenuated.

CHAPTER 5
Oral Narratives about Órgiva

The narratives offered by Órgiva's inhabitants shed light on the tensions and ambivalences that are part of coexistence in the town and the dynamics that occasionally lead to public rejection vs. forms of peaceful mutual recognition. The participant observation and interviews that I conducted in Órgiva—focused on three groups: *orgiveños*, converts to Islam, and Maghrebi migrants—offer alternate narratives regarding its form of cohabitation. My analysis of these narratives (spoken statements together with patterns of behavior) indicate that Órgiva's migration memory and its Maghrebi migrants, precisely the elements missing from the accounts offered by *Radio Gaga* and many of the other television shows, are two of the key elements in the practice of tolerance in the town. In what follows, I will detail the social actors found in Órgiva and the modes of interaction and attitudes toward each other that they express. Their individual narratives illuminate the power dynamics and identity narratives that are part of coexistence.

"THE LOCALS": ALPUJARRANS AND ANDALUSIANS WHO HAVE LIVED IN ÓRGIVA FOR A GENERATION OR MORE

The group that I refer to as *orgiveños* is principally made up of individuals who were born and raised in Órgiva, although it may be that their families hail from other smaller towns in the Alpujarra. Due to emigration from Órgiva and a low birth rate, there are relatively few adult *orgiveños* whose parents were born in the town. One interlocutor, Enrique, who was born in Órgiva as was his father and some of his grandparents (with the rest of his family hailing from elsewhere in the Alpujarra), estimated that only 30 percent of the Spanish nationals resident in Órgiva who are not part of the Muslim convert community or the alternative communes have been in Órgiva for more than one or two generations. The community of *orgiveños* also includes some individuals from other parts of southern Andalucía who have lived most of their adult lives in Órgiva (whether they moved there for family reasons or because of a job opportunity) and who primarily socialize with *orgiveños* born and raised in the town, and not, for instance, with the Spaniards within the Sufi or alternative communities. The individuals that I group as "orgiveños" may also identify with another town or village in the region, as well as with the *comarca* or smaller region (*alpujarreño* or Alpujarran), the province (*granadino* or Granadan), and/or the larger autonomous region (*andaluz* or Andalusian), and also—depending on the context—as Spanish or as European. Aside from social networks, what primarily marks them as *orgiveños*, in contradistinction with the Spanish residents of Órgiva who are from outside of the Alpujarra and of Andalucía, is their dialect of Spanish. Although the most obvious manifestation of language politics in the town arises from the use of English vs. Spanish, ideologies regarding the "correct" or "cultured" Spanish of Spain's non-Andalusian metropolitan centers (e.g., Madrid, Barcelona, Bilbao) are clearly part of the relations between *orgiveños* and residents from elsewhere in Spain. Though in Spain the Andalusian accent is seen as "colorful" at best, or "ignorant" at worst, the Alpujarran accent is particularly marked as "backward."

When I asked *orgiveños* how they would describe the confluence of different cultural and religious groups in Órgiva, the expressions that came up all pointed to the groups living side by side with little friction, but also little interaction: "juntos pero no revueltos [together, but not mixed up]," "cada uno va a su rollo [everyone does their own thing]," and "hay vida paralela [we lead parallel lives]." Through these often-repeated expressions, my interlocutors sought to explain that the social lives of the different communities were parallel and seldom intersecting. Differing concepts of leisure activities contribute to these typically separate spheres between *orgiveños* and those that they refer to as *extranjeros* (foreigners), *guiris* (foreigners from the US and Northern Europe, especially tourists), *forasteros* (foreigners/outsiders; typically used more by those age 60 and up), or *ingleses* or another national denomination. For instance, Ana, an *orgiveña* in her forties who works in the local government, complained that the British transplants rarely attend events organized by local organizations or the town hall. As an example of how they socialize separately from *orgiveños*, Ana mentioned that on Tuesday nights a large group of British residents of Órgiva gets together at a specific bar to play a board game. In a different conversation, Elena, a 50-year-old from Granada, who about 25 years before had moved to Órgiva where she works in an office of the municipal government, made a similar observation. Elena could only think of one incomer couple, a British man and woman, whom she considered truly "integrated" into local life: they're active in municipal politics and the man is part of one of the *cofradías* for Holy Week (no doubt she was referring to Bailey and his wife Sarah).[1] Elena herself is not a practicing Catholic, but she deemed participation in the Holy Week processions, which require months of preparation, as an indicator of involvement in the pastimes common among *orgiveños*, particularly older ones.

In keeping with the comments made by other *orgiveños*, *Padre* Antonio Heredia, a Catholic priest of *gitano* (Gypsy/Roma) origin, stated that in Órgiva "cada uno está en su espacio [each group is in its own space]." Father Heredia was born and raised in Órgiva and then left to enter the priesthood, first serving in an impoverished neighborhood of *gitanos* and immigrants on the outskirts of the city of Granada and now in the neighboring Alpujarran town of Lanjarón. But he returns to Órgiva frequently to see family and tend to his farmland there. I had been curious to meet Father Heredia because I remembered his grandfather, the local *curandero*, or folk healer, who had treated my back decades before. And indeed Father Heredia has developed a role akin to that of a healer, serving as a resource for labor migrants, most of them from North and West Africa, when they need help with finding work, securing lodging, or completing myriad legal and administrative steps in Lanjarón, Órgiva, and surrounding areas.

When I asked Father Heredia to describe Órgiva, in addition to noting how much it had changed during the last decades, he stated that "each group is in its own space" and then added the following expression: "all that glitters is not gold [todo lo que brilla no es oro]." He elaborated on these statements by stating that there is a lack of "true connection" in Órgiva and although there is "acceptance," there is no "integration." He then emphasized that he saw this as a superficial or rhetorical form of tolerance by critiquing the much-touted concept of "the Spain of the 3 religions [la España de las 3 religiones]" as a sham. He pointed out that "if they impose Christianity and types of clothes, that is not tolerance or *convivencia*," making indirect reference to the forced conversion and persecution of Jews and Muslims, and prohibitions on their customs, under Christian rule in medieval and early modern Iberia. Father Heredia went on to lament what he saw as there being "no forum for dialogue [mesa de diálogo]" between the cultures in the town and stated that "the barrier to it being a true meeting place [punto de encuentro] is a lack of familiarity [el desconocimiento]." As I was saying good-bye to Father Heredia, he greeted a Moroccan immigrant whom he knew with "al-salamu ʿalaykum," demonstrating his own commitment to trying to connect with minority communities in the town.

With regard to relations between *orgiveños* and the European incomers, the lack of familiarity or ignorance about each other to which Father Heredia referred is largely produced by the language barrier. One of the factors that clearly limits social interaction and creates friction is the large number of non-Spanish transplants that have marginal communicative ability in Spanish. Although many of the residents from outside Spain do make a clear effort to learn Spanish and communicate in it, the majority of Anglophones do not. Perhaps because of their high number, they do not feel as motivated to learn Spanish. The result is that there are two overarching linguistic communities in the town: the Hispanophone and the Anglophone.[2] When

I broached the topic of Northern European incomers among *orgiveños*, or when *orgiveños* were spontaneously recounting an interaction with such an incomer, the issue of the language barrier usually arose, although individuals varied in how they presented it. For instance, a 40-something-year-old *orgiveño* who works in law enforcement, when recounting a work-related interaction, expressed exasperation with the foreigners who had lived in Órgiva for more than 20 years and still hadn't learned any Spanish. Pedro, an *orgiveño* in his thirties who works in a public-facing job in the service industry, happily recounted what he did when his clients insisted on speaking to him in English. While chuckling, Pedro reported to me that when clients immediately spoke to him in English without first attempting to communicate, or at least greet him, in Spanish, he purposely responded in Spanish using a thick Alpujarran accent. Due to the circumstances of his upbringing, Pedro normally spoke with a standard or neutral Andalusian dialect, something of which he was very proud, seeing it as a sign of being cultured and educated. According to his narrative, when confronted with someone who seemed to be asserting linguistic superiority through their exclusive use of English, Pedro used his ability to code-switch with the Alpujarran accent to make himself (even more) incomprehensible and have some fun with the offending incomer. On the one hand, most of Pedro's clients were transient (tourists not residents), so he didn't need to cultivate a clientele in the same way as other types of businesses. On the other hand, what he perceived as his correct Spanish had a central role in his construction of identity and this led to him conveying his annoyance with the imposition of English via a portrait of himself as rejecting English through his linguistic prowess. Aside from the actual nature of the interactions, the way he presented them indicated that he saw them as small acts of resistance against monolingual Anglophones.

When I asked Elena about these linguistic tensions, her perspective was that in the 1980s through the '90s, the *orgiveños* were very happy to sell their *cortijos* (farmhouses) to foreigners at inflated prices and made a killing off of the British and other Europeans, sometimes taking advantage of them by selling them houses that were in terrible condition. For that reason, there was no rejection of this influx of people from outside Spain. Now, when there is less of a financial bonanza tied to the non-Spaniards, there is annoyance with people who have lived in the area for 20 years or more and don't speak any or much Spanish, and with people who *orgiveños* perceive as coming from abroad to benefit from Spain's less expensive healthcare. Elena summed the situation up with a reference to the biblical metaphor of "vacas gordas y vacas flacas [fat cows and skinny cows]": in the years of plenty the local residents didn't notice the lack of integration, but in leaner times the same behaviors irked them. Elena's assessment was borne out in Enrique's attitude. Enrique, a member of the *orgiveño* landowning class in his early fifties, is currently still enjoying years of plenty. He owns a small business in the service industry, and noted that 30–40 percent of his clients were foreigners from other parts of Europe. Appreciating the importance of these clients, he has purposely hired staff (all *orgiveños*) that speak another language or even more than one (English, German, or French), and business is booming. In extensive conversations, Enrique recounted, often with amusement, efforts at communicating across languages, and he took pride in the number of languages spoken by his staff. Indeed, it is fairly common in local businesses connected to a higher socioeconomic level (the bookstore, financial services, etc.) for the staff to at least try to speak with customers from other parts of Europe in English to accommodate them. For those *orgiveños* who are still aware of, or are still receiving, economic benefit from the more affluent Europeans' arrival, and are not invested in maintaining an identity based on linguistic skill, the incomers' role in improving their personal finances and the local economy as a whole is a lubricant that goes a long way in easing the frictions of living in parallel worlds that, by force, must intersect in the context of local services and institutions.[3] In this sense, the *orgiveños*' financial gain from the metropolitan and Northern European incomers supports the basic tolerance (absence of violent or public rejection) that they demonstrate toward these newcomers. However, the process of negotiating how to put up with those town inhabitants whose lack of efforts to speak Spanish or lack of participation in local activities is perceived as rudeness, yet upon whom many rely for their income, creates an overall sense of ambivalence among *orgiveños* toward the Northern European arrivals.

Elena also remarked that there is a generational difference: The children of these British and other European newcomers who are 30 years old or younger, grew up in the area and are pretty much like any other young person from the town. According to her, they are fully "integrated," and several have married into the local community. Elena mentioned that a few of these marriages have involved sons of Muslim converts who married *orgiveñas* who had converted to Islam. Her use of the term "integration" suggests that she views the local Spanish-speaking culture as the dominant culture to which others will assimilate, but the example that she gave of the children of incoming Muslim converts marrying *orgiveñas* suggests that while a linguistic assimilation toward Spanish may be occurring, sometimes the more recent arrivals' religious and even cultural norms are prevailing. Interestingly, probably because Elena is not a practicing Catholic, she didn't view *orgiveñas*' conversion to Islam as running counter to integration.

Although there are smaller, multi-lingual private elementary schools mainly attended by incomers, the public schools in Órgiva do serve to linguistically acculturate many incomers' children. Currently, communication between parents from different communities at the public schools is limited by the language barrier. More than one resident of the town recounted that the bilingual children of non-Spanish-speaking parents translated between their parents and others. With time, more and more residents of Northern European origin will be native speakers of Spanish (with varying degrees of bilingualism). But their religious and cultural practices may diverge sharply from the Catholic, Andalusian and specifically Alpujarran practices identified today as markers of being *orgiveño*. Evidently, Órgiva is on the cusp of an era of greater contact between its different communities and a new definition of what it means to be a "local." It will be interesting to see to what extent, and how, the linguistic, religious, and cultural communities in the town merge and what factors (if any) motivate *orgiveños* to tolerate remaining differences (in the sense of putting up with them) or even to build greater recognition-based tolerance.

For the time being, there is limited recognition-based tolerance on the part of *orgiveños* toward the metropolitan and Northern European incomers. Nonetheless, as I shall explain in the next section, the *orgiveños* do not exclusively hold the dominant societal position associated with tolerators in a permission-based toleration dynamic. This is significant because it indicates that the *orgiveños* and other constituents of the town are putting up with each other and the fact that no one group has clear dominance contributes to equilibrium, and potentially recognition, in the town. The different types of power held by the various stakeholders in the town stand to make the exchange dynamics of toleration more visible. The ways in which *orgiveños* talk about the Northern European incomers and their linguistic difference reveals that *orgiveños* are aware of their economic dependence on the incomers, but feel empowered to impose Spanish in educational and governmental (though not business and social) realms. Superficial portrayals of tolerance in the town do not capture these tensions and ambivalences, which ultimately can be productive in the establishment of greater recognition-based tolerance.

THE FIRST OF RECENT INCOMERS: LIFESTYLE MIGRANTS AND ALTERNATIVES FROM NORTHERN EUROPE AND METROPOLITAN SPAIN

The incomers from Northern Europe and metropolitan Spain that started to arrive in Órgiva in the late 1970s, with a strong uptick in the 1990s, can best be understood as lifestyle migrants, in contrast with the phenomenon of economic/labor migration. These lifestyle migrants include European expatriates, primarily Britons, as well as residents from other regions of Spain, primarily Madrid and Catalonia. On the basis of national and European identifications, and some aspects of lifestyle, this group largely overlaps with that of the "alternatives" and, as a result, I will address the alternatives within this section. The incomers from Northern Europe and metropolitan Spain also overlap in terms of national and European identities with the Muslim convert community, but with distinct boundaries created by religious observance and accompanying cultural norms. Thus, I will address the convert community in a subsequent section. Although these sets of somewhat overlapping communities are defined by common metropolitan and (Northern) European identities, they are differentiated by the factors that brought them to Órgiva and how they live there. The non-Andalusian Europeans who sought a back-to-the-land experience, or simply a warmer climate with a lower cost of living, purchased and restored properties in the area that were vacated by the Andalusian emigration of the 1960s–70s or by townspeople who had given up on farming. In this sense, labor migration paved the way for lifestyle migration and these metropolitan incomers are the agents of transnational (or transregional) rural gentrification.

While, as noted above, these property-owning European lifestyle migrants enjoy a high degree of basic or permission-based tolerance on the part of *orgiveños* because of the former's revitalization of the local economy, this doesn't correlate with the *orgiveños* having the dominant social position typically associated with the community that grants permission-based tolerance. Rather, the *orgiveños* remain marginalized in terms of civilizational hierarchies, and sometimes class hierarchies as well. Although the *orgiveños* are the preexisting community that tolerates more recent arrivals, given the civilizational and class dynamics, rather than the *orgiveños* operating like a dominant host culture tolerating incomers, the dynamic is instead an ambiguous one, that includes elements of the colonial encounter, in which the "primitive" colonized culture (in this case, that of *orgiveños*) is tolerated by the more "superior" incoming culture (in this case, that of Northern Europeans and metropolitan Spaniards).

While some lifestyle migrants voice appreciation for the farming knowledge of *orgiveños* or have collaborated with them in local politics, others express a palpable attitude of superiority toward the *orgiveños*. In this sense, the attitude expressed by Brenan toward "his" village is alive and well among some incomers. British interlocutors

Susan and John, who have lived in the town for 18 and 22 years, respectively, recounted separately the disdain with which most of their fellow expats viewed the major local festivities, such as the celebration of the *Cristo de la Expiración*, which some of the British residents refer to sarcastically as "The Big Bang" because of the shouting and fireworks that it entails.[4] However, Susan later explained that the 30-something-year-olds (and younger) of British parents who were raised in Órgiva consider themselves Spanish and are intermarrying with *orgiveños*. Susan noted that this contact is changing *orgiveños*' perspectives on the newcomers little by little. When I then asked if she saw the *orgiveños* as tolerant, she replied "Tolerant? They let things slide." In other words, rather than tolerant out of a conscious decision to accept difference, she saw them as being so laidback or careless that they lack the initiative to take action regarding their disapproval of certain behaviors. Although Susan reported that most British incomers demonstrated attitudes of superiority, her comments about intermarriage and carelessness reflect an understanding of the British as already open-minded, and of the *orgiveños* as in need of broadening their horizons. The linguistic hierarchies created by language ideologies (the higher cultural and symbolic capital of English and of standard Peninsular Spanish) and the enduring local Catholic customs that some perceive as "primitive" come together—in sometimes uneven and contradictory ways—with broader civilizational hierarchies that position the Northern European and metropolitan incomers as more "civilized" than the *orgiveños*.

When I asked Tom, a British resident who had been in the town for two decades, owns property there, and has more conservative political positions, how the different religious groups in the town get along, he replied "There doesn't seem to be any sort of friction." Like Elena, he noted that there is "quite a lot of integration going on" in the form of relationships between local Spanish "girls" and Muslim converts. Tom described the *orgiveños* as "tolerant" and "friendly." When I asked if he saw potential tensions along other lines in the town, echoing Elena's assessment and Enrique's attitude, he replied with a big laugh: "As long as people [the foreigners] keep spending money, the tolerance will remain [. . .] Younger businesspeople want to see people in their shops, and their bars, and cafes." Like various *orgiveños*, Tom also described the town as made up of separate spheres: "Many foreigners [. . .] tend to stick within their own groups, and you notice this with the Dutch, and mostly the English, and the Scandinavians, and the Germans." While these comments manifest a vision of the town as still organized according to national groupings, other interlocutors pointed to regional and urban vs. rural boundaries.

One interlocutor of metropolitan Spanish origin complained to me about problems with the local infrastructure and what he viewed as mismanaged efforts at restoring buildings and public spaces. When I asked why he thought such things occurred he responded "porque son unos catetos [because they are hillbillies/country bumpkins]." He then went on about their "ignorance," noting that although he is a prominent figure in the town, no one from the local government had ever come to ask for his input. His categorization of the *orgiveños* as *catetos* reveals the positionality that is part of the toleration process in Órgiva: some of those perceived as the most "civilized" (the Northern European and metropolitan Spanish incomers), tapping into the vestiges of the *Leyenda Negra* and conceptions of the Alpujarra as primitive, view the *orgiveños* as ignorant and close-minded. Exemplifying the dynamic criticized by Brown, the civilizational logic at work here leads to a form of toleration in which the behavior of the tolerated is viewed as abhorrent and primitive, yet this very judgment serves to reinforce the "civilized" group's moral superiority. In other words, the marginalizing judgment gives the group perceived as civilized the opportunity to magnanimously tolerate (that is, put up with) and thus boost their image as civilized, thereby reinforcing the established hierarchies.

At the same time, those "primitive" *orgiveños* tolerate (at least in a permission-granting way) the incomers—in spite of being aware of the incomers' perceptions of them. One of the most awkward moments of my fieldwork occurred when, a few hours after hearing that metropolitan Spaniard rail against the *orgiveños* as *catetos*, an *orgiveño* used this same term. While speaking with Carlos, a late-forties *orgiveño* who works in a small business, I asked whether he would describe Órgiva as a space of tolerance. He replied that, more than that, he would describe it as "surreal," because of the various contrasting elements that came together there. Carlos referenced the Spanish absurdist comedy film *Amanece, que no es poco* (Dawn breaks, which is no small thing) (1989) and, after describing the film's surrealism , he glossed his sense of surrealism in the town by saying that in Órgiva "hay muchas cosas que se juntan que no tienen nada que ver [there's all sorts of things that get put side by side that have nothing to do with each other]." Among these surreal pairings, he noted that he was amazed by the fact that people who had traveled and seen so much of the world were drawn to the remote corner that is Órgiva. Carlos thought that maybe it was because no one could feel "extraño [strange/like a stranger]" there, noting that there are "so many foreigners [*extranjeros*] and strange people [*extraños*] here" that no one stands out. He then went on to say that the only people who annoyed him were the ones from Madrid who talked down to him, "like they think I'm a *cateto*." As I focused on holding my tongue so as not to reveal that, indeed, so-and-so had just used that term, I considered that perhaps the non-Andalusian Spaniards feel the need to differentiate themselves from the *orgiveños*, to establish that they are not "backward," but rather cultured Spaniards. The result is that some of the strongest tensions in Órgiva occur intra-nationally, between Spaniards from major urban centers and *orgiveños*.

In addition to making sense of the transformations and tensions within the town by placing them within the framework of the surreal, other ways in which *orgiveños* negotiate the changes around them, and the entwined civilizational hierarchies, include assertions of tolerant superiority through humor and the rejection of the label "tolerant." Among *orgiveños*, permission-based tolerance often takes the form of humor, as witnessed by a joke that Elena told me that an *orgiveño* friend of hers liked to tell: Órgiva is the best zoo in the world because it has animals of every species. Although the joke doesn't ascribe nonrational, animal-like characteristics to any particular group, its humor is based on zoos' recognized goal of establishing a comprehensive collection of forms of animal life. While today's zoos justify collection and captivity through the institutions' scientific and conservationist aims, the element of spectacle remains. In this sense, the joke about Órgiva as a zoo conveys a sense of amusement with the human diversity present in the town, while placing those who comprise that diversity in the position of object to be observed. In that way, those who share the joke establish a sense of superiority over "the animals on display," while giving them permission to congregate as long as they provide voyeuristic entertainment.

Another way of processing the town's transformation is the outright rejection of the label "tolerant." Some *orgiveños*, those that identify more strongly as Catholic and as socially and politically conservative, reject the characterization of the town as "tolerant." Marta, a 50-year-old *orgiveña* who is very active in the Catholic Church, supports right-of-center political parties, and runs a small business, demonstrated this attitude. Another contact had put me in touch with Marta and, as I waited for Marta to finish with her clients—all *orgiveños*, mostly women over the age of 60, she and her clients chatted about which *cofradías* (associations for religious devotion and Holy Week processions) they each belonged to. When I asked Marta how she would describe Órgiva, she responded with a narrative that seemed very staged: after a dramatic pause with a strategically placed faraway look, she replied "un pueblo frío [a cold people/town]." After glossing that the "character or idiosyncrasy" of the *orgiveño* was to be cold, she stated that even after 30 years of living in Órgiva someone from another part of Spain was still considered "un forastero [a foreigner or outsider]." When I made a comment about how Órgiva is known nowadays for its confluence of cultures she said "They say that the people [of Órgiva] are tolerant, but that's a lie. As long as the newcomers don't get in the way [mientras no estorben], they are put up with." It is noteworthy that no one else described the town to me in this way. This suggests that while many *orgiveños* are aware that they are supposed to be tolerant, according to prevailing conceptions of being civilizationally advanced, and that they should embrace tolerance as a virtue to aspire to, or at least aspire to project outwardly, others push back against the changes in the town by rejecting the characterization of Órgiva as tolerant—while nonetheless practicing some form of permission-based tolerance. Marta's description of "putting up with" the foreigners, although she denied that it was tolerance, is actually a textbook definition of tolerance—not recognition-based tolerance, but certainly permission-based tolerance. The question, of course, is where she and her like-minded townspeople place the limit of what will be put up with. So far, that limit has only been reached with regard to the most radical hippies, alternatives who are street-dwellers or live off-grid, outside conventional society and its infrastructure.

In addition to tensions related to civilizational standing, which include linguistic differences and friction between Spaniards across metropolitan/rural and regional boundaries, another fault line in Órgiva is that of the relationship with the alternatives. Most residents of Órgiva refer to the alternative groups in and around the town as "hippies" (using this as an English loanword in Spanish), or as "alternatives"/*alternativos* (depending on the language of expression), which is considered by some to be the more politically correct term. Although many of the alternatives overlap with the metropolitan Europeans in national/regional origins, and often in lifestyle choices (interest in various healing modalities, natural foods, sustainability, etc.), the major distinguishing feature is that they are not typically property owners, or if they do own land, they don't live in conventional dwellings. Instead, they live in communes, campsites, yurts, abandoned crumbling farmhouses, or lodging received in exchange for work. Given their counterculture outlook, this segment of the inhabitants of Órgiva and its environs has a reputation for being tolerant towards others, but rejecting conventional rules. Ironically, the alternatives provide the sub-group that unites some other constituents—and especially those that are property owners—in their intolerance towards this sub-group: the street-dwelling and off-grid alternatives.

Residents of Órgiva from various communities within the town expressed concern or even disapproval of the most anti-establishment members of the alternative community: people with no fixed lodging and no defined or legal source of income (other than begging),

Figure 7: A member of the alternative community passes next to the town hall (inside the 16th-century palace of the Condes de Sástago) and the church.

or members of the alternative communes who are not integrated into the local utility system. More conservative, land-owning *orgiveños* referred to all unkempt alternatives as *pies negros*—black feet, in reference to the dirt on the soles of their bare feet—and complained generally about the lack of cleanliness in the town as a way of voicing rejection of the alternatives. Two *orgiveños* of working-class and middle-class backgrounds jointly reported that they had no problem with any of the groups in town, except for the hardcore hippies, like the ones in Beneficio who "are basically a cult [una secta]." But other residents of Órgiva limited their disapproval to those that they perceived of as vagabonds, the street-dwellers who live off of begging or dumpster-diving, while others defended even this group's presence as part of the "biodiversity" of the town, as long-term resident John put it. When I asked Tom, another long-term British resident referred to earlier, about attitudes in the town toward the street-dwelling and off-the-grid alternatives, he replied:

> It's getting harder. They're [the local government] toughening up on people that are living without making any contribution to society [. . .] There's a lot of people living in vans, and yurts, and tipis, with no sanitation. You gotta play by the rules at some point in your life. You just can't keep on being irresponsible. It's a tricky one. Everyone wants to have a free life and a lot of people move here for that reason.

While Tom's comments reflect a conservative positioning within the town, they also reveal the broader uncomfortable tension—"hard" and "tricky"—between different understandings of rights, responsibilities, and freedoms in the town. Indeed, they point to one of the main tensions regarding defining what is not permissible and what is—the haram and halal of Órgiva.

The presence of the more off-the-grid alternatives is the most contentious issue in the town: what to do, as a community known for its tolerance, with inhabitants also known to espouse a "live and let live" philosophy when some other inhabitants disapprove of their lifestyle? The roots of this issue go back to at least the early 1990s. A few *orgiveño* interlocutors mentioned a demonstration in Órgiva that took place some time during the 1990s, in which townspeople protested the hippie element's presence in the town. I've concluded that they must have been referring to the strike and demonstration that took place on November 6, 1991 that protested the establishment of a center for the rehabilitation of drug addicts. This protest made the national news which reported that "practically all the townspeople of Órgiva (Granada) supported [. . .] the call for a general strike to protest against the placement in this town of an *El Patriarca* rehabilitation center for drug addicts" (R. López). *Le Patriarche* (*El Patriarca* in Spanish) was the name of an association created in France in 1974 that combatted drug addiction through centers in which addicts lived and worked together. The association established many such centers throughout Europe and the Americas and, as noted by Rafael López's article in *El País*, a month prior to this demonstration had opened a center in a farmhouse two kilometers from the middle of Órgiva.[5]

The article stated that the day-long strike in which the whole town participated led to the closure of businesses and schools. This civic action also included a march through Órgiva's streets, in which more than 2,000 people (about a third of the town's population) participated and which blocked the main road into Órgiva, causing a traffic back-up that stretched for kilometers. The peaceful protest began to turn violent when a van belonging to the *Patriarca* association forced its way through the blockade and in the process ran over two protesters. In the melee, *orgiveños* started to shake the vehicle and hit it with rocks, bars, and fists. At another point, the event's organizers, through heated discussion and a physical struggle, stopped a group of protesters who wanted to direct the march toward the *El Patriarca* center itself. The organizers were concerned that this would turn into a physical confrontation. Indeed, the *Guardia Civil* (the national law enforcement agency) set up security at the entrance to *El Patriarca*'s farmhouse in order to prevent vandalism on the part of the townspeople. Town councilors from the local government supported the protest and stated that the center was functioning illegally, as it had not acquired the necessary permits to open. As reported in *El País*, one councilman in particular stated that the town hall would not grant said licenses and that it was best that the Association leave "before we kick them out" (R. López). Members of *El Patriarca*'s center in Órgiva acknowledged that they were still processing the permits, but stated that they planned to continue operating there, not allowing fear to keep them from going into the town when they needed to (R. López). This *El Patriarca* center was, in fact, shut down.

El País reported that the townspeople were opposed to the facility because it didn't have enough security measures in place and they were concerned about the contagion of AIDS or hepatitis (R. López). However, local memory frames the forceful protest differently. Within a section titled "Movilizaciones" (Mobilizations/Community Action), *Hablamos de Órgiva* mentions that on as many as 15 occasions during the last 50 years residents of Órgiva have mobilized to protest various issues and that they were usually successful in reaching their objectives ("La vida en las calles y plazas de Órgiva," 20). The section includes a list of the 13 "most important" examples of civic action taken in the town from the 1960s through 2008 and *orgiveños*' testimonials about these actions ("La vida en las calles y plazas de Órgiva," 21–22). Most of these statements are about protests related to a planned quarry, proposed projects that would affect access to water, and the protection of thousand-year-old olive trees. However, in two other chapters of the *Hablamos de Órgiva* book, cross-referenced to the "Movilizaciones" section, a few townspeople narrated their perspectives on the 1991 protest against *El Patriarca*. Although one contributor was against the closure of *El Patriarca* and another supported it, both agreed on a key element: that the protest arose from a much broader rejection of the hippie incomers. One participant described the virulent protest as the result of "a panic, a fear [un pánico, un miedo]" and noted that in the demonstration people did not carry banners saying "'Drug addicts out of here,' they carried banners with 'Hippies out of here,' it was all mixed together . . . Something like the xenophobic feelings of the town came out [. . .] [Pues en esa manifestación ya no llevaban pancartas 'Fuera drogadictos,' ya llevaban pancartas 'Fuera hippies,' entraba todo. . . Salió como el sentimiento xenófobo de la población

(. . .)]" ("La salud y las drogas" 17). Similarly, the other contributor saw the event as the bubbling-up of some residents' previously contained, underlying "hate of outsiders [odio al forastero]"; "some people do outrageous things, and the townspeople don't say a peep [la gente no dice 'ni pío']," but

> at any moment that hate can come out, like it did with the story of *El Patriarca* [. . .] People were opposed because the conditions with which they set it up were horrible, the people that were there were crowded in haphazardly [. . .] In that demonstration, where there were all sorts of people, there were banners with "Hippies out of here" [Pero en cualquier momento puede salir ese odio, como pasó en la historia del Patriarca [. . .] La gente estaba en contra porque las condiciones en que lo montaron eran horribles, la gente que estaba allí estaba apiñada de mala manera. [. . .] En esa manifestación, que había gente de todo tipo, había pancartas de "hippies fuera."] ("Los que se fueron y los que llegaron" 14).

Based on these statements in *Hablamos de Órgiva* and comments that I heard that referred to the event as an "anti-hippie" demonstration, *orgiveños* remember it as an event that reacted against the hippie element that was already visible in the town and that the townspeople either feared would increase with the establishment of the center or simply associated with the center, which became a lightning rod for accumulated rejection. Through that aggressive protest, *orgiveños* made clear where the limits of their tolerance lay: the hippie contingent and especially those that represent all that makes the hippies most reprehensible to many *orgiveños*, that is, drug use, lack of hygiene, and a lack of a formal dwelling.

In a similar vein, the town rose up against, though through more official channels, the *Fiesta del Dragón* or Dragon Festival, the event Bailey mentions in *A Chancer's Guide*. The event was a "free festival"—a multi-day mix of music and cultural activities with free admission and no central authority—that was held from 1997 to 2009 in Los Cigarrones (also known as "Ciggy"), an abandoned hamlet 2 kilometers south of Órgiva that, starting in the late 1970s, became an alternative community. The event started as that alternative community's celebration of the spring equinox, but grew to attract as many as 10,000 attendees ("La comunidad hippy [. . .]"), which led to disapproval and organizing on the part of some local residents, especially those with property at or near the site. *Orgiveño* interlocutors recounted that on a few occasions the *Fiesta del Dragón* coincided with the town's traditional celebration of the *Cristo de la Expiración*. These *orgiveños* believed that the festival was eventually banned in part because of incidents such as one in which a naked woman, one of the hippies who had arrived for the *Fiesta del Dragón*, walked through the procession of *orgiveños* bearing the statues of Christ on the Cross and Our Lady of Sorrows (*La Virgen de los Dolores*).

According to residents of Los Cigarrones involved in the festival, starting in 2002 the local government, at that time dominated by center-right councilors, prohibited the festival and tried to establish a police presence at the event. This and other types of intervention continued until mayor María Ángeles Blanco López, from the center-left PSOE party, took office in 2007 ("Dragon Festival, History"). Both the Dragon Festival blog and the former mayor indicate that under her leadership the local government attempted to work with alternatives in Los Cigarrones to regulate the event as a way to embrace it and incorporate it into the life of the town. However, the festival community rejected these efforts as an imposition of restrictions and controls that were antithetical to the nature of the event. Both sources also state that in 2009 the local authorities excavated large holes at the festival site, for a tree-planting project whose main objective was to impede the set-up for the festival. The Dragon Festival blog reports that two days before that year's festival, an order prohibiting the event was posted, subject to high fines. This led to fines being served and subsequent legal battles.[6] Since 2010, *La Fiesta del Dragón* has been held in Santa Fé, Granada. In *Hablamos de Órgiva*, statements in the two-page section on *La Fiesta del Dragón* present the general consensus that, if the event had been regulated and better managed, it could have been a great economic boon, but a few noted that it attracted people who were scary and full of "dirt [*mugre*]" ("Fiestas y encuentros" 10). The ousting of the festival on the part of the local authorities and the lingering mixed sentiments, including references to the alternatives' lack of hygiene, are another indicator of where *orgiveños* draw the line of what is permissible—what is halal, if you will—and of the towns-people's readiness to take action to put an end to what they consider intolerable.

Rejection of the more extreme alternatives is ongoing in other ways. *Orgiveños* occasionally use social media to express disapproval about the alternatives' behavior and to call for the town hall to put a stop to incidents such as alternatives stripping naked in front of the main public fountain next to the church in order to wash. At certain cafés and bars in Órgiva, the more disheveled alternatives are often refused service. These moments in which intolerance is enacted publicly lie in stark contrast with how other groups in the town are treated. The street-dwelling and off-the-grid alternatives, and certain behaviors on the part of all alternatives that run counter to the values of conventional society, are perceived as transgressive by different sectors of Órgiva's inhabitants, whether on the basis of traditional, Catholic conceptions of morality or on the basis of working-, middle-, and upper-class notions of respectability and contribution to society.

Most recently, in late January 2021, the mayor of Órgiva, Raúl Orellana of the conservative Christian-democratic *Partido Popular*, announced in a town-hall meeting that the local and regional authorities would soon put an end to illegal and informal settlements in the area. He noted that "Órgiva is an example of inclusivity/assimilation and *convivencia*, we feel proud of being a multicultural town, but we cannot confuse that with the absence of rules [Órgiva es un ejemplo de integración y de convivencia, nos sentimos orgullosos de ser un pueblo multicultural, pero no podemos confundir eso con la ausencia de normas]" ("Órgiva pretende eliminar los asentamientos [. . .]"). The reasons cited for this decision to begin enforcing existing legislation were the safety of settlements' inhabitants, and of the area in general due to the occurrence of fires and floods and the environmental impact of such settlements. Soon after, social media was ablaze with opposing viewpoints from residents of the town, in comments posted in Spanish, English, or bilingually (often with the help of Google Translate). One Facebook user referred sarcastically to the mayor, who took office in June 2019, as "the new enlightened mayor of Orgiva [el ilustrado alcalde de orgiva [sic]]." Complaints about the "traditional Spanish people" and "uptight English" in the town were countered with calls to simply "comply with the legal regulations like everyone else [cumplir con las normativas legales como todo el mundo]." The rhetoric of these comments—establishing who is truly "enlightened" and thus "civilized" based on different assessments of tradition, rule-following, and freedom—reflects the civilizational discourses at work in the struggle over this issue.

Discussion reignited when, on March 31, 2021 local police, *Guardia Civi*l agents, and representatives of Andalucía's environmental protection office visited Beneficio, in order to identify all the inhabitants and inspect the commune, part of which is situated within the Natural Park that rings the Sierra Nevada National Park. The social media discussion points included the reach of the new initiative (only the alternative settlements such as Beneficio, housing developments built without permits, or anyone living in a tent, truck, or without a legal water supply and sanitation system), the environmental impact of informal settlements vs. dense urban construction, the difference between laws, on the one hand, and ethics and justice, on the other, and how best to respond to this campaign (i.e., resist "the system," reform it, or maintain it).

When I spoke with Mayor Orellana in July 2021, I asked what the greatest challenges were that the town faced and he immediately spoke of the "asentamientos," or hippie settlements, stating that their inhabitants needed to "follow the rules" and "contribute" because Órgiva "can't be a jungle [no puede ser una selva]," thereby summoning the threat of the lawlessness of the jungle and invoking civilizational discourses.[7] More conservative members of the different communities in the town, who often identify as property-owners and taxpayers, view the more radical alternatives as choosing to be parasitic and not respect the rules, making statements such as "They want rights, without fulfilling obligations" and "They want to live outside of the system, but with all of the benefits of the system." Others who identify to some extent as alternatives defend the communes and the more radical alternatives in general, crediting them with having put Órgiva on the map by making it an attractive, unique environment. Given the paradoxical workings of tolerance, those who are intolerant toward the imposition of authority (in the words of one poster, "Many can't tolerate being dictated to about how to live their lives") unite some groups in the town in their efforts to define certain behaviors as socially acceptable or unacceptable. The ongoing debate that has resulted from this raises questions in the town about the meaning and limits of tolerance.

In this conflict, the alternatives, like the *orgiveños*, have an ambiguous position with regards to the scale of civilizational "advancement." The off-grid and street-dwelling alternatives have less power than other groups because of their lack of support from religious or municipal authorities, lack of economic capital, and, in some cases, their lack of Spanish citizenship and insufficient proficiency in Spanish, as well as in the workings of the Spanish juridical system. However, their "score" with regards to symbolic capital depends on the scale or frame of reference to which one ascribes. For others in the town who identify to some extent as alternatives or sympathize with their conception of freedom, the off-grid alternatives are enlightened precisely because of their rejection of conventional criteria for determining civilization. But for those who follow more standard conceptions of civilization, including many *orgiveños*, the more radical alternatives are rule-breakers who live in a somewhat primitive state. Viewed through this lens, these alternatives' foreignness on the basis of nationality and mother tongue is compounded by foreignness in terms of value systems. As a result, the off-the-grid and street-dwelling alternatives are largely located outside of *orgiveños*' boundaries of acceptable behavior and belonging, and occasionally this is manifested in different forms of public rejection or intolerance.

SPIRITUAL CHAIN MIGRATION: THE INFLUX OF CONVERTS TO ISLAM

Although the alternatives have been the focus of many news articles related to law enforcement, the set of communities that has featured most prominently in a range of recent media accounts of Órgiva—from television shows to news articles to travel blogs—is that of the converts to Islam. While some of the converts have also sought a rural escape, most came not so much to go back to the land as to go "back to" Islam. The largest Muslim community in Órgiva is that of the members of the Naqshbandi-Haqqani Sufi *tariqa*. There are also two other groupings of converts to Sufi Islam in the area that have some member overlap between them and a smaller overlap with the Naqshbandi-Haqqani community. These are the groups brought together by the Kutubia cultural center and the newer center, Azahara International, located at the outskirts of neighboring Lanjarón (about a 10-minute drive from Órgiva). Additionally, there are other converts who, at the time of my research, were no longer, or not yet, affiliated with any of these organizations. Aside from the very first cluster of converts, including Shaykh Umar, who were drawn by or arose from the alternative communities in the area, and a few that still follow this route (converting after arrival in Órgiva), the others have arrived through a process that can be described as spiritual chain migration: the convert either personally knew someone in the Órgiva Sufi community, was affiliated with the Naqshbandi-Haqqani *tariqa*, or had otherwise heard of this growing Sufi community and decided to move to Órgiva.

The Naqshbandi-Haqqani *tariqa*, a branch of the Naqshbandi *tariqa* within Sunni Sufism, has its headquarters in Cyprus and was founded by Nazim al-Haqqani (1922–2014), a Turkish Cypriot. One of the converts affiliated with the Órgiva Naqshbandi-Haqqani center, Amina, who was originally from Catalonia but had been living in Órgiva for decades, told me that, under Shaykh Umar's leadership, a Naqshbandi center opened in the city of Granada in the 1990s. Then there were different farmhouses in the Órgiva area that were used as gathering places and, in the mid-1990s, the group opened a center in a space with a storefront on *calle Libertad* (Liberty Street), a couple of minutes by foot from the town's church. Qasim, the owner of Café Baraka, mentioned that this center closed due to the building's poor condition. Later, around 2014, the current center was opened in a farmhouse a few kilometers from the middle of Órgiva. This mosque and center is referred to by the local Sufis and, as a result, by some other residents of Órgiva, as the *dargah*, the term of Persian origin for a shrine housing the tomb of a revered religious figure that often includes a mosque, meeting rooms, a residence for a caretaker, and related community facilities. The Órgiva *dargah* hosts gatherings every Thursday evening for *dhikr* and every Friday afternoon for the congregational prayer followed by *hadra*. On Tuesdays, a group of women from the Naqshbandi community gathers at the small mosque in town for *dhikr*.[8]

Most of the Órgiva Naqshbandis are of Spanish origin, but there are regulars and visitors from far and wide. For that reason, one of the regulars quipped that "the *dargah* is like Noah's ark." In addition to clusters of Italians and Britons, some within the community are cultural hybrids in their own right: a Spanish woman who, because her father was an Arabist, had lived in Algeria for 10 years as a child; a woman of Gulf Arab and Eritrean origin who had been living in Sweden; a few Syrian women (married to non-Syrians) who had been living elsewhere in Europe, and a few North Africans who were either women married to Spaniards or men who had been largely or exclusively raised in Europe.

Nonetheless, the Sufi community is still quite distinct from the small Maghrebi contingent in the town. When I asked a Naqshbandi community member who is of European origin whether any of the North Africans living in Órgiva came regularly to the *dargah*, she replied that they "mostly keep to themselves [se quedan en su mundo]" and didn't frequent the *dargah*. The general lack of cultural identification between the two groups was reflected in a comment made by a woman of Spanish convert origin who was living in a much larger city elsewhere in the south of Spain, but had come to celebrate Eid al-Adha

(*'Id al-'Adha*, The Feast of the Sacrifice) at the *dargah*. When I asked about the mosques in her city, she said that she didn't like to go to them because the congregation was almost completely Moroccan and "there's the woman issue [está el tema de la mujer]." She went on to explain that there was more segregation of the sexes and gendering than she found comfortable.

Based on what I observed in gatherings at the *dargah*, at their center the Órgiva Naqshbandis practice gender segregation, but, given the wide range of norms regarding this practice, some Muslims would consider it lax. At the *dhikr* and *hadra* gatherings, women sat separately from men, with the women at the unlit back of the room; a curtain divided the women's section from the men's section, but it was not completely closed, thus allowing the women to see Shaykh Umar and his interpreter while obscuring most, but not all, of the women from the men's sight.[9] The Friday service was followed by a communal lunch at long tables, with a stretch of tables for men and, perpendicular to those, another for women and children, but the groups were visible to each other and after finishing their meal they would begin to mingle.

Similarly, the covering of women among the Órgiva Sufis (both those who frequent the Naqshbandi *dargah* and others) is relatively relaxed. Both in the *dargah* and out and about, women generally wear a turban-like wrap that covers most of their hair, but leaves a bit of the front hairline and all of the ears visible, their necks either uncovered, or covered with a cloth draped over the turban piece and loosely wrapped around the neck. The women wear loose tops with three-quarter to full sleeves and ankle-length skirts. Likewise, the men wear loose pants and tunic-style shirts as well as kufi caps (topis/taqiyas). Although these women's apparel would be considered inappropriate by conservative Muslims, the converts' dress is recognized by other Órgiva residents as "Muslim clothing" and (as we shall see) opens a space for the acceptance of other types of Muslim-associated clothing.

One day, after the *jumu'a* or congregational Friday prayer, the topic of clothing practices came up spontaneously. After a Spanish woman convert told us about her recent beach vacation, Amina, the

Catalan convert who had been in Órgiva for decades, responded by asking jokingly if the woman had gone swimming in a "burkini." Amid laughter from others in this small group of women, Amina explained that when she went to the beach she swam fully clothed, as she was dressed at that moment, and didn't care what people thought. This led to complaints about how toplessness and scanty clothing are common at beaches in Spain, and questions for me about what it was like in Miami. Outside their Alpujarran Sufi community, these women's clothing practices and interest in modesty are at odds with the norms among the general Spanish population, and close to home they are even more at odds with the Alpujarra's "alternatives." Within a few days of the burkini conversation, at an alternative school in the area, two women, one from Madrid and the other from elsewhere in Europe, who were drawn to Órgiva because of their interest in an alternative lifestyle extolled the virtues of nudism. One spoke with pride about her conflict with the police when she'd gone nude at a non-nudist beach in Spain and then exclaimed "If everyone were nudist, the problems of the world would be solved! [¡si todos fueran nudistas, se solucionarían todos los problemas del mundo!]." The quest for feeling at peace with oneself and freeing oneself from materialism may be a common goal of the Sufis converts and the nudist or naturist alternatives, but it is sought in radically different ways. Given this context, more traditional Maghrebis and the Sufi converts are closer to each other in their views about clothing and modesty than they are to secular or Catholic Spaniards, and especially to those embracing an alternative lifestyle. That is, the traditional Maghrebis' and Sufi converts' conceptions of permissible and desirable clothing practices are much more likely to overlap. This unites the very diverse Muslim community in the town in their Muslimness, as much as in their rejection of alternative clothing habits (or lack thereof).

The Kutubia cultural center was founded by a group of converts to Islam from the US, the UK, and Italy, many of whom are book designers, bookmakers, and booksellers—hence the name "Kutubia," classical Arabic for the booksellers' area in a market. In conversations with Kutubia's core members, they explained the center's name, its goals, and their views on Órgiva. Their goal when they founded the center in 2016 was to create an intellectual space that would be neutral with regard to the specific branches of Sufism and conducive to fomenting connections between individuals and organizations both inside and outside of Órgiva. A few of Kutubia's core organizers are active in the local Naqshbandi group; others follow other Sufi teachers and lineages. Their center is housed in a storefront space on *calle Libertad*, even closer to the church than where the Naqshbandi center used to be. These organizers of Kutubia noted that the center has experienced "zero rejection or push back" from its neighbors, who include local residents, a corner bar, and some local businesses; rather, the neighbors have "always been very welcoming." Indeed, they described Órgiva as place where "people are more welcoming" than in other parts of Spain where they had lived.

Although the organizers' initial goals included setting up a library and an office for drop-in questions about Islam that would be open full time and, due to its location, more accessible than the *dargah*, Kutubia currently operates on the basis of donations and volunteering and they haven't been able to carry out those initiatives yet. So far Kutubia hosts films, lectures, and concerts typically linked to Islam and Islamicate cultures (e.g., lectures on Ibn 'Arabi or other aspects of Sufism and concerts of Middle Eastern and North African music) and offers classes on Quranic Arabic and Iranian music. Since the organizers want the space to be open to the community at large, the center also hosts classes of general interest such as English language, storytelling, ladies' exercise, capoeira, etc.

The Kutubia organizers who I spoke with stated that their biggest challenge was navigating the English/Spanish language divide. They had to actively reach out to the Spanish-speaking community to involve it and now they were struggling with how to be inclusive without the interruptions and time burden of simultaneous translation, or fully bilingual events. They noted that they are experimenting with different models (e.g., one language for the event, but with printed material available in the other language) to be able to achieve this. The organizers indicated that a secondary challenge was maintaining neutrality among the different Muslim groups in the area. When I asked about the involvement of local Maghrebi migrants, they noted that the Moroccans involved in Kutubia are all married to a Spaniard or other European; in that sense, the involved Maghrebis already had a foot inside a Spanish or European-centered Órgiva community. They did mention, though, that for several years, a Moroccan woman who was residing in Órgiva had led Kutubia's daily Quran recitation sessions during Ramadan. More recently, another Moroccan woman living in Órgiva had begun leading a weekly Quran memorization class at Kutubia.

The region's multi-faith history came up spontaneously when one of my interlocutors referenced hippie leatherworkers from around Bubión, a village higher up in the Alpujarra, who in the 1970s moved to Granada, converted to Islam, and then moved back to the Alpujarra. This interlocutor mentioned that they had heard stories about the residents of Bubión telling these first hippie converts in the area that they (the *bubioneros*) had Muslim or Jewish ancestors. I then probed further by asking if they saw any connections between the history of the region (Muslim Iberia, and Granada as its last kingdom) and present-day Andalucía. They responded by saying that the history of al-Andalus is a strong part of why Muslim converts come to Andalucía, although they also recognized the practical advantages of settling in Andalucía, describing it as a more "viable" place to live (i.e., to make a living) than Morocco or elsewhere in the Muslim Mediterranean. For a convert wishing to live in an Islam-infused environment with a higher standard of living, Andalucía provided an attractive option.

They returned to the Muslim and Jewish traces in Spain by referring to an event that had been held at Kutubia in February 2018: the presentation of Francisco Martínez Dalmases' book *Qandil: luces de poniente/Qandil: Lights in the Land of the Setting Sun* (Martínez Dalmases 2011, 2017), which consists of interconnected stories and essays that highlight links between 20th-century Spaniards and medieval and early modern Iberia via crypto-Muslims and crypto-Jews in Spain. The Spanish version of the book was published in 2011 and the English translation, edited by Medina Whiteman, a member of

Kutubia at the time, was published in 2017. This revisionist history of the expulsion of Jews and Muslims, which questions the official narrative that Spain was "cleansed" of its non-Catholic elements, resonates a great deal with the converts to Islam in Spain. For instance, at one point, one 70-something-year-old American founder of Kutubia mentioned the many Spanish converts to Islam that she had met that looked to her like they must have Moorish origins. On a separate occasion, within a conversation about the irrigation system (*acequia*) in the Alpujarra, the same interlocutor talked about how at the time of the Muslims' expulsion, two Muslims in each village were asked to stay because of their important know-how—one to maintain the *acequia* and the other to maintain the mulberry trees for silk. She proposed that I should research whether the descendants of those two Muslims per village had stayed in the area and whether they had maintained any Muslim traditions. She then added that "the *acequia* guy" (the person tasked with keeping the irrigation channels clean and in good repair) that she knew had "such an Arab face" that she would be surprised if he were not a descendant of Moors. These comments reveal a conception of a visible Moorish ethnicity—in other words, a North African biological difference rather than a situation of common Mediterranean phenotypes and changing religious affiliations over the centuries.

As noted earlier, at least one younger Muslim connected to Kutubia has linked her experience as a Muslim in Órgiva to al-Andalus while questioning ethnic thinking and romanticizing impulses. Whiteman, in *The Invisible Muslim*, expresses connection to the terrain of the region via al-Andalus while questioning the organicity of such connections and reflecting upon the identity formation process, but among Spanish Sufis I heard more expressions of connection to Iberia's Muslim past without any questioning or self-awareness.[10] Rather, they viewed Islam as a "natural" fit for the region.

For instance, a Spanish woman who was visiting the Órgiva *dargah* to celebrate Eid al-Adha, who was from a city about a 40-minute drive away, told me her and her husband's conversion stories. In his case, he was visiting the Alpujarran village of Juviles (about an hour's drive from Órgiva), which she referred to as the site of a famous bloody battle, and he saw a vision of that battle that moved him to convert to Islam. The way that she referred to the battle, and the effect that it had on her spouse, indicate that she was referring to a 1492 battle, part of the Catholic Monarchs' conquest of Granada, in which Juviles had a prominent role as a Muslim stronghold that eventually was taken by King Ferdinand, who ordered the destruction of the Juviles fort. (The ruins of this fort were then used in the mid-16th-century Second Rebellion of the Alpujarra as a site of *morisco* resistance.) But she may have been conflating these moments of *morisco* resistance with an earlier battle that was indeed known for being a bloodbath: at the end of the 9th and beginning of the 10th centuries, a group of *muwalladun* (Muslims of Iberian origin or of mixed Arab, Amazigh, and Iberian origin) rebelled against the Cordoban Caliphate and their last holdout was the fort of Juviles. This earlier battle at Juviles points to the historical tensions between Muslims of Iberian stock and those hailing from the Middle East and North Africa and thus, whether or not it was intentional on the part of this Spanish convert, reference to this battle adds a great deal of complexity to these Iberians' decision to embrace Islam. I wasn't surprised, given that surreal contrasts are par for the course in the Alpujarra, when a few days later an *orgiveño* happened to mention that Juviles (along with Trevélez) is one of the most renowned locales for the curing of *jamón* in the Alpujarra.

In a similar invocation of the past, Amina, a female convert originally from Catalonia whom I referred to earlier, talked to me about the mountains surrounding us and how all different types of spiritual traditions appreciated mountains as sacred places to seek refuge and spirituality. Amina then went on to say that, in Órgiva, in addition to the mountains, they were between two Muslim saints' tombs. Presumably, with the first of these tombs she was referring to the *dargah* itself. But before I had the chance to ask whose tomb the *dargah* marked, she mentioned that the *Ermita de San Sebastián*, a chapel on a hill on the edge of town, was a saint's tomb, but that they didn't know who in particular. Amina then spoke of a Muslim holy man who had walked by the *Ermita* and said he could smell the saint. When I asked another

144 • *Jamón* and *Halal*

FIGURE 8: The *Ermita de San Sebastián*, a Catholic chapel on the edge of town that may have once been a *ribat* (a combination of Muslim monastery and military outpost) and some believe to be the tomb of a Sufi saint.

member of the Órgiva Naqshbandi group about whose tomb the *dargah* was connected to, he said that in this case *dargah* simply referred to a religious meeting place, and not necessarily a tomb. Another Sufi community member mentioned that the farmhouse that had become the *dargah* belonged to a Naqshbandi community member, who lent it rent-free. Thus, the space responds more to practicality than to sacred status as the site of a saint's grave. The use of the term "*dargah*" for this space could incite disapproval among non-Sufi Muslims, given that elsewhere conservative Sunni Muslims reject shrines (sometimes violently) as a form of idolatry. But this term that typically denotes a shrine built around a tomb serves two functions: it broadly evokes the spiritual spaces of Sufism and also connects the space, through the association with saints' graves, to Sufism's historical presence in the area, from the time that Iberia was under Muslim rule. The ambiguity regarding which Sufi saints' tombs, if any, can be found in Órgiva allows for multiple, individualized narratives, some of which rest upon a spiritual connection to the local terrain via al-Andalus.

According to historians of the region, the *Ermita* was originally a Visigoth fortress, was then taken over by Muslims, and later officially incorporated into the Church in 1591 (Álvarez Pérez). Although I have not found documentation regarding this *Ermita* in particular having been a *ribat* (a combination of military outpost and Muslim monastery) or a *zawiya* (an Islamic religious school and monastery), Trillo San José (1994) states that the high number of *ribats* in the Alpujarra during the period of Muslim rule, with some villages having as many as 10 or 15, suggests that a significant religious movement was rooted in the area (363). Trillo San José goes on to note that Muslim mystics arrived in the area soon after the Muslim conquest and became particularly strong beginning in the 11th century under Almoravid and Almohad rule (363). Under Almoravid rule, the city of Almería was the capital of a Sufi movement that encompassed both Granada and Seville. Then, during Almohad rule, a Sufi shaykh, Abu Marwan al-Yuhanisi, who was born and raised in a village of the Almerian Alpujarra (d. 1268/1269 in Ceuta), practiced mysticism and traveled around the Alpujarra.[11] Thus, it is possible that the *Ermita* in Órgiva and other structures in the vicinity were originally constructed around the tombs of Muslim religious figures and it is quite certain that the Alpujarra has deep ties to Sufism that stretch back for a millennium.

The circulation of anecdotes such as Amina's about Muslim saints buried in the area, whether or not they can be directly linked to the

Ermita de San Sebastián or the *dargah*, and those referenced earlier regarding the Moorish origins of Spaniards, reflect the role of this historic location in granting the converts a feeling of legitimacy in their identities as Muslims and/or in their presence in Southern Spain. Similarly, Bahrami, in her work on converts in the Albaicín neighborhood in the city of Granada, observes that "The Albaicin gives the Spanish converts a sense of historical legitimacy by setting the tone of their identity as a Spanish romance" (131–32).

Demonstrating more affinities with the Alpujarra's alternative cultural scene, the Azahara center bills itself as an organization that promotes the "spiritual ecology of al-Andalus" (https://azahara-international.org/). A predominantly Anglophone space, Azahara follows the *tariqa qadiriyya* via a shaykh from Gambia and promotes what its organizer and members understand as the permaculture that was first established in the region by Muslim agriculturalists. That is, the organization promotes sustainable agriculture as a Muslim practice autochthonous to Spain. This is done through guest lectures, retreats, permaculture courses, and a youth summer camp.

After a *dhikr* at the center, Azahara's founder, Joanna Fatima Redstone, explained to me that she is a British convert to Islam that was drawn to Órgiva because it offered a Muslim community in a rural and eco-friendly setting. In the UK, she was part of a permaculture community, but the weather there was not suitable to growing, at least not year-round, and it could only be done in the countryside, where there was no Muslim community. Through her permaculture network, she heard about Órgiva as a place that had both a growing Muslim community and a growing community of people interested in ecological agriculture. She moved to Órgiva and lived there for several years, eventually buying the property for the center and (while commuting back and forth between the UK and the Alpujarra) began to hold events in early 2020. Her project's interest in the Muslim agricultural practices of the Middle Ages not only creates alliances with the alternative community, but gives the participants a sense of organic connection (in both meanings of the term) to the Alpujarra. In sum, the history of the region—maintained presently through a

FIGURE 9: The entrance to the Sufi *dargah* on the outskirts of town; the flyers on the right announce a concert of Turkish Sufi music benefitting the children of Palestine, and a lecture on permaculture and the Muslim agricultural tradition of al-Andalus.

sense of biological, spiritual, and/or horticultural connection between the *moriscos* and contemporary Spaniards or Muslim converts of any origin—gives the converts in Órgiva and its environs a sense of validity, organicity, and purpose regarding their presence in the area.

At the same time, the indeterminate and lower-profile nature of the Muslim traces in Órgiva allows for not only malleability with regard to converts' narratives about the town's Muslimness, but also a less protective attitude from Catholic authorities or conservative *orgiveños*. Given the contrast with the ways in which the Catholic Church has intervened in the debates surrounding the Mosque-Cathedral of Córdoba and the new Great Mosque in Granada's historic Albaicín neighborhood, it seems that the lack of a major heritage site in Órgiva, and perhaps also the predominance of social issues such as alcoholism and drug abuse for which spirituality serves as an antidote, have led the local Catholic clergy to embrace an ecumenical attitude in which they seek to work collaboratively with the other religious groups present, rather than reject the strong Muslim presence.

The priests of Órgiva's *Nuestra Señora de la Expectación* Catholic church also serve various smaller municipalities in the Alpujarra. Father Vílchez and Father España, both assigned to the parish in 2016, emphasized their work to combat substance abuse and their contact with other religious groups in the area.[12] They mentioned that they have made it a point to establish ties with other religious groups in the area (Sufis, Jews, practitioners of Subud, and Buddhists) and so far they have attended Friday prayers and the communal lunch at the *dargah* a few times on Muslim holidays, and a few Passover seders and other events at private homes on Jewish holidays (though, as Father España wryly pointed out, it was an idiosyncratic seder in that it was vegetarian).[13] Father España explained that he had met the hosts of this seder, a French Jew and a Dutch Jew, through annual music competitions hosted by the church, the largest of which takes place during the Christmas holidays, in which people from various different communities within Órgiva participate. When I asked the two priests what motivated them to meet with practitioners of other religions, Father Vílchez replied that without dialogue one can't arrive at anything new, but "through dialogue and mutual respect a further horizon can be reached [sí se puede llegar a algo más]." Earlier, Father España, like several other interlocutors from different sectors of Órgiva, had described the form of coexistence in the town by saying "people lead parallel lives" and now he commented on the importance of dialogue by adding "If there is no coming together [encuentro], we'll continue in our parallel lives." From his perspective, unlike that of many other residents, the dynamic of completely separate spheres is not sustainable or desirable.

Although there are a small number of specific events at the church that draw participants from the various communities in Órgiva, and there are many day-to-day spaces of contact (such as supermarkets, the weekly Thursday market, the plazas, the public playgrounds, and the public primary and secondary schools), the town has some distinct community spaces. While the *dargha* is a meeting place for many, but not all, the Muslims in the town, Café Baraka has a clearly defined role as the hang-out for all converts to Islam, all transplants from abroad, and tourists—especially those seeking halal food and other elements of a halal (or "permissible") lifestyle, such as an alcohol-free environment.[14] This establishment, officially named "Restaurante-Tetería Baraka" (Baraka Restaurant-Teahouse), but known commonly as "Café Baraka" or "el Baraka," was established in 2003 by Qasim Barrio Raposo, a convert to Islam who has been featured in a few of the television narratives about the town. Qasim was born as Pedro to a Galician family that had established themselves in the Basque country. Qasim recounted to me that soon after he first opened the café, an old *orgiveño* that was passing in front of the restaurant asked him "you don't sell alcohol?" When Qasim replied "no," the old man said "so what do you sell?" The elderly *orgiveño* was confounded by the concept of a café and eatery that was alcohol-free. When I asked Kutubia folks whether there were any barriers in the town on the basis of religion, one immediately mentioned the prevalence of wine, beer, and pork in social spaces; she said that that is why they meet at Café Baraka, because it offers a halal environment. Some North African residents of the town also frequent Baraka, with one telling me that she prefers it over any of the other eateries in town because at Baraka she feels very comfortable, as if she were back home or somewhere in the Muslim world. Amid the mainstream Spanish culture of socializing with cigarettes over wine, beer, and *jamón* (attested to by the high number of bars in the town), Café Baraka serves an important function as an alternative space.[15]

Although now a few *orgiveños* (from among those who do not identify strongly as Catholic and are under age 50) frequent Café Baraka, it is still mostly a gathering place for members of the other communities and (Muslim) tourists.[16] According to Qasim, every summer there are one or two Muslim families of North African or South Asian origin who have been living in Europe for years and choose Órgiva as a vacation spot because they feel very comfortable there. He explained that they are more used to being in Europe than in their countries of origin, and Órgiva offers them a crossover space where they can have halal food and no one looks twice at a woman in hijab. Qasim said that so many people were always asking him about where to go to pray in Órgiva, where to find halal meat, and so forth, that he created the "Islam Órgiva Halal" website.[17] The website includes information about some of the halal eateries in the town and one of the supermarkets that sells halal meat, the in-town prayer space, as well as points of interest related to the medieval period of Muslim rule.

Regarding the attitudes of *orgiveños* toward the converts to Islam, I still recall walking along *calle Libertad* on my way to my cousins' house during the mid-1990s and seeing for the first time the Naqshbandi center in a storefront space two doors down from a beauty salon where I had had my hair cut during the previous visit. I had recently spent a year studying advanced Arabic in Cairo, where I had seen up close a *dhikr* ceremony in the multi-colored tent of a Sufi *tariqa* at the festival for the birthday of Sayyida Zaynab, the granddaughter of the Prophet Muhammad. The Sufi center on Órgiva's *calle Libertad* was my first indication that there were Sufis living in the town and I had the distinct feeling of worlds colliding. When I asked *Tía* Conchita about it, she just replied by saying that it had opened a few months back and mentioned that there were many "forasteros" in the town now, including the new next-door neighbor, who was British—a very nice lady with whom *Tía* Conchita communicated using an improvised sign language. It wasn't until years later that I found out that this neighbor, to whom *Tía* Conchita regularly took fruit from her *huerto*, had arrived in the town as a convert to Islam. Recently, a few interlocutors confirmed my recollections and stated that when that very visible center on *calle Libertad* opened, there was no perceptible negative reaction in the town. In March 2015, when the Naqshbandi's current *dargah* had only been open for about a year, in a group conversation with the local business-owner Enrique, he made a joking comment saying that for all we knew the Muslims who gathered in their center right outside of town were "a terrorist cell." There were chuckles from some, while others protested the comment, but no one else developed the remark further and since then I've never heard such a comment again. Rather, in 2019, *orgiveños* expressed that the Sufi converts "don't bother anyone; they keep to themselves" and that "among Muslims they are the ones who place less restrictions on the clothes that women wear, on who they marry." Although there may have been initial discomfort or apprehension related to the Sufi community, as reflected in the terrorist comment, now *orgiveños* refer to the Sufis as amicable practitioners of a "lighter" form of Islam, with the implicit message that Sufi Islam is so far from the predominant images of Islam that it is more compatible with 20th-century Spanish cultural norms.

THE OTHER MUSLIMS IN ÓRGIVA: MIGRANTS FROM THE MAGHREB

While the European converts inhabit a difference that is chosen, or perhaps more accurately that is a chosen expression of a difference experienced internally, there is a smaller group of inhabitants of Órgiva that were not only born into Islam but also live with markers of difference that are external and fixed: accent, skin color, hair type, and/or facial features that are coded as North African.[18] The first North African immigrant arrived in Órgiva in the early 1990s, but most have arrived since about 2004. According to the *Instituto Nacional de Estadística*, there are 56 residents in Órgiva who were born in Morocco and 9 who were born in Algeria. This total of 65 North Africans does not include the children of these migrants born in Spain, nor does it include the more transient populations that I will refer to further on. The Maghrebi migrants make up a small percentage of the population of Órgiva, but their presence is significant because of Maghrebis' position in Spanish discourses about self/other, Spanish identity, and Europeanness—within which secularism and Christianity (vs. other religious, social, and political systems, and especially Islam) play a key role.

Aside from a few Maghrebis who came to Spain to pursue university studies and ended up in Órgiva, most of the Maghrebis in the town are economic migrants. However, the majority of these arrived in Órgiva, after living elsewhere in Andalucía, with enough economic capital and/or skills to have more stable, higher-tier livelihoods. This has allowed some to set up small shops and take-out restaurants and others to work as chefs in larger eateries, in contrast with the small group of low-skill labor migrants who work in small agricultural ventures higher up in the Alpujarra.[19] My conversations with the Maghrebi migrants in Órgiva revealed that not only did first living elsewhere in Andalucía or Europe give them the capital to establish themselves in Órgiva, but their experiences elsewhere contributed to them choosing to settle and then stay in Órgiva, rather than a city with more job opportunities and more anti-immigrant sentiment directed at North Africans.

For these migrants, life in Órgiva is not devoid of remnants—or resuscitations—of *moros* vs. *cristianos* thinking. For instance, in the summer of 2016 while socializing with a Moroccan immigrant, Zakiyya, in her apartment, her son Karim asked to play outside with my children. Zakiyya told Karim that it was fine as long as they stayed in the street in front of their apartment building (not further away, such as the plaza). The children went downstairs with a ball and as I was sitting near the balcony I saw that a pair of *orgiveño* boys who knew Karim had come by. One of the *orgiveño* boys asked

Karim to come play with them in the plaza. When Karim replied no, that he couldn't, the boy from Órgiva, interpreting my children to be Muslims and/or Maghrebis because of their skin tone and features (from their father's side), said "Oh, you only want to play with people from your religion? Well, we only play with Christians" and left in a huff. This misunderstanding—the *orgiveño* boy assuming a rejection on Karim's part (given that he didn't explain why he couldn't go to the plaza) and reacting to that with his own counter-rejection—reveals the at least occasional manifestation of a mindset of "us" vs. "them" along religious lines. Although on both sides of the Strait of Gibraltar some experience this *moros* vs. *cristianos* view of the world as timeless and self-evident, it is part of identity narratives from al-Andalus, the Reconquista, and the colonial era that have been partially maintained, but also revived and reformulated. In Spain, these narratives are tightly interwoven with the country's cultural and political responses to North African immigration, which include xenophobic ethno-nationalism. Nonetheless, the narrative that the North African immigrants tell about Órgiva is one of a high degree of inclusion and respect, and the figurative language that recurred among migrant women was that of family and home, as contexts of caring.

Karim and his family had arrived in Órgiva about a year before the incident recounted above, when his mother Zakiyya was in her late twenties. Zakiyya (who may or may not have heard about the incident from Karim) told me in 2019 that in comparison with other parts of Andalucía in which she had lived beforehand, the people of Órgiva were the ones who helped her the most and that there she experienced "ahsan muʿamala"—the best treatment. Zakiyya, who wore a hijab that covered all her hairline, ears, and neck, said that any day-to-day tensions were due to personality ("tabiʿat al-insan"), not to place of origin or religion. She went on to say that she "felt like [she] was among family [wust ʿaʾilati]." When I asked why she thought that Órgiva was like that, she referred to the number of different nationalities present in the town, people from not only Morocco and Spain, but various other countries. Her response suggests that with so many regional and national identities present, it is more difficult for nationalist narratives to dominate.

Another Moroccan migrant, Malika, had moved to Órgiva 12 years before we met in 2019. When I asked how she and her family had ended up in Órgiva and why she had decided to stay, Malika, who was in her mid- to late forties, explained that at first she didn't like Órgiva because she felt like she was in the middle of nowhere and she didn't want to raise her children among "dirty hippies." Then she grew to like it because of the high number of Muslims living there. "It feels like one big family [ʿaʾila kabira]. I don't feel like a stranger [ghariba] here," she explained. Later in our conversation, Malika mentioned that sometimes a Spaniard would ask her to translate between Spanish and Arabic for the rental of a farmhouse or something similar. She stated that this sort of request made her feel important and that people respect and trust her. She felt that they also respect that others are Muslim and don't eat pork or drink alcohol. When I asked Malika, who goes out in short sleeves and no head covering, but has Maghrebi-presenting features, if she had ever experienced discrimination she replied "Never. When you hold your head up with pride [tirfaʿa raʾsak], people in kind treat you with respect."

On a separate occasion, Malika introduced me to her friend Rachida, a Moroccan migrant who had moved to Órgiva more than 13 years prior with her Moroccan husband and children. When I asked Rachida how she would describe Órgiva she said: "It's like one big house [casa], you feel like you are all together in one big house. People watch out for my kids when they're playing somewhere else in the town." Rachida then went on to recount an experience that had clearly touched her: she said that one day an *orgiveña* had walked up the street into Rachida's business carrying heavy bags of oranges and lemons from her orchard to give them to Rachida. It was a client that Rachida didn't even know well and she was amazed by this gesture. In the context of Rachida expressing her contentment with life in Órgiva, she said she wouldn't mind if one of her daughters married a Spaniard—assuming, of course, that he would convert to Islam. That she is able to imagine an *orgiveño* converting to Islam is interesting because certainly in other parts of Spain, Europe, or the US, such a

FIGURE 10: A North African immigrant, wearing a longer headscarf and long skirt, passing in front of the town library.

scenario would not be easily imaginable. The level of tolerant coexistence in the town is sufficient for her to imagine conversion to her family's religion as a possible, and agreeable, future for her daughters.

I met another Moroccan migrant, Fatima, in summer 2016 when she heard me speaking in Arabic with another migrant in the main plaza. Fatima is one of the few migrants in Órgiva who dresses more conservatively: she wears a dark, ankle-length ʿabaya or cloak and a longer headscarf that drapes past her shoulders and only reveals her face. She had arrived in Órgiva about 11 years earlier and described it as different from all the other places in Spain where she had lived. In 2019, Fatima stated that in Órgiva "everyone is friendly and nice," in contrast, when she goes to the next town over, Lanjarón, "people look at me funny and I feel like they might throw a rock at my head [al-nas kayashufu fiyya shaufa naqsa bi-halla ghadi shiru ʿiliya bi-hajara lil-raʾs]." Although Lanjarón is considered more politically and socially conservative, I was surprised by this violent figure of speech, but no doubt Fatima's style of dress had made her the target of hostile stares—outside of Órgiva.

Another migrant from North Africa, ʿAziza, who wears a more subtle head covering (one that wraps around her head and mostly covers her neck) voiced a similar perspective when I spoke with her in 2021. When I asked ʿAziza, a native of Algeria, if she felt comfortable wearing hijab in Órgiva, she immediately said yes. In response to follow-up questions, she said that she noticed a significant difference between the large Northern Spanish cities where she had lived before and Órgiva. ʿAziza had moved to Órgiva almost five years before, as the result of her search for a more welcoming environment. She described her life in Northern Spain by recounting experiences in which she felt that Spaniards had avoided sitting next to her on the bus, or had not offered her a job, because of their Islamophobia. She felt that the city of Granada would provide a more hospitable environment and was planning to move there when she saw a video on the Internet in which the mayor of Órgiva at the time, María Ángeles Blanco, spoke about the diversity and multiculturalism of Órgiva. (Most likely ʿAziza saw the segment with the mayor that was part of *España a ras de cielo*, discussed in Chapter 4.) Although in some ways her experience in Órgiva had not lived up to her expectations, in part due to experiences that she described as discrimination along class lines, she stated that she feels very comfortable as a Muslim in Órgiva. She felt no discrimination or uncomfortable looks while wearing hijab there and she attributed this to the fact that there are so many Muslims in the town that people are used to seeing hijab. In a separate conversation, ʿAziza, using family-based language similar to that of Malika and Rachida, mentioned that she was so comfortable at work that she felt like her employer's "sister or cousin," not like an employee.

How Islamic dress is treated within Órgiva also arose in the testimony offered by Mustafa, a Moroccan who moved to Órgiva in 2016 from a town less than 40 km away on the coast. Mustafa stated: "Sometimes here I go out in my *djellaba* [a loose-fitting, long outer tunic commonly used in the Maghreb] and no one looks at me funny. They might even complement my clothes. Where I lived before [elsewhere in Andalucía] I would wear it to go to Friday prayer and people would give me a mean look [shufa naqsa] . . . a racist look [maʿ ʿunsuriyya]." For that reason, he would take the *djellaba* off immediately after visiting the mosque. He emphasized that it wasn't because he wasn't proud of his culture, but that the looks were "nasty [haqira]." In contrast, in Órgiva he reported feeling very comfortable walking around in public dressed that way. The mix of religions and relatively high support for diversity found in Órgiva give Mustafa and other migrants a beneficial type of invisibility, or, inversely, an acceptable visibility: the dress from their region of origin is either not noteworthy (doesn't stand out as particularly different) or is appreciated and praised. Galeotti, in her work on theories of tolerance, explains the mechanics and significance of accepted visible difference as follows: "The public visibility of differences [. . .] represents the legitimization of their presence in public. In its turn, the legitimization of their presence in public signifies their inclusion in the public sphere on the same footing as those whose practices and behavior are "normal." This inclusion then implies the acceptance of the corresponding identity and, hence, the acceptance of those who are marked by such identities" (100–101). Thus, the Maghrebi migrants in Órgiva are not just tolerated—in the sense of being put up with—but are symbolically recognized as part of the fabric of the town and even a group that adds to it aesthetically or culturally.

The diversity and accepted visibility in Órgiva seems to attract in particular Maghrebis in mixed marriages. Another distinguishing characteristic of the Maghrebis in Órgiva is that, according to self-reports and my observations, a third to half of them are in mixed marriages and most typically these are marriages between Maghrebi women and European men, some of whom have converted to Islam and others who have not. This is significant, because for a Maghrebi Muslim woman to marry a non-Muslim is generally a transgressive act that may lead to rejection by family and friends.[20] Through a mutual *orgiveña* friend, I met Laila, a Moroccan woman married to a Spanish man from a large city in Andalucía. Laila moved to Spain in the late 1990s when she was in her late teens, met her husband a few years after, and later moved with him to Órgiva. Unlike most of the other Maghrebis in the town, Laila attended university and she does not work outside the home. Like *orgiveños* and British incomers, Laila noted that the different groups in Órgiva lead parallel lives: "Cada grupillo tiene su mundo [each little group is in its own world.]" She said that they are cordial and greet each other, but keep some distance, setting a boundary ("marcan una frontera"). When I referred to North Africans residing in the town, Laila mentioned knowing two or three Moroccan families as well as a few "mixed couples" that live in Órgiva. She then used the same expression as before—"I decided to set a boundary [marcar una frontera]"—to explain that she had chosen to maintain some distance from the Moroccan families that she knew. She clarified that it was because the Moroccan migrants she had met always ended up talking about religion, that is, Islam: "That topic is always present." Although Laila was raised Muslim, she is not a practicing Muslim, her husband did not convert to Islam, and they are raising their children with only very light exposure to the teachings and practices of Islam. When socializing with the Moroccans that she knew in Órgiva, she felt that she couldn't avoid the topic of religion and that it became awkward to try to explain her beliefs and lifestyle. Inversely, though, she felt very comfortable within non-religious Spanish circles in Órgiva.

At the beginning of Laila's relationship with her husband, both sets of parents were opposed to the relationship, with her husband's mother once telling Laila that she had never wanted her son to have a "mora" girlfriend. Eventually, Laila's parents reached a degree of acceptance and her husband's family ended up treating Laila like any other member of the family. As a very non-religious Moroccan, the high number of Muslims in Órgiva has never been a factor that drew Laila to the town; nonetheless, her experiences as someone who entered what she referred to as a "mixed" marriage make Órgiva an excellent setting in which to live, work, and raise a family. With so many people from around the world, a diversity of faith practices alongside the non-religious outlooks of most *orgiveños* under 50, as well as a relatively high percentage of other Maghrebi-European couples, Laila's family blends right in—especially if they maintain a boundary with the "fully" Moroccan families in the town.

Interestingly, when I asked Laila how she would characterize Órgiva, she was the only Maghrebi migrant to reference the *convivencia* of Muslim Iberia. When I specifically asked for adjectives that she would use to describe the town she said "unique," "multicultural and peaceful." And then she spontaneously added that she feels that Órgiva "reflects the way that people lived in this region centuries ago, under the Muslims, if it was like people say it was [. . .] It reflects al-Andalus, how the different groups lived together." For her, rather than offering a Muslim enclave in Spain, Órgiva offers diversity—a third space that is neither Morocco nor standard Spain, a space of mythical Andalusian *convivencia*. In Laila's case, although she is somewhat skeptical of the well-known *convivencia* narrative, it offers her a way to conceptualize and find positive meaning in her culturally transgressive choices and the life she has built in Spain.

In terms of what draws Maghrebi migrants to Órgiva, Mustafa, who recounted his experiences wearing a *djellaba* in Órgiva vs. other parts of Andalucía, also noted that where he had lived before elsewhere in Andalucía, there were other Moroccans who were always loud and goofing off. He said it bothered him because it feeds negative stereotypes about Moroccans and reflects badly on all Moroccans, affecting him negatively. He explained that, in part, he came to Órgiva to get away from other Moroccans. In a separate conversation, I asked Rachida's husband what had drawn him to Órgiva and he said that though there were few job opportunities, he was attracted by the lower cost of living, in comparison with the city of Granada or other similar locations. The comments from the Maghrebi migrants presented above, as well as the arrival trajectory of most of the Maghrebis in Órgiva, indicate that they are a self-selected group: although they arrived in Spain as economic migrants, as a lifestyle choice, they have elected to live in Órgiva rather than the typical sites of Maghrebi immigration in Spain. They have chosen Órgiva for its low cost of living and (from the women's perspective) its small-town support system, for its acceptance of Islam and even respect for it. Additionally, they have chosen this Alpujarran town because, in contrast with Andalusian cities with many Maghrebi laborers, or areas of Almería with many Maghrebi agricultural workers, Órgiva has a low number of working-class Maghrebi migrants and as a result it offers less concern regarding the image of North African migrants in the eyes of Spaniards.

Within the linguistic panorama of Órgiva, in addition to the fact that Arabic is the language of a much smaller minority than English, outside of Muslim spaces such as the *dargah*, the Kutubia center, Café Baraka, etc., Arabic is at the opposite end of the language spectrum as English, with regard to civilizational prestige. Although the converts to Islam value the Arabic-language skills of the Maghrebi migrants for religious reasons (something I discuss further on), outside of the convert communities, spoken Arabic carries no prestige and is occasionally mildly rejected in public. Maghrebi migrants were clearly comfortable speaking in Arabic in public areas of the town, but when I asked a question about it, they described some small tensions. One evening as I sat outside on the side of a small street chatting with Malika and friends, an *orgiveño* boy came out to the balcony one floor up from the street level. Malika started cracking up and asked if he was going to say the same thing as before. She then recounted a humorous incident in which she and the same Maghrebi friends were in the same spot boisterously telling stories in Arabic and the same little boy had come out to the same balcony. He had been awoken by their voices and said that they were "talking funny [hablando raro]" and not letting him sleep. As we laughed about this episode, I asked the Maghrebis about how other townspeople responded when they heard Arabic. First, Malika and her friends said that there were no negative reactions and that they tried to be considerate and switch to Spanish if someone who didn't speak Arabic joined the group. Then Malika went on to say that occasionally an *orgiveño* who overheard her speaking in Arabic said as a joke: "You're in Spain, speak Spanish!" She noted that they expressed it as a joke, but underneath they probably meant it. Malika continued by saying that sometimes when that happens, she quips: "Will you speak Arabic when you go to Morocco?" Thus, though outside of Muslim contexts Arabic is lightly rejected, the environment in the town is conducive to the Maghrebis gently pushing back against such attitudes.

Given this situation, and the realities of making a living, the North African migrants in Órgiva are generally quick to make efforts to learn Spanish and many reach high levels of proficiency. As a result of the North African immigrants' command of Spanish, where they often work (in public-facing businesses and/or with *orgiveño* colleagues), and where they generally live (in apartments within the town, rather than farmhouses on its outskirts), they have more contact with the *orgiveños* than most of the monolingual Anglophones or some of the converts to Islam. Consequently, in comparison with other groups, the parallel world of the North Africans is more connected to that of the *orgiveños*. This is certainly a contrast with parts of Spain in which there are large Maghrebi immigrant populations and high anti-immigrant sentiment.

Like Bailey's 2020 memoir, almost all of the television narratives about Órgiva present the town as an idyllic space of tolerance. At the same time, none of these accounts address the immigrants from North Africa who are part of town life, and several do not even address the Sufi convert community that is so prominent in other narratives. On the one hand, the stories told by Moroccan migrants render Órgiva as a uniquely welcoming space in which they are shown—or are able to establish—respect. The negotiation of recognition and respect in which the migrants engage, and which is absent from most of the televisual and written narratives about Órgiva, sheds light on the creation and maintenance of spaces of tolerance. It reveals the conditions and work that are part of deeper, more equitable forms of tolerance. This is particularly clear in the relations between the Maghrebi migrants and the converts to Islam, and between those migrant families and the unaccompanied minor migrants that also live in Órgiva.

Although the "Noah's ark" of the Naqshbandi *dargah* in Órgiva welcomes all, many Maghrebi Muslims feel that it is not their space because it doesn't embody their understanding of Islam. I only met a handful of people of Maghrebi origin who participated regularly in the Naqshbandi Sufi gatherings. One was born in Morocco within a family that for generations had been involved in Sufism, albeit of a different *tariqa*, and had immigrated to Spain with his family during his childhood, one was raised in Northern Europe by non-religious parents, and another was a woman married to a Spanish convert to Islam. Thus, one was already a part of Moroccan Sufism, which has deep roots but up until recently was marginalized as non-orthodox; the second had a very secular upbringing in Europe, and the third was connected to the Sufi convert community via marriage.[21] Both of the Sufi men of Maghrebi origin interact very little with the other Maghrebis in Órgiva; instead they identify as part of the Sufi community and it is with that community that they primarily socialize. In contrast, among the migrants with whom I spoke who practice a more mainstream Maghrebi Islam, only two reported going to the *dargha* to pray and neither socialized regularly with the Sufi converts in Órgiva.

Zakiyya, Karim's mother, was in regular contact with the converts to Sufi Islam in Órgiva because she worked in food preparation; thus her interactions with them were primarily within an employment context. She felt comfortable with them and often went to the *dargha* for Friday prayers. Although this may have been conditioned by the fact that she didn't have a car with which to easily travel to the closest town with a standard Sunni mosque (the town of Motril, a 35-minute drive from Órgiva), Zakiyya talked about the *dargha* with no qualifiers or reservations. Similarly, Malika reported cheerfully that she sometimes went to the *dargah* to pray.

However, Malika's friend Rachida had a different perspective. Rachida wore a wrap that covered most of her hair and was much more akin to the types of head-covering used by the Sufi converts in Órgiva than to those seen in Morocco. At one point, while speaking with her alone, Rachida adjusted her hair wrap and spontaneously explained that she didn't cover up more, as a veiled woman would in Morocco, because of the heat, but then she conceded that she didn't cover her hair due to any religious motivation, but because she didn't like her frizzy hair. I mentioned that her hair-covering looked like that of the Sufi women in town and asked if she ever went to their mosque, the *dargah*. She replied that it was fine with her if the people there enjoy it, but she was not interested in that style of prayer; she preferred to pray at home than go to the *dargah*. In a separate conversation, Rachida's husband said that he never goes to the "Sufi mosque [jami' al-sufiyin]" to pray, not even during Ramadan. He explained that the local Moroccans go to a mosque in Motril to pray. A couple of other interlocutors among the Maghrebis in Órgiva were more specific and expressed that they didn't like the environment of the *dargah* because the Islam that the Sufis practiced didn't follow the norms and structure that the migrants considered intrinsic to Islam. Other conversations revealed additional facets to this intra-Muslim tension.

Mustafa, who enjoyed wearing his *djellaba* out in public in Órgiva and was annoyed by loud Moroccans because they negatively affect the public image of Moroccans, went into a bit more detail about the Sufi community. He started off by saying that he thinks *dhikr* is nice, but he doesn't like to go to the Sufi mosque in Órgiva for Friday prayers. On Fridays, he goes to a mosque in Motril to pray. He added that he'd never been to the Sufi mosque because it didn't interest him. He recounted that once he had sent an Arab who was visiting the town to the *dargah*. The man left before finishing his prayers and came back to tell Mustafa that the *khutba* (sermon) was strange and they prayed very fast. Mustafa explained that the Sufis practiced a "light" version of Islam that contradicted his vision of what Islam is: "They're very special [nas khasa]. They say that they are Muslim, but they don't follow the Sunna or the Quran." Mustafa's tone alone revealed that he was not sympathetic towards the Sufis, but he went on to tell anecdotes about people that he thought were Sufis smoking marijuana and drinking alcohol. He added that, among the Sufis, relationships between men and women were more liberal and that their children had less restrictions. He concluded his remarks by saying that he tried to maintain some distance from the Sufis and to raise his children well in order to maintain their values, but that on a personal level he had no problems with the Sufis. Particularly noteworthy here is that, in spite of his differences with the Sufis regarding dogma and lifestyle, Mustafa closed by emphasizing that it was enough for him to keep a distance—to mark a boundary line, and that he had nothing against the Sufis. That is, he concluded by indirectly stating that he was willing to tolerate the Sufis and their definition of what is halal. Although not explicitly acknowledged by Mustafa, these same Sufis made a positive contribution to the quality of life that he and other Maghrebi migrants enjoyed in the town. This mix of disapproval and contribution to quality of life made the relationship between Mustafa and the Sufi community one marked by ambivalence.

'Aziza, the Maghrebi migrant who explicitly acknowledged that the presence of the many Sufi converts had made Órgiva a more hijab-friendly environment than cities in Northern Spain, had a similarly conflicted relationship with the Sufi community. Over the course of various conversations, 'Aziza told me about her views regarding the Sufi convert community, whose *dargah* she had visited on numerous occasions. On the one hand, she was aware that the community was viewed by some non-Muslim Spaniards with suspicion. She noted that a couple of *orgiveños* had asked her if the local Sufis were "a cult [una secta]" and stated that the local Naqshbandi community members knew that they were under surveillance by the Spanish authorities for potential terrorism. On the other hand, although she found the idea that the Naqshbandis were a cult laughable, and found the authorities' suspicions to be absurd—simply an example of Islamophobia—she admitted that she didn't like certain aspects of Sufism. She believed that the "dancing" or rhythmic movements that are part of Sufi worship (in contrast with *dhikr* itself), are "bida'a," innovation or invented heresy, but quickly added that you "need to respect others and their beliefs." She also said that the Sufi interpretations of scripture sought the *batin* or esoteric, figurative meaning, rather than the *zahir* or readily apparent, more literal interpretation that she believed to be the correct one. At the same time, ʿAziza asserted that the Órgiva Sufis are "better Muslims" than the people in her home country because the Sufis in Órgiva live simply, are very devoted to God, give generously to charity, and make an effort to help the less fortunate.

Right after ʿAziza talked about the Sufis' way of interpreting the Quran, she expressed concern about what I might write about it. I reminded her that, as I had told her previously, I would change names and remove or change any identifying information so that no one would know who had told me something, but she explained that she was more worried about how this would affect the image of Islam as a religion. She emphasized that they were all Muslim: that even though there were small frictions between some Sufi community members and some Maghrebi community members, they needed to be united as Muslims because that bond remained. I then explained to ʿAziza that my assessment was that the Sufi converts and the Maghrebi migrants had a symbiotic relationship and gave her the classic example of the crocodile that holds its jaws open for the little bird to pick out food particles from between its teeth—the crocodile gets clean teeth and the bird gets food. ʿAziza immediately chuckled and said that the Maghrebis were that little bird—the vulnerable ones—and the Sufi converts were the crocodile. Although she emphasized that what united the Sufi converts and many of the Maghrebis was precisely that they were all concerned about the image of Muslims and Islam, she also identified the power differential within this mutualistic symbiotic relationship.

As per Brown's critique, discourses about tolerance mask the social power that constitutes difference. However, some forms of difference are self-chosen and self-demarcated: to wit, that of the converts to Islam and that of Laila, the non-religious Moroccan migrant who socializes almost exclusively with non-Maghrebis. Moreover, in spite of the masking role of liberal rhetoric about tolerance, a recognition-based toleration process can also allow social actors to assert and exercise power and even to constitute an identity as tolerant, one which confers higher community status. If nothing else, the newcomers (rural gentrifiers, converts, and migrants included)—and the *orgiveños* too—have the power to leave. Awareness of their potential mobility allows them to weigh the things that they tolerate in Órgiva against those that they wish to change, even if leaving is the only possible change. But clearly many choose to stay. Maghrebi migrants who settle there have chosen the locale and have not ended up there by default (as would be the case for the port of arrival), or because of the many job opportunities. Although tolerance on the part of minorities is certainly conditioned by their societal status and the benefits that they stand to gain, it is important to acknowledge that the "guest" also makes a choice regarding what, how, and why they will tolerate the "host"—and other "guests." That is, there are conditions and practices that contribute to inter-minority tolerance.

In Órgiva, Maghrebi migrants seize their limited power to demonstrate that they too are capable of recognition-based tolerance. Despite the strong differences between most of the European converts' Sufi Islam and the Islam of the vast majority of the Maghrebi immigrants, Maghrebi immigrants by and large recognize the Sufis as Muslims and support them in their pursuit of religious devotion, in exchange for the normalization of Islam in the town that the converts' presence creates, and that makes the migrants' daily life more comfortable. Although the North African migrants do not necessarily feel at home in the specifically Muslim spaces in the town (the *dargah* and Café Baraka), the Sufis contribute to the migrants feeling at home in Órgiva overall. The migrants tolerate the practices of those who straddle the perceived East/West and Muslim/Christian divides in order to reap the benefits of their presence. The conceptualization of tolerance as a multi-directional process can help reframe tolerance not as a gift that can only be offered to someone with less power, but as a practice bartered with by both the socially and/or economically empowered *and* disempowered community members, in order to reap individual and community benefits.

But the working- and middle-class Maghrebi migrants in Órgiva do not all readily recognize one group of Muslim residents as making a beneficial contribution to their quality of life. Mustafa was more hesitant regarding another group in Órgiva that others are likely to associate with North Africans like himself. In Órgiva, it is fairly common to see two or three male North African teenagers walking through the town or hanging out in the plaza or the *poli* (short for *polideportivo* or community sports center). Their limited command of Spanish distinguishes them from teenagers who are the children of Maghrebi migrants but have already completed several years of schooling in Spain. These young Maghrebis with limited Spanish are a more transient group of migrants who are not included in the statistics on the national origins of the town's residents. They are the unaccompanied minor migrants ("MENAS," according to the Spanish acronym for *Menores Extranjeros No Acompañados*) who live in the government-funded center on the outskirts of Órgiva.[22] It seems that the coordinators of the collaborative, community oral history *Hablamos de Órgiva*, found the topic of the center for MENAS (established a few years prior) too sensitive, too potentially divisive: in the 500-plus pages of the book produced by the project, there is not one mention of the center or its adolescent immigrant residents. Although, given their protected status as minors, I did not carry out interviews with any current center residents, through conversations with staff members at the center and other town inhabitants, including the Maghrebi migrants, I endeavored to gauge how the MENAS are viewed in the town.[23]

Órgiva first became home to a facility for MENAS when a *Centro de Acogida Inmediata* (CAI), or initial shelter for unaccompanied minor immigrants, opened in July 2006 in the same space as the current center. In approximately 2010, the CAI was turned into a *Residencial Básico*, a middle-stage residential center for MENAS, and then in October 2012 it became a *Centro de Orientación e Inserción Laboral*, or Center for Orientation and Job Placement. For this reason, the facility is known locally as either "el CAI" or "el Centro." The center's current director, Javier Talavera, explained that when the facility was a CAI it had about 20 minors in residence at a time and currently it has approximately 30. The center is run by an NGO that has an agreement with the *Junta de Andalucía* (the regional government of Andalucía) that is renewable annually. It is officially designated as a center for the protection of minors, not necessarily foreign minors, but in practice more than 90 percent of the youths at the center are MENAS. These are primarily from the Maghreb and various countries in sub-Saharan Africa. In the late 2000s, as a CAI, the MENAS were 80 percent North African; now as an integration center, there are more sub-Saharan Africans, but Maghrebis are still the majority. These adolescents arrive at the center after three to six months in a CAI in the province of Granada, though potentially from CAIs anywhere in Andalucía. It is almost exclusively under-age males that arrive unaccompanied in Spain and the government agency that works with the Órgiva center has designated it to receive only males. Typically, they arrive at the center at 15 or 16 years of age and they stay until they turn 18. The director noted that previously 6–8 youths per center was considered ideal, but that's not possible now because of the rising number of MENAS and the lack of resources.

Unaccompanied Maghrebi (and mostly Moroccan) minors began to arrive in Spain in the mid-1990s and their numbers climbed in the first years of the 2000s (Plann, 1 and 7). The Órgiva center's director estimated that in the last three years, the number of MENAS in Spain had tripled. Indeed, a 2019 news source indicates that the number of MENAS entering Spain doubled between 2017 and 2019, on top of a 60 percent increase from 2016 to 2017 ("Cuántos menores [. . .]"). According to the Spanish Ministry of the Interior, there are more than 12,300 MENAS in Spain, but the actual number is higher. As in the United States, the issue of what to do with unaccompanied minor migrants is a political flashpoint that reflects deep ideological differences. In Spain, this situation is complicated by the fact that while each Autonomous Community is responsible for the custody and protection of the MENAS, the main point of entry for them is Andalucía, but upon arrival the minors often travel from their port of entry to other Autonomous Communities. Elections and the need to form political coalitions as part of Spain's parliamentary system lead to some politicians trying to withhold specific data regarding the MENAS ("Cuántos menores [...]"). On a national level, the sharp tensions surrounding current MENA policies, in which these youths are sheltered in Spain funded by the Spanish government, is evident in protests against the building of MENA centers, physical attacks on MENA centers and on the young men themselves, and some politicians—from both right-wing and center-left parties—calling for a change in policy to shift toward repatriation of the MENAS.[24]

According to Susan Plann, the most common ways for Moroccans to "burn" (*harag*), or emigrate clandestinely, are to hide under or inside a vehicle bound for Spain via ferry, or to sneak into the ferry itself (4). The undocumented immigrants, or *harraga*, primarily cross the Strait of Gibraltar on ferries that travel between North Africa and the Andalusian cities of Algeciras, Motril, and Almería. Motril, which is a 35-minute drive from Órgiva, is the only major seaport in the province of Granada. Connected by ferry service to the Moroccan ports of Tangiers-MED, El Hoceima, and Nador, as well as the Spanish North African enclave Melilla, Motril is likely the port of entry for most of the adolescents in the Órgiva Center. Stowing away in a truck or directly onto a ferry can lead to gruesome accidents or, if intercepted before departure, a beating by the Moroccan police. But the other method for crossing the Strait is still more dangerous: crossing on a small boat, known in Spanish as a *patera*, with the trip organized by a human smuggler. This method could land the *harraga* anywhere on the Andalusian coast, but it could also leave them dead at the bottom of the Strait.[25]

Plann notes that before leaving Morocco, the typical MENA had not been "living on the street," but rather with their parents (16). However, "*Harraga* minors were typically from the lower socioeconomic classes" (4) and the former MENAS whose accounts she gathered "came almost exclusively from the humbler classes, with families often living in poverty" (16). Before departure from Morocco, about a third of the young men with whom she spoke "had left school entirely, often to perform menial labor" (20). Plann observes that although many

Spaniards think that Moroccan families urge their sons to emigrate, many of the young men who spoke with her "insisted [their parents] knew nothing about their intentions" to emigrate clandestinely (45). If they did know, "very few parents were supportive of their son's plans," and in some cases parents suspected their son's plan to emigrate, but didn't bring themselves to acknowledge it until after the son's departure. Plann concludes that "In nearly every case, the decision was made by the boys themselves, in an unmistakable show of agency and self-determination" (45). Emigration in general is very common in Morocco, with the government promoting it since the 1960s as a way to quell socioeconomic and political unrest (Brand 45–47). But the phenomenon of young men from marginalized socioeconomic classes emigrating clandestinely has taken on the dimensions of a rite of passage (Plann 35 and 154), one that confirms one's determination, courage, and street smarts—in a word, one's manliness.

As a result of these circumstances, MENAS often arrive in Spain not only undernourished, but with a low education level and a high sense of self-efficacy or, at least, a self-image as adventurous and autonomous. At the same time, there is rising, vocal sentiment against the Spanish government's sheltering of MENAS. The Spanish care system, then, has its work cut out for it. The director of the Órgiva center indicated that the goals of the center were to orient the MENAS, to have them complete their education through 16 or 18 years of age, and to help them with job placement.[26] These goals are accomplished through a team of psychologists, social workers, tutors, and Spanish/Arabic interpreters, as well as through close collaboration with a team in the local high school. In 2019, of the 15 staff members (including the director) at the center, the majority were *orgiveños*. Similarly, most of the ATAL (*Aulas Temporales de Adaptación Lingüística*—Temporary Classrooms for Linguistic Adaptation) team at the high school, which focuses on Spanish-language instruction, integration, and academic support, is from the town or the Alpujarra region. The young men are placed in internships at local businesses (supermarkets, restaurants, etc.) and also carry out job training in the vegetable garden at the center itself. The center focuses on agricultural training because the center's location lends itself to that and there are more job opportunities in that industry. The director proudly noted that in 2019, seven youths from the center had graduated from ESO (the mandatory secondary curriculum that ends at approximately age 16). Antonio Rodríguez Ruiz, the principal of the public high school in Órgiva, IES Alpujarra, mentioned that when unaccompanied minors turn 18, they are transitioned out of the center; thus, if the MENA student turns 18 in the fall, it can be difficult for him to complete the school year and graduate.[27] For that reason, it's not uncommon for local teachers to take in these young men, so that they can stay in Órgiva and complete their advanced high school diploma. Rodríguez Ruiz noted that in 2019 two teachers did this to make sure that two young men would be able to complete the high school *bachillerato* program that would allow them to pursue tertiary education.[28] The high school principal mentioned that the school makes concerted efforts to support non-Spanish students (whether from elsewhere in Europe or from the Maghreb) academically, to integrate them socially, and, in response to the high number of Muslims at the school, to educate the school as a whole about Muslim practices and holidays such as Ramadan. The level of support that the Muslim and MENA students receive, mostly from local educators and social workers, is remarkable, particularly in the context of increasing national sentiment against both Islam and unaccompanied immigrant minors.

The youths from the Órgiva center go into the town to attend the high school, to carry out internships, and for other specific activities (e.g., to take a computing workshop, to swim in the pool, or participate in soccer tournaments at the *poli*, etc.). A few *orgiveños* mentioned to me that at the beginning, when the facility first opened as a CAI, there were some tensions with the town due to petty crimes. But these tensions disappeared, probably around the time when the facility became a center for integration and job placement, as the director was careful to point out that the youths who go to the center in its current incarnation are carefully vetted ["tienen que cumplir con un perfil específico"]. The previous mayor (María Ángeles Blanco López), current town councilors, and *orgiveños* with whom I spoke did not recall any opposition on the part of the town hall or the town residents to the establishment of the initial facility in 2006. The former mayor noted that, on the contrary, the municipal government had always had a cordial relationship with the center, in which they tried to cooperate with any incident that required police intervention (e.g., an escaped minor) and with job training and placement. This means that the residents of Órgiva had a much stronger, more visible reaction against the street-dwelling and off-the-grid alternatives and the *Fiesta del Dragón* than against the unaccompanied Moroccan minors.

Indeed, the independent immigrant minors seem to experience the town as a welcoming space. One of the center's staff members noted that many of the adolescents find jobs in the town and stay there after turning 18: "They stay in Órgiva [. . .] because they feel accepted [acogidos] and because it's easy." When I asked why they felt accepted in the town, my interlocutor referenced the high number of different nationalities in the town: "So, one more, one less [. . .] The Spaniards are almost the odd ones [los anormales]." When I asked specifically about incidents of discrimination, he stated "The kids have never mentioned to me that someone treated them in a discriminatory or racist way." On a different occasion, I asked another center staff member about discrimination and she immediately mentioned discrimination among the MENAS themselves: the North Africans sometimes discriminated against the sub-Saharan or black Africans. When I asked follow-up questions, she indicated that both groups of MENAS suffered discrimination, but not in Órgiva "because [in Órgiva] there are people from all over. It's a place with a lot of tolerance." She added that in Órgiva mistreatment was limited to occasional suspicion: when something happened, people sometimes suspected the kids from the center. For that reason, the staff tried to bolster the youths' image by making sure that they were well dressed and groomed.

A small-scale interaction that I observed confirmed the goodwill shown toward the MENA youths in Órgiva and suggested that, at least in part, this warm reception is facilitated by the community of Muslim converts. In Café Baraka, where the owner and a few of the staff are Spanish converts to Islam, the owner explained to me that the provincial government (*la diputación*) had asked him to give two youths unpaid job training for a few months. One of them was a Moroccan adolescent from the center who had only been in Spain for about 6 months. The restauranteur noted that so far the internship was going well. Later, I happened to be at the restaurant when the young man stopped by with three friends, also from the center. It was the intern's day off and the youths from the center were celebrating the birthday of one of them. The intern, the restaurant owner, and the waitstaff warmly greeted each other, the four young men sat down for a celebratory snack, and a very friendly atmosphere surrounded the visit. Interestingly, some of the Moroccan migrants who had arrived in Spain with some level of capital and/or skills did not display as much warmth in their words about the unaccompanied minor migrants.

Although a few of the Maghrebi migrants in Órgiva stated that they had not had any contact with the Moroccan MENAS, Malika said that she often interacted with them through her small business. What stood out most to her was that they complained a lot, for instance, about the food that was served at the center during Ramadan because they weren't eating the special dishes that are prepared in Morocco for the holy month. But she also told, with a tone of compassion, the story of one particular unaccompanied migrant who had arrived at the facility several years ago. He was much younger than the typical unaccompanied migrants and she saw him sitting in the plaza crying for his mother, whom he missed terribly. She recounted that he would often talk with his mother on the phone and was homesick. Malika speculated that he didn't realize what he was doing when he left, or that maybe someone took him across the Strait under false pretenses. When he turned 18, he went to visit his family in Morocco for the first time since he had left, but then he came back to Órgiva and eventually married a girl from the town and had stayed to live there. Malika's story served to underscore the level of contentment of Moroccans in the town that she wished to convey to me.

Mustafa, who enjoys wearing his *djellaba* in Órgiva but is wary of how other Moroccans might affect the public image of Maghrebis, had no heartwarming story to share about the MENA kids and only focused on their ingratitude. He said that he knows a Moroccan who works in the center and tells him that the kids are not very grateful, that they complain about the food. Mustafa explained this by saying that this attitude probably has to do with the way that they lived before, with the ignorance and poor upbringing brought on by their difficult circumstances. He mentioned that he knew that some did internships or stayed to work in the town. His tone throughout suggested that he clearly had some reservations about the MENAS, but wanted to be nice about it and demonstrate understanding.

When I asked Laila, the secularized Moroccan married to a Spaniard, about the youngsters from the center, she said that she didn't hear people say anything negative about them, but she also became visibly tense, sitting back and more upright in her chair. She noted that they go to the high school in Órgiva and that she didn't like that much. She has told her husband several times that she would like to move away from Órgiva before their children go to high school, because she doesn't want them to go to school with those kids. Laila clarified that it was not because they are Moroccan, but because they come from very disadvantaged or marginalized backgrounds. It was clear to her that they received little to no education before arriving in Spain. She explained that she knew this because she overhears bits of their conversations when they are in the town. Laila happens to not look typically North African and given that she dresses like any Spaniard, she figured that the youths from the center assumed that she didn't understand them as they spoke Moroccan *Darija* and so they continued to express themselves freely even when she was nearby. Laila didn't like the kinds of things they talked about and how they talked. She recognized that all adolescents have their attitude, but felt that the MENAS were particularly bad, making statements that demonstrated "hate toward non-Muslims." She said she was familiar with the kind of mentality in which they had been raised, one in which they think that it is all right to rob or cheat someone who is not Muslim. Clearly, this perturbed her. Laila's comments point to differences between secular ways of viewing the world and a type of religious outlook that pits the in-group against an out-group that is perceived as an antagonist. Her comments, together with Mustafa's and to a lesser extent Malika's, point to the effects of socioeconomic class difference between the Maghrebis resident in Órgiva and the Moroccan adolescents at the MENA center. These Maghrebi migrants' narratives about the unaccompanied migrants from Morocco manifest a concern with a lack of gratitude and certain values that may either victimize non-Muslims or reflect poorly on other Maghrebis by calling into question their gratitude toward their new country or even their level of education and respectability. This apprehension toward the MENAS seems to be rooted in either concern regarding the MENAS reflecting badly on the other Maghrebis residing in the town, or concern regarding the MENAS introducing tensions between religious groups in a space that has heretofore offered a respite from such tensions experienced elsewhere. That is, this apprehension toward the MENAS arises from concerns regarding how they may negatively affect the high quality of life experienced by the Maghrebis in Órgiva.

In the summer of 2019, one or more of the unaccompanied Moroccan youths voiced his perspective through graffiti. Although it is common to see graffitied slogans on the outskirts of Orgiva, these are always in Spanish or English. In contrast, this phrase, spray-painted in dark green on an asphalted road, stood out because it was in Arabic script. On a residential street that serves as a short-cut to the MENA center, someone painted "al-ghurba saʻiba," which could be translated as "life as an émigré is difficult." The expression *al-ghurba saʻiba* is very widespread among North Africans and may have started with the first massive waves of emigration to France from Algeria, and later Morocco, in the first half of the 20th century. Within the array of North African cultural production that depicts or reflects upon migration, the phrase *al-ghurba saʻiba* appears in various songs. These songs focus on the North African cities that have lost so many people to emigration and, especially, on the migrants who nostalgically lament the loss of their homeland. For instance, the world-famous Algerian Rai singer Cheb Khaled has a very popular song "Wahran Wahran" (1996), whose lyrics include the phrase "al-ghurba saʻiba wa-ghaddara [life as an immigrant is difficult and treacherous]."

176 • *Jamón* and *Halal*

FIGURE 11: The Arabic graffiti stating "al-ghurba saʿiba" meaning "life as an émigré/being a stranger is difficult."

The phrase *al-ghurba saʿiba* and its variants reflect the mythology surrounding the *harraga*, that is, the tendency to romanticize those who make it to the other side. The risky act of clandestine migration is often presented as a bold, heroic action that is accompanied by the bitterness of having to stay away from home until one's legal status is normalized by acquiring new travel documents. The phrase glorifies the male rite of passage of clandestine immigration as a bold act that condemns the migrant to long for home in order to help his family through remittances. Those struggling in North Africa may understand the voicing of this sentiment as a warning that migration is not as wonderful a solution as it may seem to be, or they may view the difficulties of *al-ghurba* as a desired privilege. Either way, and for both migrants and those thinking about leaving, the phrase demonstrates that *al-ghurba* is an integral part of North African life.[29]

In the summer of 2021, through a friend of a friend, I met a young man, Nabil, who had arrived in Spain from the Maghreb on a *patera* as an unaccompanied minor and had been placed in the Órgiva center 3 or 4 years before our conversation. Nabil lived in the center for a few years and by the time he turned 18, he had a local girlfriend and a contract for a job-training internship in the area. When he first arrived, he didn't like Órgiva because the people seemed closed-off and set in their ways ["el pueblo parecía muy cerrado"]. He explained that initially he had decided to stay only because of his girlfriend and job, but now he likes living in Órgiva and feels a comfortable sense of community there. When I asked about any instances of discrimination, he said he had only felt discriminated against by a *gitano*, which just made him laugh since that person "wasn't even Spanish," meaning, he clarified, that others didn't consider him Spanish, that he was also marginalized.

Nabil and I met at a restaurant-bar and I had noticed that when Nabil sat down and the waitress took his order (a Heineken), he had immediately told her that he didn't want a *tapa*. I wondered why he would refuse food that was included in the price of the drink and later in the conversation the reason emerged: he refused the *tapa* because of possible pork contamination. In response to my questions about his religious observance, he stated that he drinks beer and smokes tobacco, but doesn't eat pork. He doesn't pray five times a day, but he does fast during Ramadan. His rationale was that he drinks and smokes because he did these things in his home country (though not in front of his parents, he added), but he doesn't eat pork because he didn't do that back home. He mentioned that his friends in Órgiva were very accommodating: when he ate with them, they would prepare a separate dish without pork.

Nabil went on to say that he had been having some doubts about *tapas*, and a couple of months ago he asked a friend who works in a restaurant who confirmed that sometimes pork dishes came into contact with other dishes or were fried in the same oil. Since that day he had stopped eating *tapas*. I asked whether that meant that he never ate out and he said no, that he would eat out, but ordered grilled meat, the idea being that preparation on the same surface was different from being on the same grill, where the fire purified the grill. I asked if he limited himself to places that served halal meat and he said no, that if he did that he would starve. I acknowledged that it would be difficult and he reiterated that he ate any other kind of meat, but wouldn't eat pork and then observed with an ironic smile that we were in the center of Spain's *jamón* production. Although Nabil said that he had had no contact with the Sufi convert community, his dietary habits mirrored that of some of the converts. A British convert to Islam, Aya, had mentioned to me that in the Alpujarra, convert Muslims are more flexible than back in the UK: in the Alpujarra, they will eat non-halal chicken or turkey with the idea that "well, at least it isn't *jamón* . . . ." Nabil's practice of Islam is idiosyncratic, but well-reasoned: it combines the maintenance of de facto Maghrebi lifestyle patterns with unorthodox food rule innovations. No longer plagued by doubts, Nabil is content with the limits that he has established in a setting that is both *jamón* and alcohol heavy and also accustomed to difference. Nonetheless, I was happy to be able to inform him that the new restaurant at which we had met, Alquimia, established in 2020 by an Iranian and a Spaniard, serves alcohol as well as halal meat (no pork!). At least at one Órgiva eatery, Nabil would not have to forego *tapas* with his beer!

Towards the end of our conversation, I mentioned to Nabil the graffiti that I had seen nearby, which by then was almost completely faded: "al-ghurba saʿiba." With an intense look on his face, he immediately said "It's true," and then explained that it was difficult to arrive in a place where one didn't know the language and didn't know anyone. He said that he still misses his family and added that his family was the only thing that he misses. Although he has created a community of friends and worked out a way of practicing Islam that suits him and his setting, some feeling of strangeness persists.

A more literal translation of *al-ghurba saʿiba* would yield one of two options: "being away from home is difficult," or "being a stranger is difficult." The network of related meanings from the Arabic root *ghayn-ra-ba* includes: *ghurba*—separation from one's place of origin, homesickness and alienation, life or a place away from home; *ightirab*—estrangement and alienation, and *gharib*—strange or odd, foreign, a stranger or a foreigner, an émigré. Avtar Brah, in her work on the South Asia diaspora, helps us to understand the intersection between immigrant estrangement and existential estrangement. Brah states: "'home' is a mythic place of desire in the diasporic imagination" (188). The idealized home is a place where one, rather than feeling strange, feels a sense of sameness and connection known as belonging. As Brah points out, "The question of home, therefore, is intrinsically linked with the way in which processes of inclusion or exclusion operate and are subjectively experienced under given circumstances. It is centrally about our political and personal struggles over the social regulation of 'belonging'" (189). To be a stranger, then, is to not belong, to not feel at home. But the fact that this can occur without ever leaving the place called home indicates that "home" sometimes exists more as a desire than as a reality. In this sense, the phrase *al-ghurba saʿiba* connects the Maghreb's intimate relationship with migration to the feeling of being a weirdo or oddball, a misfit in search of one's spiritual or alternative community. The psychoanalytic conception of estrangement posits that for all people, difference is already present in the self and the recognition of this disrupts the illusion of a coherent, stable self.[30] However, for some people the feeling of being strange, the awareness of estrangement, motivates a spiritual conversion journey, or the search for an alternative lifestyle—a process which results in bringing their inner "strangeness" to the surface. Whether brought on by an existential or spiritual search, or a migration journey, Órgiva's residents are connected by their (multiple types of) strangeness.

As detailed in Chapter 2, basic tolerance is coexistence without violence or public rejection, but with the marginalization that is part of permission-granting; whereas sustainable and socially empowering tolerance is based on recognition as well as awareness of the power dynamics that are part of the exchange of tolerance. Órgiva is characterized by relative social categories and an ambiguity regarding who is tolerating who—that is, who has power over who. Given the relativity of the categories of dominant/mainstream and minority, and the different perspectives on civilizational hierarchies at work, who is a minority in Órgiva? Numerically, and thus politically through voting power, the *orgiveños* represent the majority culture. But civilizationally, in terms of the prestige carried by metropolitan or non-Andalusian European identities, it is the incomers from other parts of Europe (especially those that are property-owners) who are the dominant majority in terms of economic, cultural, and symbolic capital. This group that is dominant civilizationally includes the European converts to Islam. While there is covert prestige among *orgiveños* in their identification as Alpujarran and Andalusian, some also aspire to a European identity characterized by open-mindedness and tolerance. At the same time, some conservative *orgiveños*, if they even subscribe to tolerance as an ideal, do so with a narrow definition of its limits. The Maghrebi migrants, and within that group the unaccompanied minors, are the most marginalized group in the town, in the sense that they start out without Spanish and European Union citizenship and are usually perpetually marked as an ethno-racial other who is low on the contemporary scale of civilizational hierarchy. However, as Muslims born into Islam and Arabic-speaking Muslim-majority cultures, some of the Maghrebi migrants claim authority regarding Islamic orthodoxy. The fact that majority group and minority group, or dominant and marginalized cultures, are in many cases relative categories in Órgiva, together with spaces of recognition for even the most marginalized, results in more equitable tolerance that is defined by the opportunity for the most marginalized—and the "most" Muslim—to participate in the gift exchange that is the negotiation of toleration.

Órgiva's relative social categories and power differentials highlight the presence of power in toleration processes while they can also create or exacerbate feelings of estrangement, but this estrangement can pave the way for recognition. The following chapter examines the mechanisms that support peaceful coexistence in Órgiva and, as part of that, considers how strangeness is integral to tolerance. It traces specific connections between different communities within Órgiva and assesses how these connections—through strangeness—promote tolerance.

CHAPTER 6

Bridges between Parallel Worlds: The Creation of Shared Narratives Via Estrangement

Given the tensions that do exist in Órgiva—arising from language differences, dialectal differences within Spanish, and language ideologies; class, conventionality, and respectability; civilizational identities; and conceptions of proper Islamic practice—how is the town's high level of peaceful coexistence (in comparison with nearby manifestations of intolerance) achieved? Living in parallel worlds creates an ambiguous relationship with permission-based and recognition-based tolerance. Functioning in separate spheres can make it more likely for a particular community to feel grudgingly put-up-with and marginalized when tensions arise. Although some interlocutors stated that they liked the dynamic of parallel lives, if there is no positive contact between groups, the small frictions that are bound to arise in any space of everyday interaction (supermarket, sports center, etc.) can easily escalate. With the passage of time, the school system in Órgiva will probably be the focal point of increased contact between groups and a testing ground for the maintenance of parallel worlds or a transition to more hybridity. But, at present, it is the positive points of contact between the largely separate spheres that allow for community members to feel respected and offer a promising context for recognition-based tolerance.

There are specific alliances that create connections across the separate communities in Órgiva. The three main alliances that bridge otherwise disparate groups are: 1) migration memory, 2) women's issues and feminist identities, and 3) Islam and the imposed label of *moro*. I use the term "migration memory" to refer to the migration-related experiences of *orgiveños*, many of whom have never lived outside of Órgiva or the Alpujarra. The term seeks to include the effects of migration on those who were mobile as well as on those who were immobile—that is, on the non-movers who stayed behind. Departures, especially when they are followed by regular return visits, have an important role in the lives and outlook of those who stayed. The mobilities paradigm promotes the study of the relationship of "mobilities to associated immobilities or moorings, including their ethical dimension; and it encompasses both the embodied practice of movement and the representations, ideologies and meanings attached to both movement and stillness" (Sheller, 1). When viewed through a mobility studies lens, the deeper layers and lasting resonances of population shifts in the Alpujarran region come to the fore and it becomes apparent that migration memory makes many *orgiveños* identify to some extent with economic migrants.

In spite of being a mountainous region that is difficult to access, the layers of population movement in the Alpujarra are deep. After being colonized by Iberians, Celts, Romans, and Visigoths, the Umayyad Caliphate arrived, bringing Imazighen and Arabs to the Alpujarra. But after a few centuries, the Arabo-Amazigh population underwent a radical shift. Pozo Felguera explains that in response to the second Rebellion of the Alpujarras (1568–71), starting in 1570 Castilian authorities sent approximately 64,200 *moriscos* to other parts of the peninsula. Meanwhile, between 1572 and 1595, the Christian authorities encouraged people from other parts of Andalucía, Castile, Galicia, and Extremadura to settle in the houses and lands left by the *moriscos*. This was followed by the expulsion decrees (1609–14) mandating the departure of the *moriscos* and more official efforts to resettle the area with Galicians and other Christians from the peninsula. Then, for almost 300 years, the Alpujarra had a very stable population, until some intrepid inhabitants of the region became part of a wave of Spanish emigration at the turn of the 19th century, primarily to Hispano-America. These émigrés, mentioned by Brenan in *South from Granada*, mostly went to Argentina, Brazil, and Algeria.[1] Then the Spanish Civil War (1936–39) violently reduced the population of the Alpujarra, site of some of the last Republican holdouts, and of Órgiva in particular. Although the town itself was under Nationalist control, the front line between Nationalist and Republican forces ran just south of Órgiva. In addition to those who perished in the conflict, some Republicans went into exile in other parts of Europe and in Latin America, during and after the war.

In more recent memory, economic migration affected the population of the Alpujarra. In the 1950s, alongside an overall Spanish trend of movement from rural to urban areas, an emigration wave took people from the most economically depressed parts of Spain—the regions of Andalucía, Extremadura, and Galicia—to urban centers in other parts of the country that were experiencing economic growth: Madrid and (for Andalusians in particular) Barcelona. Additionally, the Franco government's 1959 *Plan de Estabilización* (Stabilization Plan) authorized extranational emigration. This produced an exodus from Andalucía and the other depressed regions to other Western European countries (mainly France, Switzerland, and Germany) during the 1960s and early 1970s. As noted by Jiménez-Díaz, in the decade of the '70s the Alpujarra in particular contributed to this exodus because of a local agricultural crisis (227). According to *Hablamos de Órgiva*, between 1950 and 2010, more than 2,000 people left Órgiva ("Los que se fueron y los que llegaron" 3). With changing economic circumstances on the individual and regional levels, some of these labor migrants returned after several years in Catalonia or elsewhere in Europe. For these reasons, in the second half of the 20th century, emigration became one of the defining characteristics of not only Andalusian, but specifically Alpujarran, culture.

If a given *orgiveño* did not emigrate (and return), he or she certainly has family members, neighbors, and friends who did emigrate. Some who left returned after several years, with children who had been raised outside of Andalucía; though they sometimes spoke Spanish like any other *orgiveño*, those children would be known from then on by the place of the family's emigration: *el alemán, la catalana* (the German guy, the Catalan girl), etc. Many of those who left settled outside the region permanently, but for decades came to visit their home village on a regular basis. In Órgiva, up until the early 2000s, busloads of local families who had emigrated to Barcelona would return to the town annually at two points in the year: for the Christmas holidays and for the celebration of *El Cristo de la Expiración* leading up to Holy Week. Up to three chartered buses full of émigré *orgiveños* would arrive in the town plaza and be greeted with great fanfare.[2] Many of the same émigré families would return (trickling in by family unit) for the summer, when the population of the town would swell. With time, aside from a few return migrants, the generation that had been born in Barcelona became rooted there and no longer visited the town regularly. However, because of this experience of emigration with decades of regular visits, *orgiveños* above the age of 30, whether they left and returned, or stayed behind, are very aware of the dynamics of labor migration; it was a part of their familial and social lives.

This labor migration is not a Castilian or metropolitan Spanish story, rather it is primarily an Andalusian and Extremaduran story. In the particular case of Órgiva, it is a story that revolves around the encounter between rural, working-class, less educated individuals who come from a region long considered to be backward and primitive and an urban society considered to be more advanced. It is the story of an encounter between "barbarism" on the border with North Africa and "civilization" in cities (whether in Spain or elsewhere) that are considered fully European. And this encounter is echoed in interactions within Órgiva in which a metropolitan Spaniard looks down at an Alpujarran as a *cateto* or hillbilly. *Orgiveños* carry the cultural memory of active migrant ties from the 1960s thru the early 2000s in which the émigrés were at an economic and social disadvantage and in which broader, very mobile, hierarchical discourses were at work.

My conversations with the return migrant Mari Carmen, together with comments made by the small business-owner Enrique, shed light on the dynamics of migration memory (memories of labor migration and return, or of contact with loved ones who were labor migrants). After being born in Órgiva, Mari Carmen was raised in Barcelona, where her Alpujarran parents, like so many others, had gone to work around 1960. Mari Carmen recalls growing up with a steady stream of house guests: friends and relatives from Órgiva who stayed with Mari Carmen's family as they looked for work and their own lodging as part of their labor migration process. Although her father was a barely literate manual laborer and her mother was illiterate, Mari Carmen worked hard and had built a successful career in Barcelona. She jokingly acknowledged that it was not "nostalgia for my hometown [nostalgia por mi pueblo natal]" that had brought her back to Órgiva as an adult, but rather family circumstances. When I asked if she felt like more of an *origiveña* or a *forastera*—which community she felt more a part of—her response was to say that she has two best friends in the town, one from Órgiva and the other from Switzerland. From her vantage point straddling two communities, she described the townspeople as "supportive [solidario]" and "welcoming [acogedor]," but also noted that those *orgiveños* who have stayed in the town have limited "empathy," in the sense that they have a hard time accepting those who have a different opinion or custom: they aren't able to put themselves in the other's shoes.

In conversations with Enrique, I saw the limits of empathy, the line at which tolerance began to fade, but it was a bit further out than one would expect for someone of his socioeconomic standing and political affiliations. Recall that Enrique is a successful small business-owner and part of the land-owning class in the town. In keeping with this, his politics are center-right to further right. He has never lived outside of Órgiva, but has first cousins that emigrated to Barcelona and neighbors that emigrated to Germany and returned. One evening, while sharing dinner with Enrique and a group of *orgiveños*, the conversation turned to politics and the recent national elections of April 2019, in which the ultra-conservative Vox party, whose political campaign called for a new Reconquista and a rejection of Islam, had won more than 10 percent of the votes and thus had secured the fifth largest number of representatives in the Spanish Congress.[3] It was one of various occasions in which I have heard Enrique complain about the arrival of undocumented immigrants on *pateras* (simple vessels carrying Maghrebis and sub-Saharan Africans from the shores of North Africa). This evening, Enrique cited that these immigrants drain the Spanish economy and criticized center-left and left immigration policies that he saw as giving too much government assistance to immigrants. Then Enrique gestured with his hand toward a small business on the plaza run by a Moroccan who is commonly referred to by *orgiveños* as "el moro de la plaza"—the Moor of the plaza. Drawing a distinction, Enrique said: "Here you have the Moor, who pays his taxes... God bless him! [¡Bendito sea!]" After making clear his approval of this fellow small business-owner's presence by wishing him blessings, Enrique then continued with: "We're also immigrants, all the people who left for Germany...." This local narrative, along with Stewart's references to Alpujarran emigration in his third memoir, *The Almond Blossom Appreciation Society*, demonstrates that migration memory creates an identification with economic migrants that can even take the form of feelings of solidarity toward the North African migrants in the town. Perhaps due to the temporally overlapping experiences of labor emigration, an influx of relatively affluent Northern Europeans, and labor immigration (North African immigrants), the *orgiveños* have been more tolerant of the legal, working migrants from the Maghreb. Migration memory leads some *orgiveños* to identify with the process of labor migration—though they may reject clandestine immigration.

Feminist identities, or at least a broader concern for women's issues and a desire for sisterhood, create another bridge across communities in Órgiva. Through local women's associations, the concern for women's rights and the desire to support other women creates bonds between women from various communities in the town. On International Women's Day in 1991, a group of local women with leftist political affiliations founded *la Asociación de Mujeres de Órgiva* (the Women's Association of Órgiva), now known as the *Asociación de Mujeres por la Igualdad*.[4] The association's current president stated that the main mission of the organization is "to establish real equality" among genders and that this was accomplished through its major initiatives and the very act of people coming together to work on those initiatives.⁵

The association's main initiative is its women's shelter. Since 2000, the *Asociación de Mujeres*, with funding from the *Junta de Andalucía*, has run a women's shelter whose official name is *La Casa de Acogida para Mujeres con Graves Problemas Sociales y Económicos* (The Shelter for Women with Serious Social and Economic Problems). This shelter provides a residence and support services for victims of domestic abuse and their children. An employee of the shelter explained that the women and children who reside in the facility, typically for several months, are transferred there from centers in other parts of Andalucía and often include Maghrebi immigrants (an average of one North African woman, with her children, per year).⁶ This adds to the more transient Maghrebi population, that is not reflected in the population data on the town.

In the summer of 2016, I was invited to a party at the apartment of a Moroccan woman who was a former resident of the women's shelter. After spending several months at the shelter, she had decided to stay in Órgiva. This survivor of spousal abuse was struggling to improve her financial situation, and a group of friends who were local women, including members of the *Asociación de Mujeres* who had met the Moroccan migrant through her stay at the shelter, decided to organize a gathering to support her. The group of *orgiveñas* as well as other friends whom they had invited, each chipped in to collect money for the migrant who had prepared a Moroccan meal to share with us. The gathering, which included *orgiveñas*, a few Britons, and a few Spaniards who had moved to Órgiva from elsewhere in Spain (with only one man among them), was jovial and welcoming. In addition to Maghrebi food, there was music and singing, including Spanish folk favorites and North African pop music. This grassroots fundraiser for a Moroccan migrant, organized by and for women, demonstrated not only a will to help and an interest in inter-cultural dialogue, but a respectful recognition of Maghrebi culture and of a shared social positioning as women.

As an organization, the *Asociación de Mujeres por la Igualdad* also parallels this level of inclusivity with regard to country of origin. According to the current president, *orgiveñas* make up approximately 60 percent of the association's membership, with the remaining members coming from an array of different countries and parts of the world. These more recent arrivals in the town have been prominent in leadership positions within the association. Up until recently, the president of the association was from Colombia, and in November 2019 a new president, Rahma Sevilla Segovia, of North African Muslim origin, was elected. Sevilla Segovia, a native of Ceuta, noted that while she was a student at the University of Granada friends spoke highly to her about Órgiva and the Alpujarra, so a few years ago she decided to move there and soon afterwards she began volunteering at the women's shelter.[7] She observed that while she didn't see the different groups in Órgiva "mix [entremezclarse]," and there may not be much day-to-day contact between them, she did see collaboration between the different communities that created "a high level of *convivencia*." Sevilla Segovia then spontaneously gave the example of the convert community in Órgiva, pointing out that it has been particularly supportive of the association's activities. For instance, on various occasions, they have provided employment for women who had been living at the shelter and decided to stay in Órgiva. Later in our conversation, she mentioned a woman from Morocco who had been a resident of the shelter in 2018 and after several months there had decided to stay in Órgiva. Now this Maghrebi woman had become a regular volunteer in the association's activities. These examples of cross-community engagement make it clear that women's interests and mutual support is a strong corridor for connections across the "parallel worlds" that exist alongside each other in Órgiva.

The third bridging identity in Órgiva is still "under construction" for those who (would) participate in it, although it certainly exists, in an ill-defined but historically rooted form, in the eyes of *orgiveños*. From the perspective of many of the townspeople, Muslimness binds together both the converts to Islam of European and Euro-American origin and the Muslim Maghrebi migrants. Although, as seen earlier, the convert and Maghrebi communities are distinct in myriad ways and even the site of intra-Muslim tensions or ambivalence, the *orgiveños* often place them in the same category, conflating *marroquí* and *musulmán*. Rogozen-Soltar (2017) notes that in the city of Granada the term *moro* is mostly used to refer to Moroccans and other Muslim migrants, and not to converts (12). Something similar occurs in Órgiva. Although the ratio of converts to Maghrebis is almost inverted in Órgiva in comparison with Granada (where today there are many more Maghrebi migrants than converts), the term *moro* carries a strong racial connotation. Additionally, since nearly all the converts in Órgiva are aligned with Sufi Islam, the term "sufí" is often used by *orgiveños* to refer to the converts. Nonetheless, *orgiveños* sometimes use *moro* to refer to both groups, as the townspeople seem to be attempting to adjust their cultural schemas to the new reality around them.

One example of the conflation of the migrant and convert Muslim communities is that when I asked an *orgiveña* if there were any more businesses in Órgiva run by Moroccans, other than the ones I had just mentioned to her, it became clear that there was some confusion regarding terminology. In her response, my *orgiveña* interlocutor included businesses run by European converts to Islam and I had to emphasize the distinction between Moroccan and Muslim in order to get clearer information. Although neither of us used the term *moro* in this conversation, I believe that the cultural schema that produces the category *moro* was at work in our interchange. The schema of *moros* vs. *cristianos* inherited from the medieval and early modern periods and the Spanish colonial enterprise in North Africa, and reworked by political parties such as Vox, persists among at least some *orgiveños* in the form of a conceptualization of identity groups that is based solely on religion—even if the *cristianos* in question are not particularly observant. My interlocutor had an easier time grouping all Muslims together, than she did separating out the North Africans in the town. It could be argued, as Pérez-Reverte attempts to do, that the conceptual category of *moro*, while inaccurate for European converts, can be separated from its historical baggage and does not necessarily entail rejection of the so-called *moros*. However, even when not used to directly express any form of rejection or intentionally invoke the hierarchical manner in which the term has historically been used, the term *moro* reinscribes religious boundaries, connects them with race or a biological essence, and in the process obscures both the diversity among practitioners of Islam and the many commonalities that traverse religious boundary lines.

The complexities surrounding the usage of the term *moro* and how it is employed to exclude and hierarchize can be appreciated in an anecdote recounted to me by the British convert Aya, whose children were born into Islam and are being raised in Órgiva. While we talked about the Muslim convert community in the town, Aya brought up the adolescents from the center for unaccompanied minor migrants. She told me that one day her pre-teen son was at the Órgiva *poli*, or sports center, when a group of *orgiveño* boys was recounting a recent incident in which "un moro," referring to one of the Moroccan youths from the Center, had thrown a rock at so-and-so. Then some of the *orgiveño* youths turned to Aya's son and asked "¿tú eres moro? [are you a Moor?]" Aware that he was or might be Muslim, the local youths were trying to determine if Aya's son was indeed Muslim, and perhaps, also who exactly the term *moro* could or should include. Regardless of the intention of the question (whether informational or pursuing a definition of categories), at that moment through that question they were establishing boundaries between "us" (Christians) versus "them" (Muslims) that implied a superior positioning of the Christians.

The conflated label of *moro* creates strange bedfellows in Órgiva: a blond youth who is bilingual in English and Spanish and whose parents have university degrees may be grouped with a brown-skinned youth who is barely literate in Arabic, is starting to learn Spanish, and whose parents back in Morocco are poor, manual laborers—not to mention the fact that they may have very different understandings and practices of Islam. Historically, in Iberia the fluidity of religious conversion led to an emphasis on purported biological difference. As the Reconquista process advanced and Muslims converted to Christianity, in some cases by force and in some cases by choice to improve social status, Christian concern over being able to distinguish between "old Christians" and *conversos* or *moriscos* grew. The Iberian concept of *limpieza de sangre*, literally "cleanliness of blood" and meaning "blood purity," viewed Jewish and Muslim lineage as a biological impurity that must be ferreted out and barred from positions of power such as religious and military orders and guilds. This form of discrimination took on legal dimensions when the first statute of *limpieza de sangre* appeared in 1449, which banned *conversos* and their descendants from most official positions, and continued to play an important role in both the Iberian Peninsula and the Americas into the 19th century. Walter Mignolo and Anouar Majid, among others, have argued that Reconquista Iberia and its concept of blood purity is the source of modern systems for codifying and rejecting difference: religious, racialized religious, and racialized difference in general.[8]

A fair amount has been written about the racialization or ethnicization of converts to Islam.[9] Rosón Lorente, in his work on converts and Maghrebis in the city of Granada, argues that "local Islam, its communities and representatives, end up being 'ethnicized' as symbols and markers of an alterity that is supposedly incommensurate with modernization and the 'Europeanization' of the culture of Andalucía" (1). However, at least in the context of Órgiva, the recalibration of the term *moro* is intertwined with the process of formulating a new conception of "Muslim," one that is separated from the concept of the Moor as racially other and civilizationally less advanced—that is, less modern and less European.

To whatever extent the converts in Órgiva are perceived or operate as an ethno-racial group, that ethno-racial marker would only last while they are wearing their distinctive clothing and head covering (hijab or kufi cap). If a convert were to choose to dress in unmarked clothing (any type of mainstream Spanish dress), the visual ethno-racial marking would disappear. All that would remain, aside from practices such as abstention from alcohol and pork and observance of Ramadan, would be their (adopted) Muslim first names. For Maghrebi migrants, this is typically not the case. Although some Maghrebi immigrants and their children don't have any physical traits associated in the Spanish imaginary with North Africa and by extension with

Islam, many do have such physical characteristics. For these people of Maghrebi origin, no matter what they wear, regardless of whether or not they have a notable accent in Spanish, and irrespective of whether or not they choose to go by a Christian first name, they will be interpreted by the majority culture as Maghrebi, Muslim, and Other. Thus, any ethnicization of European converts is very contingent in comparison with that of Maghrebi migrants, even when the migrant is not a practicing Muslim.

While the converts to Islam in Órgiva are marked by their clothing and head-covering, adopted names, and food-related practices, the names and food-related practices overlap with those of the Maghrebis in the town and the clothing and head-covering share some elements with, or at least are perceived as being related to, those of the Maghrebis. For centuries in Spain such attire, names, and food practices have been labeled as *moro*. *Orgiveños*, while grappling with the redefinition of the term *moro*, are attempting to understand how that which is marked, especially in the context of the borderland of Andalucía, as European and modern (whiteness and standard Spanish or being a native speaker of English) can intersect with that which has been marked as African and primitive (certain names, the attire associated with Muslims, and abstention from alcohol and pork). Additionally, most of the European converts are land-owning and of a middle to high socioeconomic background, in contrast with the image (and often reality) of the economically struggling Muslim migrant.

For these reasons, in Órgiva over time Islam may become decoupled from race. While the term *moro* may linger as an ethno-racial marker for North Africans, and the term "sufí" may become the way to refer specifically to white/European Muslims, in the process, the breadth of the concept of Muslim is in the midst of transformation. An important factor in this emerging dynamic is that the *orgiveños* are "less European" than most of the converts to Islam. Within the existing civilizational hierarchy, Alpujarran Spanish and monolingualism in Spanish do not carry the prestige of dialects that are seen as more correct—that is, those of Madrid, Barcelona, and other metropolitan centers outside of Andalucía—as well as bilingualism with

English. In other words, according to prevailing indexes of European-ness, the converts to Islam are more "European" and "modern" than the local "catetos" or country bumpkins. This situation may lead to a reformulation of the concepts of "European" and "Muslim" among *orgiveños*. That is, the delimiting of the concept of *moro*, may occur alongside a broadening of the concept of *musulmán* that entails an erasure of ethno-racial, linguistic, and socioeconomic markers previously tied to Islam.

The policing of *limpieza de sangre* and racialization of religion that began in the medieval period was a response to Muslim conversion to Christianity in Christian-ruled territories. The regulation of who could be considered a "true" Christian served to limit the power of converts and, in the process, racialized religion. The case of European converts in Spain, however, represents a reverse conversion trajectory: one from Christianity to Islam and from the religion (or at least cultural affiliation) of the majority to that of what has become a minority. The conversion of Christians to Islam, again sometimes by force and sometimes by choice, was fairly common in the earlier periods of Muslim rule in Iberia. The Muslims of Iberian descent, or of mixed Arab, Amazigh, and Iberian origin, who lived in al-Andalus were known as *muladíes*, from the Arabic *muwalladun* for "born and raised," in the sense of "born and raised among Arabs, though not of Arab origin." Although those converts were converting to the dominant religion, the situation of the *muladíes* can help illuminate one aspect of the situation of the modern-day converts. The case of one *muladí* that left an extensive written record is that of Ibn García (died 1084).[10] His full name was Abu ʿAmir Ahmad Ibn García al-Bashkunsi (the Basque). Born into a Christian Basque family, Ibn García was taken prisoner in his childhood and raised Muslim. Ibn García became an Arabic poet in the Taifa Kingdom of Denia (Daniyya), a Muslim kingdom that existed on the Valencian coast discontinuously from 1010 to 1244. This convert-poet became a leading figure in the *shuʿubiyya* movement of al-Andalus through a letter that he wrote in courtly Arabic. From the Arabic for "peoples," through the *shuʿubiyya* movement, the non-Arab peoples of Islam rejected the privileged position of Arabs within the Muslim community and sought equal power and status. Ibn García is the Andalusi proponent of the *shuʿubiyya* movement, which first arose among Persian Muslims in the 9th and 10th centuries. In his letter, Ibn García asserts the superiority of non-Arab Muslims. However, as indicated by Monroe (1970b, 14), Ibn García glorifies non-Arab Muslims by using all the techniques of Arabic high literary style, including rhetorical ornamentation and allusions to the Arabic literary canon. Thus, Ibn García presented a rejection of Arab dominance while demonstrating integration into Arab culture and high literature, and one could argue that it is precisely because he was able to demonstrate mastery of Arabic—as a literary language and also as the language of the Quran and the Prophet Muhammad—that he was able to express his protest safely and effectively.

What about the Ahmad Garcías and Muhammad Smiths of Órgiva? Today's converts in Iberia are not *muladíes* (reared among Arabs): they live in a larger Christian-dominant society that looks upon them as oddballs and sometimes even as cult-like or potential invaders or terrorists (as witnessed by the *Diario Vice* episode). As a result, they are drawn to Órgiva, where their sheer number normalizes them. They are also not *muladíes* in the sense that, for the most part, they are not fluent in Arabic. While struggles regarding the relationship between Islam and the different cultures and languages with which it has been intertwined are ongoing, Arabic maintains an unparalleled status as the language of Islam. Converts and non-Arabic literate Muslims negotiate some type of access to Arabic in order to further their practice of the faith. For these reasons, to be viewed as (peaceful) Muslims, and not members of a heterodox cult-like offshoot of Islam, and also to access the sacred texts of their faith, they need the acceptance and input of "native-born," Arabic-speaking Muslims. On the one hand, the *shuʿubiyya* movements and their echoes in later periods demonstrate the ethnic and linguistic tensions inherent within the Muslim *umma*, or religious community, and the North African migrants themselves may identify more as Amazigh than Arab. But, on the other hand, the two groups sometimes brought together under the label *moro* know that they are viewed as one from the outside and find that living side by side has mutual rewards.

In Rogozen-Soltar's 2017 work on the city of Granada, she found that both Maghrebi migrants and European converts emphasized the differences within the Muslim community: "Muslims in Granada consistently answered my questions about their relationships with *non*-Muslims by broaching the issue of differences *within* the Muslim community. This was especially the case when Muslims discussed their efforts to represent Islam positively in Spain" (158; emphasis in the original). Rogozen-Soltar argues "that Muslims in Granada experience their efforts to represent Islam to wider Spanish publics as hinging on their ability to manage tensions within the city's diverse Muslim population" (159). Rogozen-Soltar discusses the pressure to represent Muslims placed upon Muslims in the West (2017, 159–61) and notes that the Muslim migrants in Granada express concern that the converts' strict practice of Islam will be associated with extremism, or that a more relaxed practice also gives the wrong impression to non-Muslims (178). The two groups' efforts to "disassociate from one another" (159) included converts making arguments about the need to distinguish between true Islam and the cultural traditions of Morocco and migrants accusing converts "of exclusionary social practices and religious inauthenticity." In both cases, they worried about "the other's potential contribution to public perceptions of Muslim extremism" (159).

In Órgiva, although some Maghrebi migrants clearly disassociated themselves from the converts, neither group expressed concern with the other being perceived as extremists. The vast majority of the converts in the town practice Sufi Islam, a form of Islam associated with peacefulness and the pursuit of mystical experiences—not violent politics. For this reason, the converts are experienced by the Muslim migrants, rather than as a threat to the image of Muslims, as a boon to the image of Muslims. With regard to the Sufis' attitudes, they ascribed differences in religious practice and the interpretation of scripture either to cultural factors or other Muslims' lack of knowledge and openness. However, they were very welcoming of any who may wish to join them at the *dargah* or at the Kutubia center. Given the particular circumstances in Órgiva, the tensions seen between (and among) migrants and converts in Granada regarding representation, minority politics, and the definition of Muslim identity itself (Rogozen-Soltar 2017, 174–87) are not palpable in the Alpujarran town. Muslims in Órgiva, in spite of their occasional judgments regarding each other's religious practices, benefit from each other and from being grouped together as Muslims by *orgiveños*.

With regard to the Sufi converts, their "image problem" is compounded by issues of authenticity. Some outside the community view them as cult-like, a fringe form of Islam. Moreover, based on my interactions with community members, some Sufi converts experienced their lack of Arabic language skills as an impediment to legitimacy and/or spiritual practice that they wished to overcome. Here, the Maghrebis have cultural and especially linguistic knowledge to offer. For instance, Zakiyya, the mother of Karim who was accused of not playing with Christians, prepared North African food for the Sufis. More importantly, as mentioned earlier, the Kutubia group hired Moroccan women to contribute to the converts' spiritual journey with the migrants' Arabic language skills. These Moroccan migrants led Quranic recitation sessions and taught a Quran memorization class. In addition to the ways in which this contributes to the converts' spiritual life, the cultural and linguistic content, and the very interaction with "native" Muslims—that is, Muslims from Arabic-speaking, Muslim-majority countries—give the converts greater legitimacy as Muslims outside of the sphere of Sufis.

With regard to the Maghrebi migrants, their concerns are rooted in their precarious position as non-citizens and an undesirable visibility as *moros*. In other words, they are navigating a larger Spanish and European environment in which Maghrebi migrants are a hot-button topic associated with economic concerns and a threat to conservative visions of nationhood. In such an environment, their position as noncitizens (whether documented or undocumented immigrants) makes it difficult to assert their voices and needs. When the migrants are sought out for their linguistic and religious knowledge and contribute to the European converts' spiritual growth, this is a great enhancement to the migrant's self-image. Bahrami mentions a Moroccan woman in the Albaicín of the 1990s (when there were still relatively few migrants in Granada) who "admitted that she enjoyed her special role in the Albaicín as a Moroccan and a Muslim by birth. This gave her a degree of self-respect she had not experienced in other European circles" (128). Similarly, Muslim migrants in Órgiva referred to situations in which they were called upon to share their knowledge of sacred texts in Arabic with Muslim converts and recounted such interactions with pride. Even when there were differences of interpretation (*zahir* versus *batin*) the migrants felt certain of their knowledge and this enhanced their sense of self.

For the Maghrebi migrants (as well as for the converts), the presence of the large number of converts in Órgiva also makes it easy to be a practicing Muslim without standing out in a negative way. It is easy to find halal food in local supermarkets and there is awareness of Ramadan and Muslim holidays in the public school system and elsewhere. As discussed earlier, some of the Maghrebi women wear a hijab (whether in a stricter or more relaxed style) and Fatima in particular mentioned feeling safer doing so in Órgiva than in the next town over. One of the men, Mustafa, mentioned that he liked to wear his *djellaba* on Fridays and, as opposed to the hateful stares that he experienced in other parts of Andalucía, he felt that such attire was not only accepted but celebrated in Órgiva. Thus, the presence of the convert community allows the migrants to follow North African and Muslim practices from food to fasting to clothing with a level of normalcy or accepted visibility that the North African migrants enjoy.

Furthermore, as European and Spanish citizens, the converts are well positioned to promote Muslim interests and the migrants stand to benefit from this. For instance, around 2011, the local Naqshbandi Sufi group requested of the municipal government that a section of Órgiva's cemetery be designated as a Muslim cemetery where the specifications of Muslim burial rites (graves perpendicular to the direction of the Qibla in Mecca, the deceased laid in the grave without a coffin and facing Mecca, etc.) would be followed. The request was fulfilled with no evident objections. Whether or not the Maghrebis wish to be buried among Sufis, the political agency that the converts were able to exercise can be useful to the migrants in a practical, material sense and also created a positive recognition of Islam in the town.

Given the fact that there was no preexisting Maghrebi community network in Órgiva when the current migrants arrived and that it is still a small and somewhat loose community, the convert community's presence is even more important to the migrants. The Sufi community's presence gives the migrants opportunities for boosting self-esteem and opportunities for recognition—that is, for the valuing of difference and cultural knowledge, rather than its stigmatization or disregard. In other words, the presence of the converts creates an environment in which the Maghrebis are appreciated for who they are (for their knowledge of Arabic and the Quran, for non-Western clothing, etc.) and are not pressured to assimilate. Additionally, in the redefinition of Muslimness that is in progress in Órgiva, the converts are establishing a conception of Islam that is not associated with a racial or economic threat. This is in stark contrast with the situation of Maghrebis and Muslims in other parts of Spain, including towns only a short drive away. The sense of well-being—the feeling that Órgiva's migrants reported of being a big family in one big house—to which the presence of the converts contributes is strong enough for the migrants to tolerate the low-level discrimination—the remnants of *moros* vs. *cristianos* mindsets—and discomfort with Sufism that they encounter in Órgiva.

In sum, for the Maghrebi immigrants and the European converts and Sufis in Órgiva, there are mutual benefits to living side by side. Both groups conceive of themselves as distinct communities, but they are grouped together by *orgiveños* under the label *moro*, or the emerging, more heterogeneous conception of *musulmán* (Muslim). The mutual benefits that each group offers the other in material matters related to the observance of their faith, in their self-image, and in their public image as Muslims in Europe, creates a high degree of inter-minority tolerance among them. Thus, in spite of the persistence of some *moros* vs. *cristianos* thinking and a widespread lack of identification between the migrants and the Sufis, in Órgiva, Islam and concerns regarding external perceptions of Muslims create a bridge—albeit a (still) shaky one—between the convert community and the North African migrants.

At one point, I asked the Moroccan migrant Malika about the term *moro* and, true to her spunky attitude, she acknowledged that sometimes she heard people use it to mean "Muslim," but said that that was just due to "ignorance [jahil]." She said that it didn't bother her because people who used *moro* that way didn't know enough to distinguish between Muslims in general and North Africans. With time and greater interaction between Muslim converts and others in Órgiva through the school system, this ignorance may be replaced by awareness of the similarities and differences between the Muslims of European origin and residents of Maghrebi origin, who may or may not be practicing Muslims.

Interestingly, what may aid the town in transitioning toward a more nuanced understanding of identities is also one of the factors contributing to identification among converts to Islam and Maghrebi migrants, as well as beyond. Even if the Sufi converts and the Muslim migrants don't find points of contact in their conceptions and practices of Islam, if nothing else, they share an interest in a life that is guided by a faith-based outlook and spiritual concerns. This also loosely connects both the Sufi converts and the Muslim migrants to the broader interest in spirituality shared—or at least understood—by many in Órgiva. There is a synergy between the recently decreased religiosity of *orgiveños* and the high interest in spirituality on the part of many newcomers. On the one hand, the majority of *orgiveños* age 55 and under are not regular churchgoers; for them, religion is a cultural practice that (at most) takes the form of participation in the celebration of the *Cristo de la Expiración* and the *cofradías* of the Holy Week processions. Yet, they are typically the first generation in their families to have this more secular, less religiously fervent outlook, since (depending on their age) their own parents or grandparents were not just "observant" (mass on Sundays, adherence to Lent, etc.), but "fervent": they participated in prayer groups that circulated a small statue of the

Virgin Mary from house to house and practiced mortification of the flesh by wearing cilices (coarse hairshirts or, more typically, spiked metal chains worn around the thigh). Given this close familiarity with religious worldviews, the *orgiveños* who do not identify as practicing Catholics still understand and (to varying degrees) respect the role of visible religious practices as a source of cultural identity and a question of faith, but, at the same time, they are not concerned with proselytizing or maintaining strict Catholic codes of conduct. On the other hand, many of Órgiva's newer residents—specifically the alternatives and the Muslims, whether of European or Maghrebi origin—are in agreement in their view of Órgiva as a haven for spirituality.

In particular, the converts to Islam and Muslim migrants stated that spirituality was a defining and positive characteristic of Órgiva. In a conversation at Café Baraka, Yasir, who has resided in Órgiva for about 15 years and is a convert to Islam affiliated with the Naqshbandi group, noted that there are no tensions between the different communities in the town; having lived in other parts of Spain and Europe as well as the Americas, he described Órgiva as "One of the places that I've seen in the world with less prejudices." Yasir said that although in the town "There's everything, in the positive and the negative sense," what draws people to Órgiva is "the search, the spiritual element [la búsqueda, lo espiritual]." Similarly, in a separate conversation at the *dargah*, Rachida, a convert from another part of Andalucía who had been living in Órgiva for about 2½ years, said that she likes the town "because it has people from various religions. What its people have in common is their spiritual search [su búsqueda espiritual]." The Moroccan migrant Fatima made a similar statement when I asked her why she felt that Órgiva was different from other places in Spain where she had lived. She said that Órgiva had "ruh al-qadasa [a spirit of sacredness]." Although the convert and Maghrebi Muslims are (thus far) clearly separate communities, this view of the sacred and the spiritual as the binding and distinctive character of Órgiva unites these two groups as well as others following different spiritual paths in Órgiva.

The three cross-cut alliances present in Órgiva—migration memory, women's issues, and Muslimness as well as a broader concern with spirituality—come about because of the acknowledgment of common strands in identity narratives and, in the process create recognition, the element needed for more egalitarian forms of tolerance. These transversal alliances demonstrate healthy tolerance in the sense that horizontal recognition of the Other's worth is present alongside the vertical process of putting up with practices or presences that are deemed undesirable. Boundaries and bridges are both central components of Órgivan coexistence: maintaining distinct cultural identities instead of imposing or seeking assimilation, but also having intersections between communities that facilitate and enhance recognition as equals. In this way, the same practices that build and maintain group identities also bolster inter-group tolerance. Yet, these bridging alliances also counteract exclusionary essentialisms by acknowledging and augmenting points of contact in established identity narratives.

Those who cross bridges between groups are examples of the "dual identity model" which posits that:

> the combination of subgroup and superordinate identities is most promising for developing harmonious intergroup relations in plural societies. Dual identities would reduce subgroup identity threat, and the shared superordinate identity would stimulate positive attitudes and cooperation with other subgroups [. . .] Out-group members will be evaluated more positively when they are seen as part of a shared superordinate category through processes that involve pro in-group bias [. . .] This is especially likely when the superordinate category is represented as a dual identity that affirms subgroup distinctiveness in the context of common belonging [. . .] (Verkuyten and Yogeeswaran 84).

The cross-community bridges in Órgiva create dual identities that link the separate social spheres and enhance recognition, thus allowing for the circulation of power and a more sustainable intergroup tolerance.

Significantly, loss and the estrangement that it entails is part of each of the three cross-community bridges. Outside of the uses of the term "tolerance" in immunology (e.g., in the context of autoimmune disease) and financial investments (e.g., with regard to risk tolerance and loss tolerance), tolerance is not often connected to loss. Yet in many, if not most, cases, toleration requires not only self-restraint, but the endurance of a loss of familiarity, a loss of the givens that are central to one's narrative of identity. Williams is one of the few scholars who notes the role of loss in toleration. He points out that when we ask someone to be tolerant:

> They will indeed have to lose something, their desire to suppress or drive out the rival belief; but they will also keep something, their commitment to their own beliefs, which is what gave them that desire in the first place. There is a tension here between one's own commitments, and the acceptance that other people may have other, perhaps quite distasteful commitments: the tension that is typical of toleration, and which makes it so difficult (Williams, 19–20).

Barbara Henry connects this loss with the original, literal meaning of tolerance: "the relative capacity to withstand an unfavourable (external) factor" without being changed (78). The fear that sometimes makes tolerating so difficult is the fear of loss of self: "the (not necessarily well-founded) fear of losing oneself, of becoming blurred and blended into the surrounding environment as a result of excessive receptiveness (alias tolerance) to external unfavorable factors," that is, external cultural and religious groups (101–2).

Through the sense of loss created by defamiliarization and the destabilization of one's identity narrative that can seem to threaten one's very self, the process of toleration makes one feel strange. Thus, estrangement is part and parcel of toleration, as well as of migration, as the migrant minors' graffiti reminds us: *al-ghurba saʿiba*. Accepting difference includes the discomfort of accepting the presence of people and practices that make one feel un-home-liness, a sense of estrangement from home—however constructed that feeling of wholeness and belonging referred to as "home" may be. For this reason, in expanding upon Appiah's 2006 formulation of cosmopolitanism, the historian Thomas Bender adds the experience of unfamiliarity that leads to self-reflection. Bender observes that "New experience for the cosmopolitan is moderately unsettling. Such an unsettling stimulates inquiry into the novelty or difference. But—and this is the main point—it also prompts introspection by the cosmopolitan. The cosmopolitan is open to the unease of forming a new understanding of both one's self and of the world when invited by the confrontation of difference" (117). When Bender states that "Tolerance is a considerable virtue, but if it is cosmopolitanism, it is cosmopolitanism-lite, as it does not demand self-reflexivity" (119), he is referring to a permission-based tolerance that remains superficial because it doesn't consider and question power dynamics and how to access—recognize—a common human bond. "The experience that makes a cosmopolitan," and, I would add, a participant in recognition-based toleration, "is at once a partial understanding of the other and an enriching partial reunderstanding of one's self" (121). The discomfort of estrangement is integral to self-reflection and the rewriting of one's identity and the concomitant opening-up of the possibility of recognition.

Each of the three cross-community alliances in Órgiva has estrangement as one of its constitutive elements. In migration memory, first- or second-hand experiences of economic difficulty, separation, and longing promote respect for the earnest livelihood motives of migrants. With regard to Órgiva's women's groups, estrangement from cultures dominated by patriarchal (Catholic or Muslim) systems is the driving force behind organizing as women. As for the more tentative bridge between convert and migrant Muslims, although there is a conflation and historical baggage with which the two groups are uneasy, the conflation and lingering past themselves point to how both groups are alienated in a predominately secular, Christianity-based culture. Additionally, these two groups experience a parallel (though distinct) estrangement process through religious conversion and migration. Estrangement leads one to view the world and oneself from a different angle, from outside the frameworks that create a sense of normalcy. This, in turn, opens the door to awareness of identities as myths or cultural narratives.

Indeed, Henry proposes that the fear of dissolution of one's self-perception can best be mitigated by "cultivating [. . .] a sense of wonder at one's own collective imagination and that of other cultures" (102). That is, an attitude toward the foundational cultural myths that create group identities which both appreciates the myths as elaborate and beautiful, and acknowledges that they are constructions, is a safer route than sanctifying the myths or pretending that they no longer operate in society. Carlos, the *orgiveño* who spoke about being looked down on as a hillbilly (*un cateto*), pointed out that in Órgiva no one can feel strange because everyone is a stranger. Like Qasim, the convert featured in *España a ras de cielo* (among other television series) and Suniya, the convert featured in *Radio Gaga*, explain, in Órgiva they have found comfort in the company of other "weirdos." Whether it is the result of an existential or spiritual search or a migration journey, the residents of Órgiva are connected by their multiple types of strangeness. While the company of other "strangers" can create a new kind of belonging, the experience of strangeness is integral to tolerance. Strangeness can support connections, even across distinct communities, because it creates an askance perspective that brings to light unexpected points of contact in identity narratives. Moreover, strangeness, through its outsider viewpoint, encourages an awareness of identity narratives as wondrous constructions. Feeling strange, being aware of one's alienation, enables the tolerating of strangers, because both self and other are understood as the products of fantastical tales. The transversal alliances in Órgiva point to common threads in identity narratives and the ideologies that produce them. In the process, they make community members more aware of the constructedness of group boundaries and the types of differences that are rejected. This awareness gives community members an active role in evaluating what they are tolerating and what gifts (other acts of toleration) they receive in exchange.

CHAPTER 7

Conclusions: Accepting Estrangement, Building Bridges, and Two-Way Tolerance

Through the 1950s in particular, but even up to today, narratives about Órgiva and the Alpujarra have represented the area as a space of primitiveness—whether this was sought after as an antidote to modernity, or considered in need of development—and, intertwined with this, as a site of the vestiges of medieval Muslim Iberia. As Órgiva received many newcomers, starting in the late 1990s British residents' memoirs, the *Hablamos de Órgiva* project, and several television shows appeared, offering new narratives about the area. In many of these narratives, and particularly the televisual ones, the presence of tensions regarding language and lifestyle, of groups rejected elsewhere in the country as antithetical to Spanishness (Muslims and Maghrebi migrants), or of *orgiveños*' ties to labor migration are minimized or completely erased. This impedes the narratives' ability to consider the dynamics involved in the practice of tolerance in Órgiva—and the sites at which that dynamic gives way to rejection. At the same time, some of these new narratives about Órgiva point to the migration memory of *orgiveños* and the role of estrangement in the convert experience, elements of the town's cohabitation dynamic that were echoed in my fieldwork.

The local narratives of lived experience in Órgiva that I gathered point to the ongoing negotiation of difference in the town, the positioning of the different community groups vis-à-vis civilizational hierarchies, and the role of power within coexistence. These oral narratives about life in the town also point to the bridges or spaces of mutual recognition that foster connection, self-reflection, multifaceted identities, and more sustainable tolerance. Most of the television depictions of Órgiva, by mobilizing the narrative of happy harmony that has been built around the concept of *convivencia*, have labeled the town as tolerant or as an example of *convivencia*. This oversimplification obscures from view the tensions and ambivalences that are part of the texture of coexistence in the town and may make the work of toleration—open discussion of differences—more difficult to enact. A community that is labeled or self-labeled as tolerant, but doesn't question the extent or workings of that tolerance, may avoid the process of recognition, estrangement, and self-reflection and be less likely to reach sustainable tolerance.

As seen in the preceding chapters, tolerance in Órgiva is built through layers of outbound and inbound migration. The departure of *orgiveños* as economic migrants created the conditions of possibility for Britons and other Europeans to settle there. The hippie or "alternative" movement served as an incubator for the start of the convert and Sufi community, which in turn has made Islam (by virtue of being viewed as an "Islam-lite" and of being practiced by Spaniards and other Europeans) less threatening to the townspeople, and created a more familiar (and welcoming) environment for Maghrebi immigrants. At the same time, the alternative movement has brought to the town certain behaviors that have been much more of a rallying cry for local protest than working immigrants and even unaccompanied migrants from the Maghreb.

Many outside accounts of the town engage in different forms of *convivencia*-washing and, whether or not they reference the Sufi community, they omit the particular dynamic between Maghrebi migrants, converts to Islam, and *orgiveños*' use of the term *moro*, as well as the active rejection of street-dwelling or off-the-grid alternatives that arises every so often. On the one hand, invoking the *convivencia* model can be a useful reminder that diversity itself is an Iberian tradition. On the other hand, it has led to concentrating attention on the confluence of religions, with negligible attention to intra-Muslim issues and the deep differences in lifestyle—and conceptions of tolerance—between alternatives and others in the town. The focus on internationalism (referred to in the shows as "cosmopolitanism") and religious harmony—without noting the issues between those who embrace rules-based governance and accept at least to some extent the capitalist system, and those who reject as much as possible the capitalist system—has led to a limited portrait of the town and an underdeveloped conceptualization of difference and tolerance.

Even in a town that is relatively peaceful compared to nearby locales, there are some hotspots of friction—some types of difference that community members have a hard time tolerating and occasionally publicly reject. Tolerance is weakest in Órgiva, and occasionally finds its limits, at the juncture of class and lifestyle aspirations: those who are dwellers interested in maintaining state authority and dominant understandings of progress reject the most extreme members of the alternative community who live off-grid. Interestingly, of the other three most notable friction points, two are intra-national and two are linked to linguistic tensions. Some metropolitan Spaniards view *orgiveños* as ignorant hillbillies (*catetos*) and the *orgiveños* are aware that they are largely marked as such by their far-from-standard regional dialect. Also related to language and the prestige accorded to certain dialects or, in this case, languages, the *orgiveños* are irked by the incomers who insist on speaking to them in English, or are incapable of basic communication in Spanish. And last, there are some tensions—or more precisely apprehensions—on the part of the Maghrebi migrants toward the unaccompanied minor migrants from Morocco, apprehensions stemming from concerns regarding potential negative effects on the Maghrebis' quality of life in Órgiva. Thus, the friction points at which tolerance is most vulnerable, or where it finds its limits, are largely intra-European or intra-national: between all other inhabitants and the most anti-establishment alternatives; between *orgiveños* and residents from urban, cosmopolitan areas of Spain associated with progress, or from other parts of Europe—primarily

England—that are similarly located in terms of civilizational prestige, and finally between Maghrebi immigrants and the undocumented immigrant youths who the adult migrants see as a threat to their image and/or to the inclusive diversity they find in Órgiva.

Therefore, while some elements of the *moros* vs. *cristianos* mentality do arise, what divides the residents of Órgiva the most is not religion, but social class and conceptions of civilizational prestige, in which some extra-local groups display a presumption of greater sophistication that can be understood as a form of colonial attitude, while other groups (the Maghrebis) fear losing the modicum of acceptance that they have attained because of a lack of urbanity or tolerance on the part of the MENA youths. All these differences are publicly tolerated, except for, occasionally, the tensions with the street-dwelling and off-grid alternatives.

The specific factors that create more egalitarian tolerance in Órgiva are the bridges between communities, primarily those of migration memory, feminism or women's issues, and Muslimness or broader spirituality. These alliances are based on and enhance the perception of common strands in identity narratives and, thus, facilitate recognition-based tolerance. Contrary to the cultural schemas of *moros* vs. *cristianos* thinking, it is the last of these that is most tentative.

Since 1492, the Alpujarra has served as a refuge for Muslims fleeing and/or resisting the imposition of Catholicism in Iberia and the rising nationalism of the Catholic Monarchs. Soon after the *morisco* rebellion was quashed, the region also became a refuge for the impoverished from other parts of the Iberian Peninsula, especially Galicians. In a similar trajectory, today the Alpujarra is a refuge for Northern Europeans and metropolitan Spaniards, European converts to Sufi Islam, and a small contingent of Muslim economic migrants from North Africa. In Órgiva in particular, the residents seek to build community in order to have a space in which to take refuge—whether from a moribund, depopulated rural setting; from modern urban life in a consumerist, capitalist system; from a national Catholic culture that rejects converts to Islam; or from discrimination against North African migrants elsewhere in Andalucía. The converts and North

African immigrants specifically seek different forms of visibility and invisibility (accepted visibility and normalcy). These two sectors of the community, while both are placed by *orgiveños* in the same category of *moros*/Muslims, actually differ greatly in terms of religious and cultural practices.

However, the presence of the convert Sufi community allows the North African immigrants to find a culture of acceptance, a refuge from Islamophobic attitudes found in other parts of Spain—specifically through the converts' and others' recognition of the migrants and the migrants' own practice of tolerance toward the converts. The Sufi converts welcome the immigrants as Muslims and as potential bearers of authenticity and linguistic knowledge, whereas the Muslim immigrants, while often not agreeing with the Sufis' religious practices or conceptions of what is halal, at least appreciate the spiritual outlook of the Sufis (one shared by many in Órgiva), and benefit directly from the Sufis' presence as community members who help to normalize Islam and the cultural practices of Islamicate societies. For these reasons, rather than refuse to share their knowledge of Arabic and Islam, or reject openly and without mitigating statements the Sufis' claim to being Muslims, the Maghrebi migrants who are practicing Muslims tolerate practices of which, to varying degrees, many do not approve.

Órgiva has long been the site of many forms of inter-cultural contact and population movement. The latest of these layers is one in which the presence of an unusually large number of European converts to Islam helps a relatively small number of Muslim migrants from the Maghreb enjoy a higher level of tolerance—visibility with acceptance. Maghrebis may not seem significant as a small minority within the town; however, North Africans are a sizable, visible, and often rejected minority group in the rest of Spain and Europe. Observing how they live and how they are treated in a setting in which they do not represent a demographic threat sheds light on issues that go beyond perceived economic impact. In Órgiva, recognition is a crucial element of equitable toleration that is more viable in the long run. Moreover, by highlighting or creating dual identities, Órgiva's cross-community bridges allow for the circulation of power and a more sustainable type of intergroup toleration. These bridging alliances allow for two-way recognition and toleration between otherwise strongly bounded identities. Rather than impose assimilation, the toleration process in the town allows groups to live side by side with transversal alliances that, interwoven with various types of estrangement, heighten awareness of identities as myths or cultural narratives. The bridging dual identities highlight common threads in identity narratives and the ideologies that produce them. In this way, they make community members more aware of the constructedness of group boundaries and the role that each community member plays in evaluating what will or will not be tolerated and how they participate in the multi-directional exchange of acts of tolerance, in which community members can both exert power and be empowered.

Additionally, the toleration dynamic in the town, and specifically the ongoing redefinition of the concepts of *moro* and *musulmán*, are working to recalibrate existing conceptions of Christian Europe as the hallmark of tolerance. European and Maghrebi Muslims have an active role in asserting and exercising power within the toleration process. Acknowledging this shakes assumptions about civilizational differences on the basis of levels of tolerance, or the ability to tolerate. Moreover, the category of Muslim is being redefined outside of ethno-racial categories. This means that while liberal discourses of tolerance take advantage of the power dynamics that are part of toleration without recognizing them, in Órgiva the process of reconfiguring essentialist East/West identities is also recalibrating the established correlation between modernity, Europeanness, and tolerance, and inversely, Islam and intolerance. Toleration in this Andalusian town breaks down essentialist East/West identities by both redefining the concept of "Muslim" and providing examples of toleration among community members of a multiplicity of faiths, including Islam. The practice of toleration in Órgiva is creating a new relationship between tolerance and established civilizational orders: East vs. West, Islam vs. Christian Europe.

Given its deep associations with al-Andalus and a pre-modern timelessness, the Alpujarra is simultaneously isolated and unique, and a concentrated version of Andalucía and Spain, as frontier zones between North and South and East and West, between modernity and "primitiveness." Today, Órgiva's residents are made up of survivors and seekers: dwellers who, though they may have never left the region, were nonetheless affected by migration, and journeyers of different types. Both the "backwards," "primitive" dwellers and the journeyers of many stripes, including the Maghrebi migrants and the converts to Islam, participate in the toleration dynamic of the town. The town's ongoing toleration process reveals that being able to tolerate "feeling strange," to the extent of becoming aware that one's community identity is a narrative subject to change, helps those with more power establish broader limits to their toleration. This is a transactional understanding of tolerance, but if mutual recognition of each other's worth is part of the process, it is an empowering form of trade in which each actor has something to offer and the "capital" that is accumulated is a sense of self-esteem that is built in part by identifying as equitably and appropriately tolerant. *Al-ghurba sa'iba*: like emigration (or religious conversion), toleration is difficult, but if one wants what it has to offer, one needs to manage its estrangement well to make sure it doesn't become treacherous—that is, a source of oppression and discontent. The community dynamic in Órgiva teaches us that tolerance is a multidirectional process (not a one-way street) that is intertwined with power, personal interest, and experiences of estrangement at all levels.

Órgiva is surrounded by rivers and mountains. Since the time when mules transported people in and out of the town, the main route between Órgiva and the winding road that leads to all points north and west had been a one-lane bridge spanning the Río Chico. When another vehicle arrived at the bridge first, one had to pull one's own vehicle over and yield the right-of-way before continuing to cross. Now that has changed. It was determined that the single-lane bridge was no longer structurally sound and, in August 2019, construction of a new bridge began. The new, two-lane bridge was completed on January 31, 2020. In its official inauguration on February 13, 2020, by the president and other representatives of the *Junta de Andalucía*, the *Junta*'s president emphasized the bridge's importance to the local Alpujarran infrastructure and the *Junta*'s commitment to investing in improving all of Andalucía's infrastructure.[1] While regional politicians used the bridge as a showpiece of transportation infrastructure, it also serves as a symbol of the community structures and dynamics that support tolerance in the town: two-lane bridges facilitate two-way tolerance and the new bridge, while strange and unfamiliar, is a reminder of improvements that make life safer and more functional. This new bridge is a sign of an even more important type of progress, also gained through commitment and investment. But rather than a strictly monetary investment, the bridge is an investment in self and community and, rather than modernity per se, it creates healthy coexistence. More important than the built infrastructure of modernity, is the infrastructure of sustainable tolerance that is worked on every day by Órgiva's residents. Their new bridge serves as a symbol of how bridges between communities and the two-way traffic of recognition-based toleration that includes productive estrangement create the ongoing negotiation that is the core of coexistence.

By recognizing the power differences, ideologies, and ambivalences that are at play, we can identify the bridges that open the door to dialogue and respect-based tolerance. Perhaps humans tend to want simple, easy, automatic tolerance—but it doesn't exist. A more sustainable tolerance is reached when there is recognition of not only each other as worthy human beings, but of each party's concessions and vested interests; rather than embracing a *convivencia* rhetoric, we need to acknowledge that living together is sometimes messy and always entangled with power. Together, the multiple, sometimes contradictory, narratives about this Andalusian town demonstrate how tolerance is negotiated and debated. While *orgiveños* and lifestyle migrants emphasized a dynamic of living in separate worlds, Muslim incomers—whether European converts or Maghrebi migrants—emphasized finding a (spiritual) home in the town. While the former group of inhabitants questions how much they want to live together (*convivir*) vs. how much they want to live side by side, the latter group is keenly aware of the relatively welcoming space that they find in the town. All of these constituents are engaged in a process of weighing the benefits and losses of different modes of coexistence. To avoid us-

FIGURE 12: An *orgiveño* and a convert to Sufi Islam wait their turn at the meat counter of a local grocery store that sells both cured *jamón* (hanging from the wall behind the counter) and halal meat.

ing tolerance as a way to mask differences and power relationships, toleration needs to be recognized as an ongoing negotiation of what and how difference will be accepted—of what can be agreed upon as haram versus halal in the land of *jamón*, with its deep roots in diversity and mobility.

Notes

Preface

1. "Paca" is a pseudonym. Throughout, in order to protect identities, I have used pseudonyms and omitted or changed details that would provide identifying information. The only exception to this is that I have used the real names of interlocutors who were speaking with me in their capacity as an author or an appointed or elected official.

Chapter 1

1. Throughout, by "Órgiva" I refer to "Greater Órgiva," that is, the town itself and several annexed areas (smaller rural communities that are officially grouped as part of the municipality of Órgiva), as well as farmhouses in the areas surrounding Órgiva. An older spelling, that is still seen occasionally, is "Órjiva."
2. While the term *kufi* comes from the West African city Kufi, *topi* is the Hindi word that is used throughout South Asia, and *taqiya* is the Arabic term. Throughout, for the transliteration of Arabic into Latin script I use a simplified version of the system used by the *International Journal of Middle East Studies*: all terms that are familiar to English-language readers are presented with the spellings commonly used in English (e.g., Quran, taqiya) and the only diacritical markings that appear are ' for the letter *'ayn* and ' for *hamza*. When representing phrases expressed in Moroccan *Darija*, I attempted to reflect the pronunciation of this colloquial dialect.
3. There are approximately 6,000 registered inhabitants in the municipality, but the area has an estimated 8,000 inhabitants if one includes those that are not officially registered. According to the *Instituto Nacional de Estadística* (www.ine.es/), there are: 707 residents of Órgiva from the United Kingdom (by far the largest group), Germany, France, and Italy. This does not include more transient populations from elsewhere in the EU and Spaniards from other parts of the country who have settled in the town. The principal of the town's public primary school (ages 3–12) estimated that 3 or 4 students in every class of approximately 20 were the children of parents from outside of the Alpujarra, both "*extranjeros*" (incomers from elsewhere in Europe) and "*inmigrantes*" or economic migrants from North Africa and elsewhere. The principal of the public high school (ages 12–18) estimated that 40 percent of the students were the children of parents from outside of the Alpujarra.

The difference in numbers can be explained by the fact that 1) many of the incomers from elsewhere in Europe choose to send their children to the private Montessori or Waldorf schools in Órgiva or to the smaller public primary school in one of the annexed rural communities, 2) for secondary school there are fewer nearby alternatives to the Órgiva school, and 3) the unaccompanied minors from North and West Africa (explained further on) arrive at high school age.

4. All translations are my own, unless otherwise noted. For oral material and secondary sources, only noteworthy phrases are provided in the original.

5. See, for instance, Faszer-McMahon and Ketz, Rueda and Martín, eds. Flesler, and Ricci.

6. Throughout I refer to the autonomous community of Andalucía, that is, the region of Andalucía, with the Spanish spelling (Andalucía) instead of the English spelling (Andalusia) because there is a tendency in English and other languages to refer to medieval Muslim-ruled Iberia as "Andalusia." Although the etymological link between "al-Andalus" and "Andalucía/Andalusia" is clear, they are distinct places in time and only partially overlapping territories. My hope is that using "Andalucía" will avoid the conflation between the two. I use "Andalusian" exclusively to refer to people, places, or things related to the region of Andalucía (not medieval al-Andalus).

7. E.g., Bahrami, Carnet, del Olmo, Dietz, Dietz and El-Shohoumi, Hirschkind 2014 and 2016, Rogozen-Soltar 2017, Rosón Lorente, Stallaert 1999, and Suárez-Navaz.

8. The Alpujarra region has a horizontal spread that straddles two provinces, that of Granada and that of Almería. It is also divided by elevation into the high, medium, and low Alpujarra. As a result, this region is sometimes referred to in the plural as "Las Alpujarras." According to *The Encyclopedia of Islam*, "Alpujarra" probably comes from the Arabic "*al-basharāt*," meaning "pastures."

9. For more on the legacy of al-Andalus as a cultural symbol that is reworked in contemporary Spain, Argentina, the Middle East, and North Africa, see Civantos. On al-Andalus in Spanish colonialism in Morocco and in Moroccan nationalism, see Calderwood 2018. On the concept of *convivencia*, see Manzano Moreno, Nirenberg, Akasoy, and Pearce, 30–31 and 34. On *convivencia* and the three Abrahamic religions in the Spanish tourism industry, see Calderwood 2014.

10. Revisionist accounts of Spanish history assert that the concept of the Reconquista is problematic because there was not a unified Christian Spain before Muslims conquered the peninsula and the process of alliance building and territorial expansion took nearly 800 years. As a result, much has been written about the term *Reconquista* itself. See, for instance, Barbero and Vigil; Lomax, 1; González Jiménez 2003; Ríos Saloma; Martínez Montávez, 30, and García-Sanjuán 2018a.

11. On the cultural implications of Spanish colonialism in North Africa, the Franco dictatorship's ambivalent attitude toward the Maghreb, and the deployment of the concept of Hispano-Moroccan *hermandad*, see Calderwood 2018, Martin-Márquez, Campoy-Cubillo, Labanyi 2012, González Alcantud 2002 and 2003, and

Aidi. For critiques of Spanish Arabism, its political deployment, and its historiography of al-Andalus see, for instance, Rojo and Casares Porcel, López García, Tofiño-Quesada, Viguera, Fierro, Martín Muñoz, Rivière Gómez, and the classic study Monroe 1970a.

12. The last mine closed in 1989, but then in 2010 some mining activity began again.

13. Barrios Aguilera (1996) states that it was not until 1568, after the first Rebellion, that the Alpujarra was repopulated by Old Christians (19, 24–25). After that point, people of Muslim origin accounted for less than 10 percent of the population of the region (26). On the repopulation project in Andalucía in general, see also Barrios Aguilera and Andújar Castillo, Bravo Caro, and González Jiménez 1980. On how *moriscos* maintained their religion and customs in early modern Spain, see, for example, Perry.

14. For more on *andalucismo*, see Stallaert 1998, 70–126. On the role of al-Andalus and the Moor in *andalucismo*, see González Alcantud 2006; Martin-Márquez, 301–03; Calderwood 2014a; Civantos, 14–15, 35–36, and Duran. On *andalucismo*, historical memory, and Spanish literature and music that depicts al-Andalus, see Civantos, 98–99, 173–76, and 251–53, and Egea Fernández-Montesinos. On *andalucismo*, history, and memory, see Hirschkind, 2020.

15. For more on Infante (who is said to have converted to Islam in Morocco in 1924) and his role in *andalucismo* and the Spanish rhetoric of a Hispano-Moroccan brotherhood that supported the colonial project in Morocco, see Calderwood 2018, 116–21. On Infante's version of Andalusian history, see Stallaert 1999, 95–97.

16. See also Rosón Lorente, 91–94.

17. The term "Islamicate" (coined by Marshall Hodgson) refers to societies in which Muslims are culturally dominant and, thus, distinguishes between the practice of Islam and cultures strongly influenced by Islam, even among the practitioners of other faiths or non-believers.

18. Rosón Lorente explains that the Muslim convert community in Granada took official form first as the "*Sociedad para el Retorno al Islam en España*" (Society for the Return to Islam in Spain) and then as "*Comunidad Islámica en España*" (Islamic Community in Spain).

19. For more on the conversion phenomenon in Spain, see del Olmo, Howe, and Abend.

20. A 2005 UNESCO report states that European sources place the total number of North Africans in Europe at just over two million, but the estimates from the countries of emigration are nearly double that. More than half of these émigrés are Moroccan, and currently Spain is the country that receives the second highest number (after France) of Moroccan immigrants (Baldwin-Edwards, and Zohry).

21. On the migrant agricultural workers in Almería province, including El Ejido, see Carnet, and Lahbabi.

22. On the debates surrounding the mosque-cathedral of Córdoba, see Rogozen-Soltar 2007, 874–77; D. Fuchs; Tremlett; Keeley; Shubert; Calderwood 2015, and Wien, 64–65.

23. For more on how the original event itself was staged, see Civantos, 185. On how the public debates regarding the event continue, see, for instance, Arroyo, and Á. López.

24. See "Piden a la RAE que el término 'moro' se considere racista" and Pérez-Reverte's 2014 blog post "Moros de la morería," whose title makes reference to the opening verse ("Abenámar, Abenámar, moro de la morería") in the medieval Spanish ballad *El romance de Abenámar*.

25. There are also a few converts from the United States within this community, most of them married to other converts who are Britons or Spaniards.

26. On consuming pork and wine as proof of being a true convert to Christianity or an Old Christian, see Lea; Root, 126–27, 129, and Dadson, 79–85, 209. The 1504 Oran fatwa explained how Islamic law allowed, when necessary for survival, that Muslims dissimulate Christianity and perform normally forbidden acts, such as consuming pork and wine (Harvey, 60–62). Before that time, crypto-Muslims abstained from wine and pork and quickly drew suspicion.

27. For more on the Alpujarran dried ham industry, see: González Blasco (2001).

28. On Faysal Mrad Dali and his Balkis Gourmet's halal *jamón*, see Frayer.

29. Órgiva's church of *Nuestra Señora de la Expectación* was built in 1500 on top of a destroyed mosque. After being severely damaged in the *morisco* rebellion the church was rebuilt in 1580. Close to its entrance a wrought iron cross is displayed with a plaque that explains that it was donated by Don John of Austria, half-brother of King Philip II of Spain, to commemorate the end of the Reconquista. In the 16th century, one of El Gran Capitán's descendants built a palace in the mudejar style (the decoration and ornamentation derived from Islamic art and architecture, such as calligraphy, intricate geometry, and vegetal forms, used in the Iberian Christian kingdoms, mainly between the 13th and 16th centuries) which came to be known as the *Casa Palacio de los Condes de Sástago*. According to the local tourism office its tower has the honor of being the only one in the Alpujarra that was never conquered during the *morisco* rebellion ("Oficina de Turismo de Órgiva," https://Órgivaturismo.wordpress.com/que-ver/). The *Ermita de San Sebastián*, or chapel of Saint Sebastian, located on a hill on the northern edge of town and said to have been originally built by the Visigoths, is today a Catholic sanctuary. The worn-down ruins of a Muslim citadel (*hisn* in Arabic) built in the 10th or 11th century and known today as the *castillejo* (small castle) of Órgiva, is on a promontory about 3.5 km south of the town. A more prominent, and better-preserved, Muslim fortress is located in the neighboring town of Lanjarón.

30. At least two of the children of converts who were largely raised in Órgiva (Muhammad Scott and Yasin Maymir) have established a tourism business that caters to Muslims from abroad wishing to visit the Andalusian sites that are part of the cultural legacy of al-Andalus. Services include guided tours with content geared toward a Muslim audience and meals at restaurants that serve halal food. Part of one of the Granada packages is an excursion to the Alpujarra with a stop in Órgiva for a meal at Café Baraka (discussed further on).

31. As explained in more detail in Chapter 4, through the term *orgiveño* I refer principally to individuals who were born and raised in Órgiva, although their families may come from smaller towns in the Alpujarra, as well as some from other parts of southern Andalucía who have lived most of their adult lives in Órgiva and primarily socialize with *orgiveños* born and raised in the town.

32. The *orgiveños* in leadership positions included: the former mayor, María Ángeles Blanco López (in office from 2007 to 2019), the current mayor, Raúl Orellana, two of the current town councilors, the head of the *Centro Municipal de Información a la Mujer de Órgiva* (the office for women's issues that is part of the municipal government), the principals of the town's public primary school and public high school, the priests from the local Catholic church, and employees of the *Centro de Orientación e Inserción Laboral* that serves unaccompanied migrant minors, as well as the director of this Center who is from the city of Granada and resides there. I also use "townspeople" to refer to *orgiveños*, and "local" as an adjective usually to refer to *orgiveños*; I trust that the context will make any exceptions to this clear. My interactions with Spaniards all took place in Spanish (though my Latin American accent marked me as a foreigner), and, depending on the origins of the converts, our interactions either took place in Spanish or in English. When interlocutors were balanced bilinguals (e.g., the child of Britons born and raised in Órgiva), I invited them to choose whichever language they preferred. My interactions with Maghrebi migrants mostly took place in Arabic (primarily with me speaking Levantine Arabic and the migrants Moroccan *Darija*). But depending on the situation (the presence of monolingual Spanish-speakers in the group, migrants who wished to demonstrate their command of Spanish, migrants who had native-like fluency in Spanish, etc.) some interactions were in Spanish or a mix of the two languages.

Chapter 2

1. I address the use of the related term "conviviality" further on.
2. On "tolerance" and "toleration," see Murphy, 595, and Forst 2004, 315. For different perspectives on tolerance and Islam, see Friedman and Shah-Kazemi. On the performance of toleration and invocations of *convivencia* among North African and Arab elites, see Boum.
3. See also Žižek's 2008 discussion of Brown.
4. See for instance, Forst 2004, 315–18; Verkuyten and Yogeeswaran, 85, and Fernández 2009.
5. See for instance, Forst 2004, 316–17; Verkuyten and Yogeeswaran, 83, and Fernández 2009.
6. On the relationships between conviviality, cosmopolitanism, and creolization, see Hemer et al.
7. For more on the positions of Forst and Brown on the relationship between power and tolerance, see Brown and Forst 2014.
8. See Bourdieu 1977, 183; 2014, 122, and 1991, 128 and 167.
9. See Benveniste, 336–35.

Chapter 3

1. Examples of this recent travel writing about Órgiva include: "El paraíso hippy de Europa," Sánchez Alonso 2015a; "Órgiva, a Culture Hotchpotch in the Alpujarras," Piegsa-Quischotte; and "The Alpujarra: An Unlikely Cosmopolitan Hub in Spain's Sierra Nevada," Threadgould. Thus far, published works in Arabic about the Alpujarra and/or Órgiva are limited to histories and historical novels about the Rebellion of the Alpujarras and a few Internet articles about the Naqshbandi Sufis that have settled in Órgiva.

2. See, for instance, Ferguson, and Heers.

3. For more on how Brenan Orientalizes the Alpujarra, see Ibáñez Ibáñez, especially 210–12.

4. On "the aesthetics of poverty" (437) in *South from Granada* and Spanish author Juan Goytisolo's relationship to it, see Henn.

5. On the Black Legend and scientific racism in Spain, see Martin-Márquez, 39–42, and B. Fuchs, 116–17.

6. On Boabdil in earlier Spanish literature, see Carrasco Urgoiti. On Boabdil in 20th- and 21st-century cultural production from Spain, Argentina, and the Middle East and North Africa, see Civantos.

7. This legend and others surrounding Boabdil were given international fame by US author, historian, and diplomat Washington Irving in his *Tales of the Alhambra* (1832).

8. On the found treasures, see Pozo Felguera 2017.

9. Known in Spanish historiography as Aben Humeya, Muhammad ibn Umayya (c. 1545–69) took the Christian name Fernando de Válor y Córdoba. As depicted in Martínez de la Rosa's play, Aben Humeya owned an estate in the village of Cádiar in the Alpujarra and initiated the revolt from there. For an analysis of the role of this play and its Arab hero in the definition of Spanish identity, see Labanyi 2004.

10. On García Lorca and the Alpujarra, see García Lorca, Elvira, and Rubio, and see also González Blasco 2004, Vol. II, 654–714, and González Blasco 2017.

11. Olóriz Aguilera never completed his projected book on "the Anthropology of the Alpujarra" (136), but he did leave an extensive diary of field notes which was later published as *Diario de la expedición antropológica a la Alpujarra en 1894*.

12. The 20th- and 21st-century historical and anthropological works on the region include: Spahni (1959), Caro Baroja (1979), Navarro Alcalá-Zamora (1981), Martín Jorge (1988), Carrascosa Salas (1992), Baumann (1995), González Blasco (2004) and Campo Tejedor (2006). Sedano Moreno's *Imagínate la Alpujarra: otro mundo, mil y una historias alpujarreñas* is a collection of columns that appeared in the 1990s in the magazine of the *Asociación Abuxarra*, a local cultural organization. Although the columns focus on traditional Alpujarran culture without dwelling on al-Andalus, the very name of the organization and its magazine reflects one of a few of the Arabic etymologies proposed for the region. Carmona Vílchez's *Clarito, un gran hombre de la Alpujarra*, is the biography of the author's father, nicknamed

Clarito, who was born and raised in different towns of the Alpujarra and lived much of his adult life in Órgiva until his death in 1997.

13. On the historical novel genre in Spain since the late 20th century, see Veres, and Fernández Prieto. On historical novels within this trend that depict Muslim-Christian contact in Iberia, see Civantos, and Flesler.

14. Two other historical novels set in the 15th- and 16th-century Alpujarra, though not specifically Órgiva, are *El rey de los moriscos* (2015) by Fernandéz Palmeral and *La tumba del monfí* (2012) by Pérez Zúñiga.

15. For more on the hamlet of El Morreón, Beneficio, and the broader context of alternative communities in Spain, see Gómez-Ullate García de León. On Beneficio in particular, see Díez Forcada.

16. His adopted name is sometimes spelled "Omar," an alternate transliteration of the name ('Umar) from Arabic script.

17. These population statistics are taken from a presentation by *Proyecto Municipio Andaluz Sostenible* at the *Jornadas Provinciales sobre Sostenibilidad Local*, June 16 and 17, 2010 (https://issuu.com/jornadas-a21/docs/orgiva__proyecto_municipio_andaluz_sostenible).

18. Personal interview with Chris Stewart, July 3, 2019.

19. For more on Stewart's construction of an inter-cultural or transcultural identity in *Driving over Lemons*, see Beaven, and Sell.

20. I will use "narrator" as much as possible in an effort to distinguish between Stewart and the persona of the first-person speaker that he creates in the text.

21. Muslim conceptions of what is permissible in the realm of money come up in a chapter in *The Almond Blossom Appreciation Society* (Stewart 2006) that recounts Stewart's quest to find a trustworthy miller for his olive harvest. Here the narrator ends up at "what's known as the 'Muslim Mill,'" explains that "There's a sizeable Muslim community in Órgiva, composed mostly of Spanish *conversos* and a miscellany of Sufis from all over the world" (191), and states that "those draconian injunctions in the Quran against usury and suchlike" made him feel like if he was being overcharged, at least "it's being done cleanly" (192).

22. Additionally, in the chapter entitled "The Almond Blossom Appreciation Society," from which the book takes its name, the narrator explains that one of the two friends with whom he goes on hikes amid blooming almond groves is an Alpujarran who had left to make money as a farm laborer in Switzerland and saved enough to buy a plot of land in the Alpujarra. One of this return migrant's projects was the establishment of an organic agricultural co-operative; however, he himself was eventually expelled from the co-operative that he had founded because of alternative "organo-fundamentalists" who had a stricter definition of organic produce (Stewart 2006, 214).

23. April 6, 2021 interview with Bailey via videocall.

24. April 6, 2021 interview with Bailey via videocall.

25. Whiteman was one of the early event organizers for Kutubia, a Muslim organization in Órgiva that I discuss in Chapter 5, "Oral Narratives about Órgiva."

26. This vision of Spanish history likely draws from Martínez Dalmases, whose book on this topic Whiteman helped to publish in English. See reference to Martínez Dalmases in this volume, Chapter 5, "Oral Narratives about Órgiva."

27. When the topic of the *Hablamos de Órgiva* project came up in separate conversations with *orgiveños*, a few of them criticized the manner in which the non-*orgiveño* coordinators carried out the project.

28. Ciudad 21 is a joint program of the *Red de Ciudades Sostenibles de Andalucía* (RECSA), which itself is the result of an agreement between the *Federación Andaluza de Municipios y Provincias* (FAMP) and the *Consejería de Medio Ambiente* of the regional government of Andalucía (*la Junta de Andalucía*).

29. PASOS: Proyecto de Participación Ciudadana "Órgiva Municipio Sostenible" https://pasos.coop/portfolio/proyecto-orgiva-municipio-andaluz-sostenible/.

30. Subsequent citations from *Hablamos de Órgiva* will only include the title of the chapter in question and the page number. Chapter titles are necessary because the page numbers are not consecutive, rather they start over in each chapter.

31. In *Hablamos de Órgiva*, the residents' statements are presented anonymously, but sometimes with identifying details included. In the case of this Algerian speaker, his statement also includes references to where he works, making him easily identifiable. Based on such details, it seems that one or maybe two Maghrebi migrants contributed to the project.

32. The PASOS webpage and the introductory chapter of the book ("Para entender mejor el libro" 11) refer to the gathering of statements and creation of the book as a first step, but I'm not aware of any subsequent steps directly building on this collaborative book.

Chapter 4

1. The entire episode is available on the Canal Sur YouTube channel: www.youtube.com/watch?v=eHkjnW-nvsM.

2. There is a 9th television program from the same time period that touches upon Órgiva. All of the episodes of the Spanish series *Búscame en el pueblo* (Look for me in a small town) focus on "neorrurales [neo-rurals]", or people who have left big city life for a rural environment. One of the 15-minute episodes is about a British artist who lives on the outskirts of Órgiva. This April 2011 episode (episode 3, season 1) presents the Argentine show host, Sofía Colombo, visiting the sculptor and his bilingual children at his home and art studio. There is no footage of the town itself and the show only mentions that in Órgiva a percentage of the population is foreigners and within that a certain number are British.

3. "Mozárabe" (and the English "Mozarab") is a term derived from the Arabic *mustaʿrab*, literally "Arabized," a modern term for the Iberian Christians who lived under Muslim rule in al-Andalus. Though they remained Christian, they were fluent in Arabic and acquired elements of Arab and North African culture.

4. My thanks to Ela Graves for pointing out the use of *manteca de cerdo* (lard) instead of oil in local sweets.

5. For interpretations of the *morisco* in *El Quijote* as an Other, see, for instance, Mancing, Corbalán, and Bolaños. For interpretations of the novel as a subtle critique of the treatment of *moriscos*, see, for instance, Johnson, Childers's review article on Johnson's posthumous book, as well as other works within *morisco* studies: Graf, Quinn, 101–32, and de Armas.

6. The "VICE en Español" YouTube channel states that it has 925,000 subscribers. For how Vice News presents itself, see "About VICE News": https://news-old-origin.vice.com/about.

7. The episode can be seen on the Vice website (www.vice.com/es/article/a3pe8j/sufis-misticos-islam-espana) and on the Vice YouTube channel (www.youtube.com/watch?v=ZmRjC4Lxw8c&t=109s).

8. This episode of *Medina* can be found here: www.rtve.es/alacarta/videos/medina-en-tve/medina-tve-comunidad-sufi-orgiva/5029907/.

9. Interestingly, the "Transcripción completa" [Complete transcription] of the episode that is provided on the same webpage as the video omits only one sentence: "Nosotros seguimos la sharía."

10. The episode was broadcast on August 17, 2015 and again on September 29, 2018. It is also available on the RTVE website: www.rtve.es/alacarta/videos/espana-a-ras-de-cielo/espana-ras-cielo-voy-pueblo/4761958/.

11. The episode of *Tierra de sabores* is available here: www.canalsur.es/television/programas/tierra-de-sabores/detalle/13413572.html?video=1680687&sec=.

12. On this occasion, the Galindo bakers make a cake called *bizcocho real* or *bizcocho de carnaval* with sunflower seed oil and note that this was the traditional wedding cake of Mozarabs (see Note 3 above on *mozárabes*).

13. The episode of *Los repobladores* can be found here: www.canalsur.es/television/programas/los-repobladores/detalle/5838836.html .

14. The episode of *Tierra de sabores* was also filmed during the pandemic (masked passersby are seen frequently). Although *Tierra de sabores* could have been made during a different period of the pandemic (a different phase of confinement measures), it never features empty spaces, but rather a market with many customers, etc.

15. The Órgiva segment of the episode, to which the time signatures cited here refer, can be found at: www.youtube.com/watch?v=996qbsv9sBY&t=32s. The entire episode can be found here: www.youtube.com/watch?v=cQIdT08ygn0.

16. Unfortunately, although I made various attempts to contact the show hosts and the director of communications at Movistar+ to ask about the genesis and development of the episode (e.g., if certain participants or topics were edited out), I did not receive a response. Two people who featured prominently in the episode described the filming process to me in separate conversations. Maryam, who at age 19, about three years after the filming, sports a few piercings on her face, but (at least while at Muslim community gatherings) wears a short-sleeved tunic and a veil of the same style as her mother, stated that the *Radio Gaga* crew carried out heavy recruitment ("fueron muy insistentes"). In other words, she didn't just happen to walk up to the microphone, as the episode makes it seem. Similarly, the waiter from Café Baraka

(the one who brings the Moroccan tea service to the *Radio Gaga* trailer) said that the whole episode was preplanned; people didn't participate spontaneously. He described it as an effective, efficient pre-production process carried out by a crew of very capable women from Barcelona who came to the town two months ahead of time to make contacts and plan everything out. He also noted that there were various scenes in which he was filmed that were cut out in the editing process.

17. None of the many internet news articles about the Sufis of Órgiva mention the presence of North African Muslims in the town either.

18. Linguistic difference only arises in *Este es mi pueblo* when the anonymous locals explain how they use gestures to communicate with non-Spanish speakers, and in *Radio Gaga* when the trio of women approach the camper and viewers witness a British woman and German woman managing, with difficulty, to express themselves in Spanish.

19. Members of different sectors of the town have different perspectives on the gravity of alcohol and drug use in Órgiva. The handful of town drunks are visibly present and, though less visible because of its illegality, many residents acknowledged that among certain communities in Órgiva recreational use of cannabis is widespread. Some interlocutors reported that there were serious substance abuse problems in the town from about 2007–09, but that the situation has improved. In the commune of Beneficio, alcohol and hard drugs are banned. Nonetheless, the parish priests asserted that substance abuse is still a major problem.

Chapter 5

1. According to both British incomers and *orgiveños* (among them the former mayor Blanco López), few residents who are from outside of the Alpujarra carry out the steps to be able to vote in local elections, or get involved in local politics in any way. Under Spanish law, legal residents in Spain from other parts of the European Union and from certain countries that have reciprocity agreements with Spain (Peru, Bolivia, Chile, South Korea, Norway, Ecuador, Paraguay, Iceland, Cabo Verde, Colombia, New Zealand, and Trinidad and Tobago) can register to vote in local Spanish elections, and can be elected to a position in those municipal elections. With Britain exiting the European Union, its reciprocity agreement with Spain will go into effect, making it the 13th country with such an agreement.

2. With some notable exceptions, most of the Britons and Americans who have settled in the area have made little effort to learn Spanish, though they are happy that their children learn to speak it. Meanwhile, the local school system is aiming to be bilingual (English/Spanish). It will be interesting to see what degree of proficiency in English is gained over time by local Spanish speakers and what the linguistic trajectory of the next generations of Anglophone transplants will be (the degree of maintenance of English, the varieties of Spanish used, etc.).

3. Analogously, when Chris Stewart's books came up in conversation with two *orgiveños* who were not directly benefitting economically from the influx of resident

Britons or tourists, they railed against him, saying that he spoke ill of Órgiva and was not "integrated" into the life of the town, but had made a great deal of money from his books. In contrast, Enrique, who has benefitted directly from the influx of incomers, mentioned Stewart without any criticism.

4. The celebration of the *Cristo de la Expiración* is a lead-up to Holy Week that takes place two weeks before Holy Thursday and Good Friday. It starts on the Thursday afternoon with the lowering of the statue of Christ on the Cross from the church altar, in preparation for its procession around town. While the statue is being lowered, *orgiveños* shout exclamations of praise and then line up to touch it. At various points, and especially the next day upon the statue's exit from the church for the start of the procession, fireworks are set off.

5. One of my interlocutors dated the "anti-hippie" demonstration as having taken place in the late 1990s and another (the former mayor Blanco López) said it had occurred in 1996 or '97. The others only referred to the 1990s in general. So it is possible that there was an additional protest that was anti-hippie in spirit after the *El Patriarca* event. However, I have not located any news coverage of the event nor is it registered in *Hablamos de Órgiva*. One other interlocutor recalled that in the early 1990s there was a small protest against the newcomers in the town that was tied to the polemic surrounding the use of dimethoate as an aerial pesticide in the olive groves. The incomers were leading a call to end the use of this chemical, while many local farmers were convinced that it was their best option. When the incomers sought to organize a demonstration against the use of this pesticide, a group of townspeople requested permission to hold a protest against the incomers on the same day. Somehow both demonstrations were combined and were held without incident. The controversy surrounding the use of dimethoate, and a passing reference to the protest, appear in *Hablamos de Órgiva* ("El campo" 26–27).

6. Another source for the festival organizers' perspective is "Dragon on a Ciggie" (SchNEWS; https://schnews.org/features/dragon-on-a-ciggie.htm).

7. Later when I asked Mayor Orellana to comment on the experience of immigration or response to it in other parts of Spain versus in Órgiva, he replied by saying that in Órgiva, there is "no illegal immigration, only the people from the hippie settlements [los de los asentamientos]." Considering that the vast majority of the adolescents in the center for unaccompanied migrants arrive undocumented through extralegal means, this comment suggests that he perceives the alternatives, given their differences in lifestyle and conception of civilization, as a much greater challenge than the MENAS.

8. This mosque is a small and unassuming space that is only marked by a small sign above the door saying "Mosque" in Spanish and in Arabic. It is managed by Qasim, the owner of Café Baraka, and primarily serves as a prayer space for his employees. But Qasim gives the keys to tourists and others who are looking for a prayer space in town.

9. Although all the recitations and chanting were in Arabic, Shaykh Umar spoke in Spanish and his interpreter (one of the Shaykh's children, Shamsuddin Margarit) translated his sermon into English. This same interpreter, Shamsuddin, also gave a

recitation of the Quran (in Arabic), a skill he developed through five years of study in Fez as a teenager.

10. On Whiteman's *The Invisible Muslim*, see this volume, Chapter 3, "Written Narratives about the Alpujarra and Órgiva."

11. For more on al-Yuhanisi's wanderings, see his biography *Tuhfat al-mughtarib bi-bilad al-Maghrib* (Qashtali 1974), translated into Spanish as *Prodigios del maestro sufí Abū Marwān al-Yuhānisī de Almería* (2010).

12. Father Vílchez passed away from Covid-19 in November 2020.

13. The Subud Alpujarra center is on the outskirts of Órgiva (about 2 kilometers from its center); Subud is an interfaith spiritual movement that began in Indonesia in the 1920s and includes regular gatherings for a group spiritual exercise. The O Sel Ling Buddhist center is a 35-minute drive further up in the Alpujarra from Órgiva and a Buddhist retirement home is being built in the center of Órgiva; both the center and the home are under the auspices of the Foundation for the Preservation of the Mahayana Tradition (FPMT).

14. "Halal" can be translated as "permissible or lawful," in contrast with "haram," meaning "forbidden." These terms in Islamic law, taken from the Quran, are commonly associated with Islamic dietary laws and in particular, the rules regarding the preparation of meat and the prohibition against pork and alcohol. But they are also used to categorize certain behaviors and activities as forbidden, such as cursing, fornication, usury, gambling, immodest clothing, and sitting with others who are drinking alcohol. See Lowry, and Hallaq.

15. One *orgiveña* pointed out with amusement that although there are only two pharmacies in the town, there are more than a dozen bars.

16. In addition to Café Baraka, there are a handful of other halal restaurants that are either take-out restaurants or were established more recently. Various supermarkets in Órgiva sell halal meat.

17. www.islamorgivahalal.es.

18. Among the Muslim economic migrants, there is also at least one Pakistani in the town. Although I heard amusing stories from the Maghrebis about how they had mistakenly assumed (because of his physical appearance and his halal restaurant) that he was North African and most *orgiveños* place the Pakistani in the same ambiguous category of "moro," I did not include him in my fieldwork. Romanians form another group of economic migrants in the town. The Romanians tend to quickly integrate into the local population, probably due to the linguistic (speaking a Romance language makes it easier to learn Spanish) and religious (they are also Christian, albeit of the Romanian Orthodox Church) similarities with the *orgiveños*. Other minorities in the town include a few Roma (Gypsy) families and one or two Chinese families.

19. Near the Alpujarran villages of Cástaras (almost an hour's drive northeast from Órgiva) and Bérchules (an hour's drive northeast from Órgiva), North African and West African migrants work in cherry tomato and strawberry farms.

20. Although attitudes and national laws vary, in Muslim-majority countries it is more acceptable for a Muslim man to marry a non-Muslim woman (and in fact

is a non-issue when the woman converts to Islam), than it is for a Muslim woman to marry a non-Muslim man. According to Islamic law, Muslim women may not marry non-Muslim men, but Muslim men may marry non-Muslim women who are "people of the book." As a result, a Muslim woman marrying a non-Muslim man is either frowned upon or is not possible legally, especially if the man does not convert to Islam. For example, in Tunisia it is only since 2017 that a Muslim woman can legally marry a man of any faith, or of none. Whereas, thus far, in Morocco a Muslim woman cannot legally marry a non-Muslim man unless he converts to Islam.

21. For an overview of the deep roots of Sufism in Algeria and Morocco and an assessment of how the government of each country is attempting to use Sufism to combat political Islam, see Muedini. He notes that since the early 1990s in Algeria and since the early 2000s in Morocco, each country's government has promoted Sufism in an effort to stem the power and violent expression of Islamism. On specific measures taken in Morocco, see Guerraoui.

22. Currently, it has become the norm in the Spanish press to normalize the acronym by writing it as "los menas." On the one hand, some see this as a dehumanizing practice, and on the other hand since it is not a frequently used acronym (e.g., laser) in English, I have maintained the capital letters.

23. The perspectives of the MENAS living in Órgiva, if the center's protocols were to allow it, would certainly enhance the understanding of the group dynamics in the town.

24. See for instance, "Polémica por la gestión de los menas propuesta por el concejal de seguridad de Colau," "Qué hay tras los ataques a 'menas,' los menores extranjeros contra los que Vox dirige su discurso," and Esparza.

25. With regard to crossing by small boat (*patera*) rather than the ferry, between the late 1990s and the early 2000s, there was approximately one fatality, usually due to drowning, per 100 migrants intercepted. Official figures show that 1,035 migrants died between 1999 and 2003 while en route to Spain. However, migrants' rights groups say that the actual number is higher (de Haas).

26. In the Spanish educational system, education is compulsory though the completion of the ESO (*Educación Secundaria Obligatoria*) program of study, typically at age 16. Completion of the additional two years of study known as *bachillerato* makes students eligible for vocational and technical schools or for university study.

27. IES (*Instituto de Educación Secundaria*) Alpujarra is the only high school (public or private) in Órgiva and for many years it was the high school that served all of the western Alpujarra. Now a couple of other towns have schools that offer the compulsory ESO degree, but IES Alpujarra is still the only institution in the broader area that offers the *bachillerato* program. Some families choose to send their children to private or charter-type (*colegios concertados*) high schools in Motril, Granada, or other cities.

28. In 2021, the Órgiva MENA center acquired an apartment in the town to house the youths who are in this limbo situation of having turned 18, but not having completed high school yet, or not having received a work permit yet.

29. I thank Nadia Naami for her help with fleshing out the cultural context of this expression.

30. See Kristeva.

Chapter 6

1. For specific figures on turn-of-the-century emigration, see Jiménez-Díaz, 227.

2. González Blasco (2004, p. 1178) reproduces photos of the arrival of these buses in the 1980s.

3. On the April 2019 election results, see Martín Plaza. On Vox's use of the Reconquista and anti-Muslim rhetoric as part of its political campaign, see García-Sanjuán 2018b.

4. In 2018 a second women's association was founded in Órgiva, *Asociación de Mujeres "La Otra Mirada" de Órgiva*.

5. Personal interview via video call with Rahma Sevilla Segovia, July 15, 2020.

6. Women typically spend six months at the *Casa de Acogida*, but the period of residence can be extended according to their needs.

7. Ceuta is a Spanish enclave in North Africa that borders Morocco. The city of Ceuta was conquered by the Portuguese in 1415 and became a Spanish possession in 1668. Spain enlarged the Ceuta enclave through its victory in the Hispano-Moroccan War, or *La Guerra de África* (1859–60). Most of Ceuta's residents are of Iberian or North African origin.

8. Mignolo, 76 and 105–6, and Majid, especially 27–28. On blood purity, the figure of Columbus, and Latino converts to Islam, see Civantos, 206–19.

9. See, for instance, Alam. For a personal account of whiteness and the convert experience, see Whiteman, whose chapter on the Alpujarra I discuss in Chapter 3, "Written Narratives about the Alpujarra and Órgiva."

10. An alternate spelling of the name, instead of reverting to the original spelling of "García," transliterates the surname as it appears in Arabic script: Ibn Gharsiya. For more on Ibn García, see Monroe 1970a, and Larsson.

Chapter 7

1. See: "Moreno inaugura el nuevo puente de Órgiva y se compromete con la zona" and "Moreno: Tenemos el firme compromiso de mejorar Andalucía."

Bibliography

Abend, Lisa. "Spain's New Muslims: A Historical Romance." *In the Light of Medieval Spain: Islam, the West, and the Relevance of the Past.* Simon R. Doubleday and David Coleman, eds. New York: Palgrave Macmillan, 2008, 133–56.
Aidi, Hishaam D. "The Interference of al-Andalus: Spain, Islam, and the West." *Social Text.* 87, 24:2 (Summer 2006): 67–88.
Akasoy, Anna. "Convivencia and Its Discontents: Interfaith Life in al-Andalus." *International Journal of Middle East Studies,* 42.3 (2010): 489–99.
Alam, Oishee. *Facing Race: White Australian Converts to Islam.* Melbourne University Press, 2018.
Alarcón, Pedro Antonio de. *La Alpujarra: sesenta leguas a caballo, precedidas de seis en diligencia.* Madrid: Imprenta de Miguel Guijarro, 1874.
"Alpujarras." *Encyclopaedia of Islam, First Edition (1913–36).* Martin T. Houtsma, Thomas W. Arnold, René Basset, and Richard Hartmann, eds. Leiden: E. J. Brill, 2011.
Álvarez Pérez, Antonio. *Santos mártires de las tahas y pueblos de la Alpujarra de Granada.* Sevilla: Punto Rojo, 2015.
Andalucía Directo, episode 4894. *Radio y Televisión de Andalucía,* September 25, 2017. www.youtube.com/watch?v=996qbsv9sBY&t=32s
Appiah, Kwame Anthony. *Cosmopolitanism: Ethics in a World of Strangers.* New York: W.W. Norton & Co. 2006.
———."Education for Global Citizenship." *The Yearbook of the National Society for the Study of Education,* 107:1 (2008): 83–99.
Arendt, Hannah. *The Human Condition.* Chicago, IL: University of Chicago Press, 1958.
———. "'The Rights of Man': What Are They?" *Modern Review,* (summer) 1949: 24–37.
Armas, Frederick de. *Don Quixote among the Saracens: A Clash of Civilizations and Literary Genres.* Toronto, ON: University of Toronto Press, 2011.
Arroyo, Javier. "Vox se apodera de la celebración del Día de la Toma de Granada." *El País.* January 2, 2020, https://elpais.com/politica/2020/01/02/actualidad/1577959762_186691.html.
Atkinson, Paul. *For Ethnography.* London: Sage, 2015.
Bahrami, Beebe. "A Door to Paradise: Converts, the New Age, Islam, and the Past in Granada, Spain." *City & Society,* 10.1 (1998): 121–32.

Bailey, Andy. *Órgiva: A Chancer's Guide to Rural Spain*. Andy Bailey, 2020.
Baldwin-Edwards, Martin. "'Between a Rock & a Hard Place': North Africa as a Region of Emigration, Immigration & Transit Migration." *Review of African Political Economy*, 33.108 (2006): 311–24.
Balibar, Étienne. "Is There a 'Neo-Racism'?" *Race, Nation, Class: Ambiguous Identities*. Étienne Balibar and Immanuel Wallerstein, eds. London; New York: Verso, 1991. 17–28.
Barbero, Abilio, and Pascual M. Vigil. *Sobre los orígenes sociales de la reconquista*. Esplugues de Llobregat: Editorial Ariel, 1974.
Barker, Martin. *The New Racism: Conservatives and the Ideology of the Tribe*. London: Junction, 1981.
Barrios Aguilera, Manuel. "Historia, leyenda y mito en la Alpujarra: de la guerra de los moriscos a la repoblación viejo cristiana." *Pensar la Alpujarra*, José A. González Alcantud, ed. Granada: Diputación, 1996, 13–55.
———, and Francisco Andújar Castillo. *Hombre y territorio en el reino de Granada (1570–1630): estudios sobre repoblación*. Almería: Instituto de Estudios Almerienses, 1995.
Baumann, Roland. "La invención de la Alpujarra." *Pensar la Alpujarra*, José A. González Alcantud, ed. Granada: Diputación, 1996, 89–104.
———. *The "Moors and Christians" of Valor: Folklore and Conflict in the Alpujarra (Andalusia)*. PhD Dissertation. Ann Arbor: University of Michigan, 1996.
Beaven, Tita. "A Life in the Sun: Accounts of New Lives Abroad As Intercultural Narratives." *Language and Intercultural Communication*, 7.3 (2007): 188–202.
Behar, Ruth. *The Vulnerable Observer: Anthropology that Breaks Your Heart*. Boston, MA: Beacon, 1996.
Bender, Thomas. "The Cosmopolitan Experience and Its Uses." *Cosmopolitanisms*. Bruce Robbins and Paulo Lemos Horta, eds. New York: New York University Press, 2017. 116–26.
Benveniste, Émile. "Civilisation. Contribution à l'histoire du mot" [1954]. *Problèmes de linguistique générale*. Paris: Éditions Gallimard. 1966. 336–45.
Bernard, Harvey R. *Research Methods in Anthropology: Qualitative and Quantitative Approaches*. Lanham, MD: Altamira Press a division of Rowman & Littlefield Publishers, 2011.
Boever, Arne de. *Against Aesthetic Exceptionalism*. Minneapolis: University of Minnesota Press, 2019.
Bolaños, Álvaro Félix. "Hispanism and Its Literary Icon's Exclusions: Moors and Indians in Reading Don Quixote Today." *Romance Quarterly*, 55:4 (2008): 255–78.
Boum, Aomar. "The Performance of Convivencia: Communities of Tolerance and the Reification of Toleration." *Religion Compass*, 6:3 (2012): 174–84.
Bourdieu, Pierre. *Outline of a Theory of Practice*. New York: Cambridge University Press, 1977.
———. *The Logic of Practice*. Cambridge: Polity, 2014.
———. *Language and Symbolic Power*. Cambridge, MA: Harvard University Press, 1991.

Brah, Avtar. *Cartographies of Diaspora: Contesting Identities*. London; New York: Routledge, 1996.
Brand, Laurie A. *Citizens Abroad: Emigration and the State in the Middle East and North Africa*. Cambridge: Cambridge University Press, 2006.
Brann, Ross. "The Moors?" *Medieval Encounters*, 15.2–4 (2009): 307–18.
Bravo Caro, Juan Jesús. *Felipe II y la repoblación del reino de Granada: la taha de Comares*. Granada: Universidad de Granada, 1995.
Brenan, Gerald. *South from Granada*. London: Hamilton, 1957.
Brown, Wendy. *Regulating Aversion: Tolerance in the Age of Identity and Empire*. Princeton, NJ: Princeton University Press, 2006.
———, and Rainer Forst. *The Power of Tolerance: A Debate*. Luca di Blasi and Christoph F. E. Holzhey, eds. New York: Columbia University Press, 2014.
Buber, Martin. *I and Thou [1923]*. Ronald G. Smith, trans. New York: Scribner, 1958.
Calderwood, Eric. *Colonial al-Andalus: Spain and the Making of Modern Moroccan Culture*. Cambridge, MA: Belknap Press of Harvard University, 2018.
———. "'In Andalucía, There Are No Foreigners': Andalucismo from Transperipheral Critique to Colonial Apology." *Journal of Spanish Cultural Studies*, 15.4 (2014a): 399–417.
———. "The Invention of al-Andalus: Discovering the Past and Creating the Present in Granada's Islamic Tourism Sites." *Journal of North African Studies*, 19.1 (2014b): 27–55.
———. "The Reconquista of the Mosque of Cordoba." *Foreign Policy*. April 10, 2015, http://foreignpolicy.com/2015/04/10/the-reconquista-of-the-mosque-of-cordoba-spain-catholic-church-islam/.
Campo Tejedor, Alberto del. *Trovadores de repente: una etnografía de la tradición burlesca en los improvisadores de la Alpujarra*. Salamanca: Centro de Cultura Tradicional Ángel Carril, 2006.
Campoy-Cubillo, Adolfo. *Memories of the Maghreb: Transnational Identities in Spanish Cultural Production*. New York: Palgrave Macmillan, 2012.
Carmona Vílchez, Antonio. *Clarito, un gran hombre de La Alpujarra*. Granada: A. Carmona, 2005.
Carnet, Pauline. "Entre contrôle et tolérance. Précarisation des migrants dans l'agriculture d' Almería." *Études rurales*, 182 (July–December, 2008): 201–17.
Caro Baroja, Julio. *Cuadernos de campo*. Madrid: Ediciones Turner, 1979.
———. *Los Moriscos del reino de Granada: ensayo de historia social*. Madrid: Instituto de Estudios Políticos, 1957.
Carrasco Urgoiti, María S. *El moro de Granada en la literatura*. Madrid: Revista de Occidente, 1956.
Carrascosa Salas, Miguel J. *La Alpujarra*. Granada: Universidad de Granada, 1992.
———. *La Alpujarra en coplas y otros poemas*. Granada: Caja General de Ahorros y Monte de Piedad, 1988.
Castro, Américo. *España en su historia: cristianos, moros y judíos*. Buenos Aires: Losada, 1948.
———. *La realidad histórica de España*. Mexico City: Porrúa, 1954.

Castro, Eduardo. *La Alpujarra en caballos de vapor*. Granada: Diputación de Granada, 2017.

Childers, William. "Cervantes in Moriscolandia." *Cervantes: Bulletin of the Cervantes Society of America*, 32:1 (2012): 277–90.

Civantos, Christina. *The Afterlife of al-Andalus: Muslim Iberia in Contemporary Arab and Hispanic Narratives*. Albany: State University of New York, 2017.

"Comunidad sufí de Órgiva." *Medina*. Radio y Televisión Española. March 3, 2019. www.rtve.es/alacarta/videos/medina-en-tve/medina-tve-comunidad-sufi-orgiva/5029907/.

Constenla, Tereixa and Ana Torregrosa. "Vecinos de El Ejido armados con barras de hierro atacan a los inmigrantes y destrozan sus locales." *El País*. February 7, 2000, https://elpais.com/diario/2000/02/07/espana/949878022_850215.html

Corbalán, Ana. "Entre la aversión y el deseo: Aproximación a la mirada del otro en las páginas de Don Quijote." *Letras Hispanas: Revista de Literatura y Cultura*, 2:2 (2005): 75–85.

"Cortegana (Huelva), Martos (Jaén), Órgiva (Granada)." *Los repobladores*. Radio y Televisión de Andalucía. February 20, 2021. www.canalsur.es/television/programas/los-repobladores/detalle/5838836.html.

"Cuántos menores no acompañados hay en España y cómo viven." *El HuffPost*. August 6, 2019.

Dadson, Trevor. *Tolerance and Coexistence in Early Modern Spain: The Moriscos of the Campo de Calatrava*. Woodbridge (UK): Tamesis, 2014.

Dietz, Gunther. "Frontier Hybridisation or Culture Clash? Transnational Migrant Communities and Sub-National Identity Politics in Andalusia, Spain." *Journal of Ethnic and Migration Studies*, 30.6 (2004): 1087–112.

———, and Nadia El-Shohoumi. *Muslim Women in Southern Spain: Stepdaughters of Al-Andalus*. La Jolla, CA: Center for Comparative Immigration Studies, UCSD, 2005.

Díez Forcada, Javier. "Los últimos hippies de España." *Las Provincias*. September 9, 2013, www.lasprovincias.es/v/20130909/sociedad/ultimos-hippies-espana-20130909.html.

"Dragon Festival, History." *Official Dragon Festival*. S.d. http://officialdragonfestival.blogspot.com/p/history.html

"Dragon on a Ciggie." *SchNEWS*. March 23, 2011. https://schnews.org/features/dragon-on-a-ciggie.htm.

DuBois, W. E. B. *The Souls of Black Folk: Authoritative Text, Contexts, Criticism*. Henry Louis Gates, Jr. and Terri Hume Oliver, eds. New York: W.W. Norton & Co, 1999.

Duran, Khalid. "Andalusia's Nostalgia for Progress and Harmonious Heresy." *Middle East Report*, 178 (1992): 20–23.

Eastmond, Marita. "Stories as Lived Experience: Narratives in Forced Migration Research." *Journal of Refugee Studies*, 20:2 (2007): 248–64.

Egea Fernández-Montesinos, Alberto. *García Lorca, Blas Infante y Antonio Gala: un nacionalismo alternativo en la literatura andaluza*. Sevilla: Fundación Blas Infante, 2001.

España en cifras. Madrid: Instituto Nacional de Estadística, 1999–2019. www.ine.es/ss/Satellite?L=es_ES&c=INEPublicacion_C&cid=1259924856416&p=12547351 10672&pagename=ProductosYServicios%2FPYSLayout&param1=PYSDetalleG ratuitas

Esparza, Pablo. "Quiénes son los 'menas' y por qué se han vuelto el blanco de ataques racistas en España." *BBC News Mundo*. December 20, 2019, www.bbc.com/mundo/noticias-internacional-50815028.

Falcones, Ildefonso. *La mano de Fátima*. Barcelona: Grijalbo, 2009.

Faszer-McMahon, Debra, and Victoria L. Ketz. *African Immigrants in Contemporary Spanish Texts: Crossing the Strait*. Burlington, VT: Ashgate, 2015.

Ferguson, Wallace K. *The Renaissance in Historical Thought: Five Centuries of Interpretation [1948]*. Toronto: University of Toronto Press, 2006.

Fernández, Christian. "'Together but Apart, Equal but Different'—On the Claims for Toleration in Multicultural Societies." *On Behalf of Others*. Sarah Scuzzarello et al., eds. Oxford: Oxford University Press, 2009, 35–60.

Fernandéz Palmeral, Ramón. *El rey de los moriscos*. Amazon, 2015.

Fernández Prieto, Celia. "La historia en la novela histórica." *Reflexiones sobre la novela histórica*. José Jurado Morales ed. Cádiz: Universidad de Cádiz, 2006, 165–83.

Fernández y González, Manuel. *Los monfíes de las Alpujarras [1856]*. Granada: Defensor de Granada, 1902.

Fierro, Maribel. "Al-Andalus en el pensamiento fascista español." *Al-Andalus/España: historiografías en contraste: siglos XVII–XXI*. Manuela Marín, ed. Madrid: Casa de Velázquez, 2009, 325–49.

Flesler, Daniela. *The Return of the Moor: Spanish Responses to Contemporary Moroccan Immigration*. West Lafayette, IN: Purdue University Press, 2008.

Forst, Rainer. "The Limits of Toleration." *Constellations*, 11.3 (2004): 312–25.

Foucault, Michel. *The History of Sexuality, Volume I: An Introduction*. Robert Hurley, trans. New York: Vintage, 1980.

———, Mauro Bertani, Alessandro Fontana, and David Macey. *Society Must Be Defended: Lectures at the Collège de France, 1975–1976*. New York: Picador, 2003.

——— and Paul Rabinow. "Truth and Juridical Forms." *[1974] The Essential Works of Michel Foucault. 1954–1984*, Volume 3. James D. Faubion, ed. Robert Hurley et al., trans. New York: The New Press, 2000.

Frayer, Lauren. "At Last, Muslims Can Savor a Halal Spin on Spain's Famous Jamón." National Public Radio (NPR). December 16, 2014. www.npr.org/sections/thesalt/2014/12/16/371018946/at-last-muslims-can-savor-a-halal-spin-on-spains-famous-jamon

Friedman, Yohanan. *Tolerance and Coercion in Islam*. Oxford, UK: Blackwell, 2003.

Fuchs, Barbara. *Exotic Nation: Maurophilia and the Construction of Early Modern Spain*. Philadelphia: University of Pennsylvania Press, 2011.

Fuchs, Dale. "Pope Asked to Let Muslims Pray in Cathedral." *Guardian* (London), December 28, 2006.

Galeotti, Anna E. *Toleration as Recognition*. Cambridge: Cambridge University Press, 2002.

García Lorca, Andrés, and Antonio S. Matarín Guil. *La Alpujarra oriental: la gran desconocida*. Albodoluy, Spain: Ayuntamiento de Albodoluy, 2008.
García Lorca, Federico. *Romancero gitano*. Madrid: Espasa-Calpe, 1928.
———, and Adoración Elvira and Fernando Rubio. *Lorca en el país de ninguna parte: Lanjarón-La Alpujarra*. Granada: Gami, 2019.
García Sanjuán, Alejandro. "Rejecting al-Andalus, Exalting the Reconquista: Historical Memory in Contemporary Spain." *Journal of Medieval Iberian Studies*, 10:1 (2018a): 127–145.
———. "Vox, la Reconquista y la salvación de España." *El Diario*. December 5, 2018b, www.eldiario.es/andalucia/enabierto/elecciones_en_Andalucia_2018-reconquista-Vox_6_843125717.html
Gilroy, Paul. "Nationalism, History and Ethnic Absolutism." *History Workshop*, 30 (1990) 114–20.
———. *After Empire: Melancholia or Convivial Culture*. London: Routledge, 2004.
Gómez-Ullate García de León, Martín. *La comunidad soñada: antropología social de la contracultura*. Madrid: Plaza y Valdés, 2009.
González Alcantud, José A. "El canon andaluz y las fronteras imaginarias." *El orientalismo desde el sur*, José. A. González Alcantud, ed. Barcelona: Anthropos, 2006, 368–80.
———, ed. *Marroquíes en la guerra civil española: campos equívocos*. Rubí [Barcelona]: Anthropos Editorial, 2003.
———. *Lo moro: las lógicas de la derrota y la formación del estereotipo islámico*. Rubí [Barcelona]: Anthropos, 2002.
———, Manuel Lorente Rivas, and Amelina Correa Ramón. *Pedro Antonio de Alarcón y la guerra de África: del entusiasmo romántico a la compulsión colonial*. Barcelona: Anthropos, 2004.
González Blasco, Juan. *Falla y Lorca en la misteriosa Alpujarra: la mazurca de Órgiva*. Granada: MCRC, 2017.
———. *Órgiva: hitos de su historia* [2003]. Volumes I and II. Órgiva [Granada]: El Puerto, 2004.
———. *El subsector cárnico del jamón curado en la Alpujarra*. Granada: Universidad de Granada, 2001.
González Jiménez, Manuel. *En torno a los orígenes de Andalucía: la repoblación del siglo XIII*. Sevilla: Universidad de Sevilla, 1980.
———. "Sobre la ideología de la Reconquista: realidades y tópicos." *Memoria, mito y realidad en la historia medieval: XIII Semana de Estudios Medievales, Nájera*, José Ignacio de la Iglesia Duarte et al. eds. Logroño: Gobierno de La Rioja, Instituto de Estudios Riojanos, 2003, 151–70.
Graf, Eric Clifford. *Cervantes and Modernity*. Lewisburg, PA: Bucknell University Press, 2007.
Guerraoui, Saad. "Sufism in Morocco 'A Powerful Weapon' Against Extremism." *The Arab Weekly*. January 4, 2016, https://thearabweekly.com/sufism-morocco-powerful-weapon-against-extremism#:~:text=Sufism%20is%20the%20mystical%20aspect,bliss%2C%20mysticism%20and%20spiritual%20rapture.&text=One%20

of%20the%20main%20influential,political%20Islam%20since%20the%20 protectorate.
Haas, Hein de. "Morocco: From Emigration Country to Africa's Migration Passage to Europe." *Migration Information Source*. October 1, 2005, www.migrationpolicy.org/article/morocco-emigration-country-africas-migration-passage-europe.
Hablamos de Órgiva: historias y reflexiones de la gente de Órgiva, sus anejos y cortijadas. Órgiva, Granada: Ayuntamiento de Órgiva, 2012.
Hallaq, Wael B. "Forbidden." *Encyclopaedia of the Qur'ān*, Jane D. McAuliffe, ed. Leiden, Netherlands: Brill, 2012.
Harvey, Leonard P. *Muslims in Spain, 1500 to 1614*. Chicago, IL: University of Chicago Press, 2005.
Heers, Jacques. *Le Moyen Âge, Une Imposture*. Paris: Librairie académique Perrin, 1992.
Hemer, Oscar and Maja Povrzanović Frykman and Per-Markku Ristilammi, eds. *Conviviality at the Crossroads: The Poetics and Politics of Everyday Encounters*. Cham: Palgrave Macmillan, 2020.
Henn, David. "Two Views of Almería: Juan Goytisolo and Gerald Brenan," *Revue de Litterature Comparée*, 65 (1991): 429–46.
Henry, Barbara. "Identities of the West: Reason, Myth, Limits of Tolerance." *Identities: Time, Difference, and Boundaries*. Aleida Assmann, ed. Berghahn Books, 2002, 7–106.
Hirschkind, Charles. "The Contemporary Afterlife of Moorish Spain." *Islam and Public Controversy in Europe*. Nilüfer Göle, ed. Burlington, VT: Ashgate, 2014, 227–40.
———. *The Feeling of History: Islam, Romanticism, and Andalusia*. Chicago, IL: University of Chicago Press, 2020.
———. "Granadan Reflections." *Material Religion: Iconic Religion in Urban Space*, 12.2 (2016): 209–32.
Honneth, Axel. *The I in We: Studies in the Theory of Recognition*. Cambridge; Malden, MA: Polity, 2012.
———. *The Struggle for Recognition: The Moral Grammar of Social Conflicts*. Cambridge, MA: Polity, 1995.
Howe, Marvine. *Al-Andalus Rediscovered: Iberia's New Muslims*. London: Hurst and Company, 2012.
Ibáñez Ibáñez, José R. "Al sur de Granada de Gerald Brenan, o la transposición de cultemas semíticos en el ámbito cultural y gastronómico andaluz." *La Andalucía rural vista por viajeros extranjeros: Campos, posadas y tabernas*, Vicente López Folgado et al. eds. New York: Peter Lang Publishing, 2013, 203–30.
Illich, Ivan. *Tools for Conviviality*. New York: Harper & Row, 1973.
Irving, Washington. *Tales of the Alhambra*. Philadelphia, PA: Carey & Lea; London: Bell, 1832.
Izquierdo, Francisco. *El Apócrifo de la Alpujarra alta*. Madrid: Editorial Azur, 1969.
Jiménez-Díaz, José F. "Una experiencia de desarrollo agrícola al sur de España: la localidad de El Ejido." *Localización: Globalización y perspectivas de la integración*

regional, Pedro Sánchez Vera and Alberto Riella, eds. Murcia: Universidad de Murcia, 2010, 225–48.

Johnson, Carroll B. *Transliterating a Culture: Cervantes and the Moriscos.* Mark Groundland, ed. Newark, DE: Juan de la Cuesta, 2009.

Keeley, Graham. "Muslims Arrested for Trying to Pray in Cordoba's Former Great Mosque." *Times* (London). March 4, 2010.

Kristeva, Julia. *Strangers to Ourselves.* New York: Harvester Wheatsheaf, 1996.

Kvale, Steinar. *Interviews: An Introduction to Qualitative Research Interviewing.* Thousand Oaks, CA: Sage, 1996.

Labanyi, Jo. "Love and Colonial Ambivalence in Spanish Africanist Cinema of the Early Franco Dictatorship." *Europe and Love in Cinema.* Lisa Passerini, Jo Labanyi, and Karen Diehl, eds. Bristol, UK: Intellect, 2012, 129–50.

———. "Love, Politics and the Making of the Modern European Subject: Spanish Romanticism and the Arab World." *Hispanic Research Journal,* 5.3 (2004): 229–43.

"La comunidad hippy comienza a concentrarse en el paraje de las termas de Santa Fe para la Fiesta del Dragón." *Europa Press.* March 20, 2015, www.20minutos.es/noticia/2410381/0/comunidad-hippy-comienza-concentrarse-paraje-termas-santa-fe-para-fiesta-dragon/.

Lahbabi, Fatima. *L'Immigration marocaine en Andalousie: vie sociale et mobilités économiques des sans papiers dans la province d'Almeria.* PhD Dissertation. Lille: Atelier national de reproduction des thèses, 2004.

Larsson, Göran. *Ibn García's Shu'ūbiyya Letter: Ethnic and Theological Tensions in Medieval al-Andalus.* Leiden: Brill, 2003.

Lea, Henry C. *The Moriscos of Spain, Their Conversion and Expulsion.* London: B. Quaritch, 1901.

Levinovitz, Alan. *The Limits of Religious Tolerance.* Amherst, MA: Amherst College, 2016.

Lomax, Derek W. *The Reconquest of Spain.* London: Longman, 1978.

López, Álvaro. "La polémica celebración de La Toma de Granada vuelve con la prohibición de 'símbolos extremistas." *El Diario.* January 1, 2020, www.eldiario.es/andalucia/granada/presencia-vox-participa-toma-granada_1_1169335.html.

López, Rafael. "Huelga general en Órgiva contra un centro de rehabilitación de drogadictos." *El País.* November 7, 1991, https://elpais.com/diario/1991/11/08/sociedad/689554804_850215.html.

López García, Bernabé. "30 años de africanismo español: el fin de la almogaravía científica (1967–1997)." *Awrāq,* 18 (1997): 11–48.

Lowe, Lisa. *Critical Terrains: French and British Orientalisms.* Ithaca, NY: Cornell University Press, 1992.

Lowry, Joseph E. "Lawful and Unlawful." *Encyclopaedia of the Qur'ān.* Jane Dammen McAuliffe, ed. July 2, 2020, http://dx.doi.org/10.1163/1875-3922_q3_EQCOM_00107.

Majid, Anouar. *Freedom and Orthodoxy: Islam and Difference in the Post-Andalusian Age.* Stanford, CA: Stanford University Press, 2004.

Mancing, Howard. "Cide Hamete Benengeli vs. Miguel de Cervantes: The Metafictional Dialectic of Don Quijote." *Cervantes: Bulletin of the Cervantes Society of America*, 1:1–2 (1981): 63–81.

Manzano Moreno, Eduardo. "Qurtuba, algunas reflexiones críticas sobre el califato de Córdoba y el mito de la convivencia." *Awrāq*, 7 (2013): 225–46.

Martín, Jorge M. *Aportaciones desde la antropología social al desarrollo comunitario de una zona rural: municipio de Ugíjar, La Alpujarra*. Granada: Casa de los Tiros, 1988.

Martin-Márquez, Susan. *Disorientations: Spanish Colonialism in Africa and the Performance of Identity*. New Haven, CT: Yale University Press, 2008.

Martín Muñoz, Gema. "A Thousand and One Histories." *Critical Muslim*, 6 (April–June 2013): 57–68.

Martín Plaza, Ana. "Elecciones generales 2019: Vox irrumpe en el Congreso con 24 diputados y se sitúa como quinta fuerza con más de 2,6 millones de votos." *RTVE*. April 29, 2019.

Martínez Dalmases, Francisco. *Qandil: luces de poniente*. Córdoba: Editorial Almuzara, 2011.

———. *Qandil: Lights in the Land of the Setting Sun*. Francisco Martínez Dalmases, 2017.

Martínez de la Rosa, Francisco. *Aben Humeya o la rebelión de los moriscos [1836]*. Barcelona: Editorial Linkgua, 2012.

Martínez Montávez, Pedro. *Significado y símbolo de Al-Andalus*. Almería: Fundación Ibn Tufayl de Estudio Árabes, 2011.

Mauss, Marcel. *The Gift: The Form and Reason for Exchange in Archaic Societies [1925]*. New York: W.W. Norton, 1990.

McKinnon, Catriona. *Toleration: A Critical Introduction*. London; New York: Routledge, 2006.

"Me voy al pueblo." *España a ras de cielo*, season 2, episode 4. Radio y Televisión Española, August 17, 2015. www.rtve.es/alacarta/videos/espana-a-ras-de-cielo/espana-ras-cielo-voy-pueblo/4761958/

Mignolo, Walter. *Local Histories/Global Designs: Coloniality, Subaltern Knowledges, and Border Thinking*. Princeton, NJ: Princeton University Press, 2000.

Monroe, James. *Islam and the Arabs in Spanish Scholarship, Sixteenth Century to the Present*. Leiden: Brill, 1970a.

———. *The Shuubiyya in Al-Andalus: The Risala of Ibn García and Five Refutations*. Berkeley, Los Angeles, London: University of California Press, 1970b.

"Moreno inaugura el nuevo puente de Órgiva y se compromete con la zona." *Granada Hoy*. February 13, 2020, www.granadahoy.com/provincia/moreno-inaugura-Órgiva-puente-rio-Chico-Alpujarra_0_1437156801.html.

"Moreno: Tenemos el firme compromiso de mejorar Andalucía," *Europa Press*. February 13, 2020, www.youtube.com/watch?v=oSE9hYyLQts.

Muedini, Fait. "The Promotion of Sufism in the Politics of Algeria and Morocco." *Islamic Africa*, 3.2 (2012): 201–26.

Murphy, Andrew R. "Tolerance, Toleration, and the Liberal Tradition." *Polity*, 29.4 (1997): 593–623.
Nhat Hanh, Thich. *Interbeing: Fourteen Guidelines for Engaged Buddhism*. Fred Eppsteiner, ed. Berkeley, CA: Parallax Press, 1987.
Navarro Alcalá-Zamora, Pío, and Emilio Lledó. *Tratadillo de agricultura popular: el medio, las técnicas y los personajes en la Alpujarra*. Barcelona: Ariel, 1981.
Navarro Velilla, Justo. *El país perdido: la Alpujarra en la guerra morisca*. Sevilla: Fundación José Manuel Lara, 2013.
Nirenberg, David. *Communities of Violence: Persecution of Minorities in the Middle Ages*. Princeton, NJ: Princeton University Press, 1996.
Olmo, Margarita del. "Los conversos españoles al Islam: de mayoría a minoría por la llamada de Dios." *Anales del Museo Nacional de Antropología*, 7 (2000): 15–40.
Olóriz Aguilera, Federico. *Diario de la expedición antropológica a La Alpujarra en 1894*. Granada: Caja General de Ahorros de Granada, 1995.
"Órgiva." *Búscame en el pueblo*, season 1, episode 3. Movistar Plus, April 2011.
"Órgiva." *Radio Gaga*, season 2, episode 4. Movistar Plus, May 3, 2018.
"Órgiva (Granada)." *Este es mi pueblo*, season 11, episode 9. Radio y Televisión de Andalucía, October 10, 2015. www.youtube.com/watch?v=eHkjnW-nvsM.
"Órgiva (Granada)." *Tierra de sabores*. Radio y Televisión de Andalucía, February 14, 2021. www.canalsur.es/television/programas/tierra-de-sabores/detalle/13413572.html?video=1680687&sec=
"Órgiva pretende eliminar los asentamientos ilegales del municipio," *Granada Digital*. January 24, 2021. www.granadadigital.es/orgiva-pretende-eliminar-asenta mientos-ilegales-municipio-granada/
The Oxford English Dictionary. J. A. Simpson and E. S. C. Weiner, eds. Oxford: Clarendon Press, 1989.
PASOS. "Proyecto de Participación Ciudadana 'Órgiva Municipio Sostenible.'" https://pasos.coop/portfolio/proyecto-orgiva-municipio-andaluz-sostenible/.
Pearce, S. J. "The Myth of the Myth of the Andalusian Paradise: The Extreme Right and the American Revision of the History and Historiography of Medieval Spain." *Far-Right Revisionism and the End of History: Alt/Histories*. Louie Dean Valencia-García, ed. New York: Routledge, 2020, 29–68.
Pérez-Reverte, Arturo. "Moros de la morería." *XLSemanal*. March 31, 2014, www.perezreverte.com/articulo/patentes-corso/908/moros-de-la-moreria/.
Pérez Zúñiga, José María. *La tumba del Monfí*. Córdoba: Editorial Almuzara, 2012.
Perry, Mary E. *The Handless Maiden: Moriscos and the Politics of Religion in Early Modern Spain*. Princeton, NJ: Princeton University Press, 2005.
Piegsa-Quischotte, Inka. "Órgiva, a Culture Hotchpotch in the Alpujarras." *Glamour-Granny Travels*. August 14, 2016, www.glamourgrannytravels.com/2016/08/14/orgiva-culture-hotchpotch-alpujarras/.
Plann, Susan. *Coming of Age in Madrid: An Oral History of Unaccompanied Moroccan Migrant Minors*. Brighton: Sussex Academic Press, 2019.
"Polémica por la gestión de los menas propuesta por el concejal de seguridad de Colau." *ABC*. July 23, 2019, www.abc.es/espana/catalunya/barcelona/abci-polem

ica-gestion-menas-propuesta-concejal-seguridad-colau-201907231414_noticia.html

Porras Carrión, José Antonio. *El secreto de la Alpujarra*. José Antonio Porras Carrión [Punto Rojo Libros], 2019.

Povinelli, Elizabeth. *The Cunning of Recognition: Indigenous Alterities and the Making of Australian Multiculturalism*. Durham, NC: Duke University Press, 2002.

Pozo Felguera, Gabriel. "La Alpujarra, Reino de las Amazonas." *El Independiente de Granada*. February 11, 2018, www.elindependientedegranada.es/ciudadania/alpujarra-reino-amazonas.

———. "Guía de fabulosos tesoros ocultos por los 'moros' en el Reino de Granada." *El Independiente*. June 25, 2017, www.elindependientedegranada.es/cultura/guia-fabulosos-tesoros-ocultos-moros-reino-granada.

Puri, Shalini, and Debra A. Castillo. *Theorizing Fieldwork in the Humanities: Methods, Reflections, and Approaches to the Global South*. New York: Palgrave Macmillan US, 2016.

Qashtali, Ahmad ibn Ibrahim. *Prodigios del maestro sufí Abū Marwān al-Yuhānisī de Almería*. Bárbara Boloix Gallardo, trans. and ed. Madrid: Mandala Ediciones, 2010.

———. *Tuhfat al-mughtarib bi-bilad al-Maghrib*. Fernando de la Granja, ed. Madrid: al-Maʿhad al-Misri lil-Dirasat al-Islamiyya bi-Madrid, 1974.

"Qué hay tras los ataques a 'menas,' los menores extranjeros contra los que Vox dirige su discurso." *Magnet*. November 7, 2019, https://magnet.xataka.com/en-diez-minutos/que-hay-ataques-a-menas-menores-extranjeros-que-vox-dirige-su-discurso.

Quinn, Mary B. *The Moor and the Novel: Narrating Absence in Early Modern Spain*. Houndmills, UK; New York: Palgrave Macmillan, 2013.

Ribas-Mateos, Natalia. "Revising Mediterranean Contexts: The Mediterranean Caravanserai." *The Mediterranean Passage: Migration and New Cultural Encounters in Southern Europe*. Russell King, ed. Liverpool: Liverpool University Press, 2001, 22–40.

Ricci, Cristián. *¡Hay Moros en la costa!: literatura marroquí fronteriza en castellano y catalán*. Madrid: Iberoamericana; Frankfurt Am Main: Vervuert, 2014.

Ríos Saloma, Martín F. "La Reconquista: génesis de un mito historiográfico." *Historia y Grafía* (2008): 191–216.

Rivière Gómez, Aurora. *Orientalismo y nacionalismo español: estudios árabes y hebreos en la Universidad de Madrid. 1843–1868*. Madrid: Universidad Carlos III, 2000.

Rogozen-Soltar, Mikaela. "Al-Andalus in Andalusia: Negotiating Moorish History and Regional Identity in Southern Spain." *Anthropological Quarterly*, 80.3 (2007): 863–86.

———. *Spain Unmoored: Migration, Conversion, and the Politics of Islam*. Bloomington; Indianapolis: Indiana University Press, 2017.

Rojo, Tito J., and M. Casares Porcel. *El jardín hispanomusulmán: los jardines de al-Andalus y su herencia*. Granada: Editorial Universidad de Granada, 2011.

Root, Deborah. "Speaking Christian: Orthodoxy and Difference in Sixteenth-Century Spain." *Representations*, 23 (1988): 118–34.
Rosón Lorente, Javier. *¿El retorno de Tariq?: comunidades etnorreligiosas en el Albayzín granadino*. PhD Dissertation. Granada: Editorial de la Universidad de Granada, 2008.
——— and Gunther Dietz. "Ethnicised Inter-religious Conflicts in Contemporary Granada, Spain." *Contested Mediterranean Spaces: Ethnographic Essays in Honour of Charles Tilly*, Maria Kousis, Tom Selwyn, and David Clark, eds. New York: Berghahn Books, 2011, 264–83.
Rueda, Ana, and Sandra Martín, eds. *El retorno/el reencuentro: la inmigración en la literatura hispano-marroquí*. Madrid: Iberoamericana Editorial Vervuert, 2010.
Said, Edward W. *Orientalism*. New York: Vintage, 1978.
Sánchez Alonso, Fernando. "Conversos sufíes: los místicos del Islam." *El País Semanal*. January 18, 2015a.
———. "El paraíso hippy de Europa." *Magazine*. July 12, 2015b, www.magazinedigital.com/historias/reportajes/paraiso-hippy-europa.
Scuzzarello, Sarah, Catarina Kinnvall, and Kristen R. Monroe. *On Behalf of Others: The Psychology of Care in a Global World*. Oxford: Oxford University Press, 2009.
Sedano Moreno, Pepe. *Imagínate la Alpujarra: otro mundo, mil y una historias alpujarreñas*. Spain: Círculo Rojo, 2021.
Sell, Jonathan P. A. "Orpheus in the Alpujarras: Metaphors of Arrival in Chris Stewart's *Driving Over Lemons*." *Metaphor and Diaspora in Contemporary Writing*, Jonathan P. A. Sell, ed. Houndmills, UK; New York: Palgrave Macmillan, 2012, 186–204.
Shah-Kazemi, Reza. *The Spirit of Tolerance in Islam*. London: I.B. Tauris in association with the Institute of Ismaili Studies, 2012.
Sheller, Mimi. "Mobility." *Sociopedia*. 2011. Sociopedia.isa. S.n.
Shubert, Atika. "Muslims in Spain Campaign to Worship alongside Christians." *CNN*. July 9, 2010.
Spahni, Jean-Christian. *L'Alpujarra: secrète andalousie*. Neuchâtel: Editions de la Baconnière, 1959.
Spivak, Gayatri Chakravorty. "Can the Subaltern Speak?" *Marxism and the Interpretation of Culture*. Cary Nelson and Lawrence Grossberg, eds. Urbana: University of Illinois Press, 1988, 271–313.
Stalleart, Christiane. *Etnogénesis y etnicidad en España: una aproximación histórico-antropológica al casticismo*. Barcelona: Proyecto A, 1998.
———. "El movimiento neomusulmán y el intento de (re)construcción de una identidad andaluza/andalusí." *Religión y cultura I*, Salvador Rodríguez Becerra, ed. Seville: Junta de Andalucía/Fundación Machado, 1999, 189–97.
Stewart, Chris. *Driving over Lemons: An Optimist in Spain*. New York: Vintage Books, 1999.

———. *A Parrot in the Pepper Tree* [2002]. London: Sort of Books, 2009.
———. *The Almond Blossom Appreciation Society* [2006]. London: Sort of Books, 2009.
Suárez-Navaz, Liliana. *Rebordering The Mediterranean: Boundaries and Citizenship in Southern Europe*. New York; Oxford: Berghahn Books, 2004.
"Sufís, los místicos del Islam en España." *Diario Vice*. Vice Media. October 26, 2016. www.vice.com/es/article/a3pe8j/sufis-misticos-islam-espana
Taguieff, Pierre-André. "The New Cultural Racism in France." *Telos*, 83 (1990): 109–22.
Threadgould, Jake. "The Alpujarra: An Unlikely Cosmopolitan Hub in Spain's Sierra Nevada." *EFE*. February 28, 2018, www.efe.com/efe/english/life/the-alpujarra-an-unlikely-cosmopolitan-hub-in-spain-s-sierra-nevada/50000263-3534197#.
Tremlett, Giles. "Two Arrested after Fight in Cordoba's Former Mosque." *Guardian* (London), January 4, 2010.
Trillo San José, Carmen. *La Alpujarra antes y después de la conquista castellana*. Granada: Universidad de Granada, 1994.
———. *La Alpujarra, historia, arqueología y paisaje: análisis de un territorio en época medieval*. Granada: Diputación Provincial, 1992.
———. "La tāʿa de Órgiva: un señorío en la Alpujarra al final de la Edad Media." *Revista del Centro de Estudios Históricos de Granada y su Reino*, IV, (1990): 49–70.
Tofiño-Quesada, Ignacio. "Spanish Orientalism: Uses of the Past in Spain's Colonization in Africa." *Comparative Studies of South Asia, Africa and the Middle East*, 23:1–2 (2003): 141–48.
Venegas, José Luis. *The Sublime South: Andalusia, Orientalism, and the Making of Modern Spain*. Evanston, IL: Northwestern University Press, 2018.
Veres, Luis. "La novela histórica y el cuestionamiento de la Historia." http://pendientedemigracion.ucm.es/info/especulo/numero36/novhist.html.
Verkuyten, Maykel, and Kumar Yogeeswaran. "The Social Psychology of Intergroup Toleration: A Roadmap for Theory and Research." *Personality and Social Psychology Review*, 21.1 (2017): 72–96.
Viguera, María Jesús. "Al-Andalus y España: sobre el esencialismo de los Beni Codera." *Al-Andalus/España: historiografías en contraste, siglos XVII–XXI*. Manuela Marín, ed. Madrid: Casa de Velázquez, 2009, 67–81.
Voltaire [François-Marie Arouet]. *Dictionnaire philosophique. Œuvres complètes*, Volume 19. Paris: Garnier Frères, 1879.
Walzer, Michael. *On Toleration*. New Haven, CT: Yale University Press, 1997.
Whiteman, Medina Tenour. *The Invisible Muslim: Journeys Through Whiteness and Islam*. London: Hurst and Company, 2020.
Wien, Peter. *Arab Nationalism: The Politics of History and Culture in the Modern Middle East*. Milton Park, Abingdon, Oxon: Routledge. 2017.
Williams, Bernard. "Toleration: An Impossible Virtue?" *Toleration: An Elusive Virtue*. David Heyd, ed. Princeton, NJ: Princeton University Press, 1996, 18–27.

Žižek, Slavoj. "Tolerance as an Ideological Category." *Critical Inquiry*, 34 (2008): 660–82.
—— and Glyn Daly. *Conversations with Žižek*. Cambridge: Polity, 2004.
Zohry, Ayman. "Migration without Borders: North Africa as a Reserve of Cheap Labour for Europe." UNESCO, 2005. http://unesdoc.unesco.org/images/0013/001391/139152e.pdf.

www.ingramcontent.com/pod-product-compliance
Lightning Source LLC
Chambersburg PA
CBHW050521170426

43201CB00013B/2036